Keeping A Horse
The Natural Way

A natural approach to horse management
for optimum health and performance

Jo Bird

Foreword and contributions by
Pat Parelli

Featuring photography by Bob Langrish

BARRON'S

First edition for the United States and Canada published by Barron's Educational Series, Inc., 2002.

First published in 2002 by Interpet Publishing

All inquiries should be addressed to:
Barron's Educational Series, Inc.
250 Wireless Boulevard
Hauppauge, New York 11788
http://www.barronseduc.com

Library of Congress Catalog Card No. 2001095153

International Standard Book No. 0-7641-5411-7

Printed in China

9 8 7 6 5 4 3

The information and recommendations in this book are given without any guarantees on the part of the author and publisher who disclaim any liability regarding the use of this material. If in doubt, seek the advice of a veterinarian or horse care specialist.

The Author

Jo Bird has owned and ridden horses for most of her life. She provides management and nutritional advice to people buying horses and has worked in an advisory capacity helping to develop new products for a leading pet and equestrian product manufacturer. She has owned horses of very different types and of all ages from very young foals to the distinctly elderly, and the proof of the success of her natural methods of horse management is the fact that all the horses in her care are extremely happy and in tip-top condition. Her philosophy of horse care is simply "think about it from the horse's point of view."

Author's Acknowledgments

I would like to thank my husband Karl, friends, relations, and colleagues for their support including: Laura Key, Gill Leage, Kate Shoolheifer, John and Myra Fuller, Angus Hudson MRICS FAAV, Edward Blundy, Jonathan Hickman, Stephanie Power, Yvonne Smith, & Dorothy Palmer.

Special thanks also to Pat and Linda Parelli, Samuel Franklin BSc MSc ARICS FAAV, David Rouse D.W.C.F., Gill Kennett, Hadham Mill Riding Centre, Wendy Jane Hines, Ingraham practitioner, S.K., Interpet Ltd, Hilton Herbs, Dodson & Horrell.

Feng Shui advice and diagram layout from Thomas Coxon Associates' website: www.fengshui-consultants.co.uk. The Feng Shui diagram on page 190 was created by Edward Blundy.

Planning and grassland management advice, CAD and photographic equipment: Sworders Agricultural, Land Agents, Chartered Surveyors and Agricultural Consultants www.sworders-agri.co.uk.

Picture Credits

With the exception of the pictures listed below, all the photographs reproduced in this book were supplied by Bob Langrish. Our thanks to him and his colleagues Sally Waters and Nicola Coombs for their unfailing help and support during the preparation of this book.

Pat Parelli: 8 top, 9, 11 right, 32-33, 39 right, 43 both, 44 top, 49, 53 both.

Kit Houghton: 181 middle, 186, 187 bottom, 192 bottom, 195 top left and right, 196, 200 bottom left.

Jo Bird: 144, 166 bottom, 168 top, 197 all, 199.

Linda Tellington-Jones, TTeam: 200 top left and top right (photographer: Ellen Van Leeuwen).

Neil Sutherland for Interpet: 61 bottom, 62 lower right, 63 lower right, 69 right, 72 top left, 79 top right, 105, 125, 171 bottom, 198 both.

Westgate Group: 61 right, 88 top left.

John Glover: 178, 187 top, 188, 191 bottom.

Contents

Warning

Riding is a hazardous pastime. Horses are unpredictable and powerful animals and even something as seemingly simple as leading a horse in from the field can potentially be dangerous. Never underestimate the situation – think ahead. It is advisable to carry a phone with you and always seek help or advice if you are unsure about any aspect of horse care or equitation.

Foreword by Pat Parelli

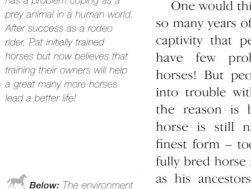

Right: *Pat Parelli has spent much of his life studying equines and realizes that despite thousands of years of breeding, an aggressive or problem horse is not a bad or untrainable horse but one that has a problem coping as a prey animal in a human world. After success as a rodeo rider, Pat initially trained horses but now believes that training their owners will help a great many more horses lead a better life!*

Below: *The environment in which we place a domestic horse is often a far cry from his natural state. By trying to curb his natural instincts, we risk putting a strain on both his mental and physical welfare.*

While there are fewer horses in use today than in centuries gone by, selective breeding and domestication have produced spectacular examples of the species.

One would think that after so many years of breeding in captivity that people would have few problems with horses! But people still get into trouble with them and the reason is because the horse is still nature in its finest form – today's beautifully bred horse remains as wild on the inside as his ancestors. That's because horses are prey animals. Their instincts for detecting danger, fleeing, reacting, and defending themselves in a split second are as sharp as ever. It's true that some horses are quieter than others, either as individuals or as a characteristic of their breed, but when it comes down to a horse feeling threatened, he'll act just like a wild horse. Horses get into trouble in the human environment because they are usually ill prepared for it. Dealing with confinement, horse trailers, and barbwire fences just isn't programmed into their genetic makeup!

This is where the dream turns into a nightmare. We buy our first horse dreaming of riding off into the sunset in perfect harmony, yet in reality this usually isn't so. So many horse-human relationships don't work out to the point that it's become the world of the disposable horse – if he's no good, sell him and get another one. Thousands of horses are destroyed because people don't know how to deal with them. They're so far from their natural state, caged in jail cells, fed unnaturally, no social interaction, not enough exercise, confined all day, all night, heads tied down, mouths tied shut, forced when they "disobey" our muddled commands to them…it's not hard to understand why a horse finally freaks out. Some horses cope with this unnatural world better than others, but the signs of disease are more prevalent than one would think. Stable vices, erratic behavior, colic, skin troubles, hoof troubles, behavioral problems…the list is far too long and it's time things changed.

An unhappy horse is definitely more of a challenge to handle than a horse who is happy on the inside, whose natural needs are attended to. Unfortunately, there's a great sense of dealing with horses in the same way "because that's the way we've always done it with horses." Difficult horses need people with more "savvy," a word that perfectly describes a level of understanding and competence that is almost instinctual. But even horses that are easy to handle and get along with will benefit from a more natural approach and more savvy in their human partner.

Left: Pat has devised a system of training that makes learning fun for the horse. There is no need for force and less chance of confusion or misinterpretation if the training mimics the games that horses themselves play in order to instigate a change in direction or gain the power of leadership. The combination of a suspicious and fearful "prey" animal being ridden by an aggressive, nervous, or unsympathetic rider requires a lot of effort on both sides if a "middle ground" is to be found where the pair can work as a partnership.

Having helped thousands of people and horses around the world improve their relationships with horses, I have discovered some important keys:

Stop "training" your horse and start "playing" with him

Horses are like kids in a classroom. They can only concentrate for so long, they hate work, they love to play, and they tend to excel under teachers who make learning fun. It's easy to knock the try and the love of learning out of a horse, so the responsibility is for us to find out what makes our individual horse tick…what's important to him. If the horse is recreation for us, how can we become recreation for him? A true partnership is mutually rewarding.

Put yourself in your horse's horseshoes

This means learning to think like a horse and trying to see things from his point of view. Having a greater understanding of the horse will help us avert problems as well as know how to do the exact right thing should the horse get emotionally upset. Think of it this way…if you knew the horse was acting out of fear, would you get firmer or do something that would help calm him? Learning how to read where your horse is coming from is a major key because all too often a horse's fearful reactions are misinterpreted as disobedience or defiance.

Both parties need to learn to use the "partnership side of their brain."

This means horses need to learn how to act less like a prey animal when with their human partner, and people need to learn to override their predator tendencies when their horse has trouble. Prey animals are designed to be eaten by predators so it's natural for them to be suspicious at some level. Problems arise when people get aggressive or get afraid (grab the rope or reins, clutch with their legs, get tight). In both cases the horse is likely to feel afraid and confused and to resist and will likely react in whatever way he feels necessary to defend himself. It would be easy to think that

66 Today's beautifully bred horse remains as wild on the inside as his ancestors. That's because horses are prey animals. Their instincts for detecting danger, fleeing, reacting, and defending themselves in a split second are as sharp as ever. 99

partnership side of the brain means that both parties are putting effort into understanding each other, overriding their instincts and so giving it a chance to work.

Give the horse his 10,000 acres

Approximately 10,000 acres is what the wild horse lives on and we think we've done the horse a favor with his 12 x 14 ft stall or five-acre paddock! Many horse owners live in the city and all they have available is the boarding stable with its barred stables. The question therefore must be "how do I give him that 10,000 acres?" You can't give it to him in physical space, but you can help fulfill some of his needs by playing with him. Most horses never get enough exercise (mustangs travel about 30 miles a day in the wild), let alone enough social interaction, mental and emotional stimulus (which is why they develop stall vices which actually cause the brain to release chemicals that act like a sedative, so they can escape their misery). So, the good news is, you're it! You need to satisfy those needs. If you can't get there every day, make sure he gets out of his stall for a good part of the day. When you are there, play with him! He needs you for this.

Love, language, and leadership in equal doses

With more and more women getting involved with horses, the happy part is that horses are getting more love these days then ever before. I have always thought that if we could pour an ounce of a man into a woman, and a gallon of woman into a man, we'd probably have the perfect horseman or horsewoman. There needs to be a balance between love and leadership or there'll be trouble in the relationship between horse and human. Too much love without enough leadership results in a disrespectful horse that will walk all over you. In their natural herd environment horses observe a pecking order, the leader being

Above: *Most of us have not got the facilities to give our horses the space, freedom of choice, and stimulation they would get living in a natural herd. Spending time with our horses – grooming them and playing games – will help to improve the animals' mental welfare and strengthen the bond between you.*

maybe the horse has a "behavior problem," but in my experience there are very few situations that aren't first provoked by an aggressive, fearful, unfeeling, or totally unconscious and accidental act from the human.

It is absolutely possible to teach horses to think before they react, and we can also learn to become mentally and emotionally fit enough to be able to calmly think through situations instead of panicking. Using the known as "alpha." When you interact with a horse, like it or not, you are entering his "herd." If you aren't alpha, your horse will try to be!

On the other hand, too much leadership without enough love can sour a horse. We've all seen the over-trained horse with no life in his eye, driven into submission. He's lost his personality (or should I say "horse-anality"!) and is usually resentful of the human or indifferent at best. Even horses in highly demanding sports can be developed in such a way that they enjoy what they do, if we know how to keep things true to their nature.

Horses are natural followers and they're looking for natural leaders. It's our responsibility to learn the appropriate leadership skills for the horse we bring into our lives and to be the kind of leader he respects, trusts, and wants to be with.

Having a language with which you can communicate with your horse is a vital part of a fulfilling relationship. If you think about it, most horses are trained to obey no more than a series of crude kicks to the ribs and pulls on the reins. No wonder there is so much resistance! Horses communicate with each other in a way much more sophisticated than we imagine, and most of it is through expression and body language. They are incredibly perceptive of the minutest changes in another horse's (or person's) look, feel, and intention, which can make it look as if they are capable of reading one's mind! For us to communicate better with horses, we don't need to teach them our language. We are

trying to get along better with them; therefore we need to learn their language. Can you imagine using a type of sign language that horses use and have your horse know exactly what you want?

Looking to the future

The next 100 years of horsemanship, I believe, are going to be incredible. In heading back to natural ways, studying the nature of horses, learning how to interact with them, and develop their talents in a fun way (as opposed to training the same old maneuver over and over and over) we're going to discover a whole new level of fulfillment from our horse-human partnerships.

There's no question that horses are good for people. Look at how much they help the handicapped, how they provide "therapy" and solace for the over-stressed and troubled. There is even thought that their electro-magnetic field influences hormonal balance in women (ever wondered why women are so drawn to horses in their pubescent and later years?). In bringing these magnificent creatures into our world, I believe we have a responsibility to make it as good for them as it is for us.

I applaud the objective of this book in helping to bring us to new levels of awareness with horses and their needs. I encourage you to embark of a lifetime of learning because even if that's not what you bargained for, your horse has plenty to teach you!

Pat Parelli
Colorado

Left: *Horses provide us with so much – companionship and sport, even a profession. Imagine how much more rewarding these achievements can be in a true, harmonious partnership.*

66 Horses are natural followers and they're looking for natural leaders. It's our responsibility to learn the appropriate leadership skills for the horse we bring into our lives and to be the kind of leader he respects, trusts, and wants to be with. 99

CHAPTER 1

Interequine Relationships

In recent years, a more natural approach to horse management has been actively promoted by welfare centers and equestrian organizations. It has become obvious that their efforts on behalf of horses have borne fruit. As owners of horses, we should realize that our moral obligation is to provide a natural lifestyle combined with good, individual care. In return, we will see happier, calmer, healthier animals, more willing and able to work and perform for us.

Keeping horses, whether it be for our pleasure, for profit, or as a professional undertaking, should never require them to be so cribbed and confined as to preclude them from enjoying social interaction with their own species.

Above: Signals gleaned from touch and smell play such a large part in a horse's life. If *only* we knew what they were saying... .
Right: There is no reason why domestic horses cannot be kept in a group environment. These foals are likely to have a mental and physical advantage over those kept solely with their dams.

Above: *As soon as they are sexually mature, wild male horses are treated as rivals by the lead stallion who will try to chase them out of the herd. These individuals often group up with others to form a "bachelor band." They seek out their own mares but are still conscious that there is safety in numbers in their fight for survival.*

> 66 Stallions lead a far more stressful life as they compete for supremacy in the herd but still remain reliant on each other for survival. 99

Unfortunately, providing company is not simply a case of turning out several animals together in a field or manège without any thought as to the likely consequences.

The Natural Behavior of Horses

In the wild there are predominantly two types of herds that roam the countryside. A typical herd consists of a lead stallion with a harem of mares accompanied by colts and fillies of varying ages. As well as the dominant stallion, there may well be a lead mare. From year to year, the "core" of the herd is likely to remain constant, although new foals will be added to the group, some elderly or weak animals will die, and some members will split off to form new herds. Although some conflict may arise when younger stallions attempt to challenge the dominant stallion in order to steal his mares, these groups tend on the whole to be harmonious, with a deep-rooted bond existing between the animals.

The other type of herd is the "bachelor band," consisting of mature and immature

males who have not yet been able to acquire a mare to establish their own family groups. These stallions lead a far more stressful life as they compete for supremacy in the herd but still remain reliant on each other for survival.

It is quite amazing how horses cope with domestication and the lifestyle that we impose on them which is so different from the way they evolved to live in the wild. However, when you consider just how simple their *raisons d'être* really are, we should consider ourselves fortunate that their needs can be catered for relatively easily.

Horses' natural basic desires are as follows:

❏ Find adequate food, water, and shelter from the elements.
❏ Be a member of a healthy herd – whether it be the leader or a follower – as an aid to survival and for social stability.

❑ Breed successfully in order to guarantee the future viability of the herd.

How Domestic Horses Behave

The innate natural desires of the wild horse still play a large part in shaping the behavior of an animal when it is born into a domestic situation.

The first necessity – that of finding food, water, and shelter – has been very much taken over by the human caretaker for a horse, who acts rather like the dominant figure in the herd. However, one must recognize that wild

horses have a great deal more individual control over their diet and physical/geographic location than a domestic horse does.

The second requirement – that of being a member of a herd – is still an important factor in managing equines today. Social interaction should be encouraged, although humans also need to establish their own position in the hierarchy of the group.

The third point – the importance of breeding for wild horses – has very much been suppressed in domestic situations because the majority of male horses are gelded and the relatively low numbers of "entire" stallions throughout the world are seldom free to seek out their own breeding partners. Although castration may seem an unnatural operation, it does encourage the animals to adopt a more acceptable lifestyle when in the ownership of the average caretaker. Young colts that are not gelded can soon actually become dangerous, incessantly mounting mares and becoming aggressive as there is rarely an adult stallion to keep them in line.

LIGHT LEVELS

Horses respond to and are affected by the hours of daylight. Mares' estrus cycles run for about six months. The urge and ability to conceive is triggered by the lengthening of days in the spring.

Above: Staying close to a water source is a high priority. There is even a pecking order when it comes to who can drink first. Usually the lead mare enjoys this particular privilege.

Left: Youngstock can expend a great deal of energy playing with each other. Competitiveness is evident even at a young age.

Above left: Some domestic stallions, such as this purebred Exmoor, are allowed to run with the herd as they would do in the wild.

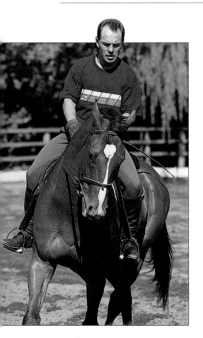

Above: *Horses can be uncooperative or "nappy" when asked to leave the herd to be ridden. Keeping all the horses together which are worked at the same time and varying the type of work undertaken can help to lessen the wrench.*

Man-making a Herd

The maximum size of a herd depends first on the space available. Conflict will almost certainly arise if animals are forced into too small an area or if food is scarce. Horses will only let trusted friends step inside their area of personal space, which is like a circle around them about two horses' lengths in diameter. They feel threatened by other horses encroaching within this area and need space to get away.

If you are turning animals out in a standard-size manège, a maximum of six ponies or four horses should be put together and this population density should always be under supervision. For temporary turnout, a 1-acre (0.4 ha) paddock could be used for three animals. For year-round turnout, though, 1.5 acres (0.6 ha) per animal should be allowed, so 4.5 acres (1.8 ha) would be required.

For owners of commercial yards of ten animals or more, the following principles can help in the formation of a larger herd.

❏ Keep animals together who obviously get along well, regardless of sex, age, or size.

> **66** Conflict will almost certainly arise if animals are forced into too small an area or if food is scarce. **99**

❏ Keep animals together that require the same dietary intake, e.g., all laminitic ponies can be monitored together or all horses/ponies receiving a short-feed could be kept together to avoid squabbling over food.

❏ In the same way, all horses worked in the afternoon can be kept separately from those worked in the morning to avoid problems of certain animals not wanting to be caught and made to leave their companions.

❏ Try to form a large herd slowly – begin with a maximum of six animals and subsequently introduce additional animals, in pairs, every couple of days.

❏ Pair-bonds should generally not be split up.

❏ Ideally, mares and geldings should be mixed provided the numbers are fairly evenly matched. However, if there are 12 geldings and one mare, it is preferable to keep the mare and a single gelding separately from the remaining 11 geldings. Be aware that some geldings do not mix well with mares as they tend to be too possessive or too aggressive.

PERSONAL SPACE
Many horses feel threatened if their personal space is invaded. They are conscious of an imaginary boundary and may only allow pair bonds or close friends within this area.

Right: *These ponies are grazing apart but are well aware of each other's proximity. Maintaining an area of adequate space around them mitigates confrontational behavior and bullying.*

❏ Elderly animals are less threatened when kept with other veteran animals or youngstock who tend to be more submissive.

❏ Horses need permanence to create a stable herd. People often unwittingly cause chaos by chopping and changing groups turned out together, a situation which is usually the cause of bullying and injury. Any new animal introduced into the herd may upset the apple cart and it can take at least a week to re-establish harmony.

When merging several small groups into one larger herd where potentially several high-ranking individuals may start to compete to be the overall leader, you are likely to see competitive displays. Vocal roars and squeals,

lashing out in front and behind, and driving away rivals will establish relative status. While this may seem an unacceptable risk for our valuable domestic animals, horses are rarely viciously aggressive and the situation should stabilize within an hour or two. In fact, the universal language used among horses ensures that each animal finds its place in the herd to ensure the future safety and stability of the unit.

Horses that are not raised with other horses are sometimes socially inept around their own kind and may never learn to fit in with a herd. These animals may have to be kept separate or with one other companion who proves compatible. Otherwise they may face a life of being bullied and made miserable by others.

Above: *Introducing any new animals will unsettle the herd until the newcomer's status is established. Try not to chop and change grazing companions or there may be displays of aggression. Disharmony can lead to stressed animals who will suffer mentally and physically.*

🐎 **Above:** *Foals learn horse "language" quickly. Although their mother is their mentor and protector, the more role models they have at a young age, the better their social skills will turn out to be.*

THREATS

When threatened or afraid, there are four choices for a horse: FIGHT the aggressor FLEE the scene FREEZE to the spot FAINT to shut down awareness – even at the sight of a veterinarian's needle!

It helps to establish a pair-bond between a nervous, submissive animal and a more dominant figure prior to their introduction into the herd (or you could remove them and re-introduce them after they have formed a partnership). This will ensure that the submissive animal is not ranked bottom of the herd. For example, if one animal has the lowest position in the herd and its pair-bond is ranked third in a herd of 15, the status of the lower horse will be raised when its pair-bond is present, and it is less likely to get bullied.

Integrating Foals into the Herd

I cannot understand why some horse breeders and stud farms do not follow nature in their methods of raising foals. They often segregate the new mother and foal for several weeks or months and then, at weaning, the foal is abruptly parted from its mother to live with a group of other weanlings or youngsters. Although breeders may feel this leads to easier handling, quite the opposite is true. It is a case of the blind leading the blind as a bunch of confused youngsters attempt to learn what is expected of them without the presence of mature horses to set an example.

A far better and more natural approach would be to integrate the new foal into the herd at the earliest opportunity (at birth or a day or so after), so that it can live in a multiage group with a variety of role models for security, stimulation, and guidance. In a herd, the mare can also more easily be separated for gentle exercise, feeding, etc., without causing distress to the foal.

As with most aspects of horse care, certain methods and practices have been established over the course of many years and they are now simply seen as the "correct" method. Breeders generally choose to wean foals at between four and six months of age, whereas in the wild, a mare would continue to feed this foal until a few weeks before she foaled again (about nine months). It is sad that many foals are sold before this time just for economic gain. The excuse that "the foal will drag the mare down" can only be attributed to poor care and feeding by the owners of these broodmares.

COMMUNICATION BETWEEN HORSES

Horses have a far more complex physical "language" than we do. I would not say it is a superior language to ours. However, it has the advantage that it is universal among socialized equines, whatever their breed, type, or country of origin.

The two senses of smell and hearing are actually far more acute than ours. Taste and touch are probably about the same as our own. However, their sight and speech abilities fall short of those that humans possess.

However, despite horses' smaller brain size and lack of complex articulated speech, their communication skills are highly refined and their sensitivity to their surroundings is far more advanced than our own. We have little fear of our surroundings. In our modern world, far less importance is placed on using our sense of hearing to warn of danger – it tends to be limited to such "dangerous" activities as crossing a road. In humans, hearing is predominantly for pleasure or social intercourse, for listening to music and speech, etc. Certainly, we do not use ear movements to communicate signals of pleasure/displeasure as horses do. We use spoken language to express ourselves with the addition of body language. For instance, arm gestures and facial expressions are used to emphasize our meaning or overall demeanor. Horses, even those in a safe domestic situation, still react as prey animals even though there is very little chance of any wild carnivorous predator

> **66** On a calm day, equines appear far more at ease when grazing. While on a blustery day, when the wind has the effect of muffling and confusing sound signals, horses often appear agitated and restless. **99**

(including a human one) stalking them from the bushes! For instance, on a calm day, equines appear far more at ease when grazing. While on a blustery day, when the wind has the effect of muffling and confusing sound signals, horses often appear agitated and restless. It would be very unusual to see horses lying down outside on a blustery day as this would leave them exposed and vulnerable to undetected predators.

The Sense of Hearing

A horse's ears are set high on the head. Each ear has 16 muscles that allow the ear to move through almost 180°, both independently of

Above: *A prey animal needs to be sensitive to external stimuli in order to react quickly to stay alive. The senses of hearing and smell are highly refined in the horse.*

Left: *Young and old meet with great interest. Young foals have little sense of fear themselves and pose no threat to adult equines.*

BRAIN SIZE
A horse's brain – small by human standards – is large for similarly sized herbivores.

THE EXPRESSIVE LANGUAGE OF EARS

We can learn so much simply by watching a horse's ears.

I'm alert and friendly

I'm relaxed

I'm attentive

I'm angry

I'm afraid

I'm in pain or unhappy

the sound and amplify it, rather in the way that cupping your hand behind your ear cuts out background noise and enhances incoming sound from one direction. The ears are usually the first of the senses to detect something interesting and the horse will swing his head and body round to face the sound with both ears pointing forwards trained on the sound while the eyes search for the visual target.

A domestic horse doing ridden flatwork will more often than not be seen with ears pointing in different directions, one forward taking in sounds in the direction that the horse is travelling and one back, showing his concentration on the rider's instructions. Advanced movements in dressage may require

Above left: *The ears are like radars, constantly picking up sounds from all directions. Their funnel shape serves to channel and amplify sounds.*

Left: *As this horse approaches the jump, his focus and ears are directed solely on the object. A few strides earlier, one ear may have flicked back to seek guidance from the rider.*

the head and in different directions from each other. They can pick up a far greater range of high- and low-frequency sounds than our own ears and have a greater ability to pinpoint the direction and source of the signal. The fur lining serves to protect the inner ear from flying insects and from foreign bodies, such as grass seeds, from dropping in while grazing. As a prey animal, it is essential for a horse to be aware of any encroaching predators and to pick up signals from the rest of the herd that may give advance warning of danger.

The ability to point an ear accurately in a specific direction and the overall funnel shape of the pinna (outer ear) serve to channel

the horse to focus his attention fully on the rider, especially when learning a new movement. A trained eye is needed to distinguish between a happy, submissive horse seeking instructions from his rider and a horse with flattened ears showing resistance to the rider and indicating poor communication skills between them.

If a pole or jump is introduced during schooling, the horse's ears will generally be pricked forward, showing concentration on the object ahead, while one ear just flicks back for a brief moment to pick up information from the rider. This also applies to cross-country, where the fast pace and obstacles to be cleared

muzzle and the area immediately above and behind the horse (and below his belly). By tilting his head to the side or moving his neck slightly, even these "blind" spots can be viewed. Horses use their eyes independently of each other and only focus with both eyes at once when looking at something directly ahead. To be able to judge distances accurately,

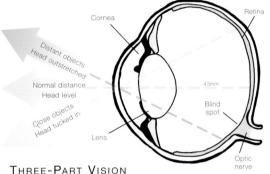

THREE-PART VISION
To focus properly the horse must either raise or lower his head depending on the distance of the object being viewed.

however, they must have the target object in front of them and be able to focus on it with both eyes.

Horses are peculiar in the way their vision functions. Humans and most animals have a concave retina in the eye and focus by altering the shape or position of the lens in relation to the cornea. This controls the angle that light hits the retina. It was thought that the dramatic way a horse raises, lowers, and tilts his head to focus properly was caused by equines having a "ramped" retina which resulted in the distance from the center of the lens to the retina varying depending on the angle that light hit it. We now think that while horses have a very wide area of vision, there is a relatively narrow field in which the vision is sharp and this is what causes the head movements as the horse tries to bring an object into this field of clarity.

mean that the horse must be primarily aware of what he is approaching and only turn this focus away for brief moments when asking for or receiving information from the rider.

The Sense of Sight

Horses can certainly recognize objects, people, and animals by sight alone but more often than not the senses of smell and hearing are needed to confirm whether it is a familiar person, animal, or object that they see approaching. They seldom rely on their vision alone, which lacks the clarity and full color spectrum of that of a human.

The eyes of a horse are set on each side of his head (a sign of a prey animal), which allows him a wider field of vision. In fact, the only spots a horse cannot see are a small area directly in front of the

> ❝ Horses use their eyes independently of each other and only focus with both eyes at once when looking at something directly ahead. ❞

Far left: *Horses use their eyes independently of each other – only focusing with both eyes together when looking directly ahead or when judging distances.*

Below: *Prey animals have eyes set on each side of their head to allow peripheral vision for early warning of approaching predators.*

Distant | Normal | Close

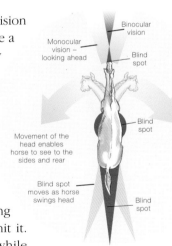

BLIND SPOTS
A horse has blind spots immediately in front of its muzzle, behind its rear quarters, and below its belly. Moving the head allows the horse to see laterally and to the rear.

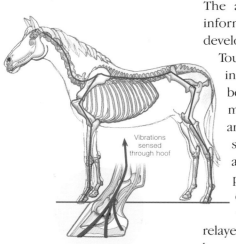

SENSING MOVEMENT
Movement can be detected from vibrations felt in the hoof and transmitted up the limbs.

Vibrations sensed through hoof

🐎 **Above:** *Touching muzzles communicates many signals, including playfulness, affection, recognition, or simple curiosity.*

The Sense of Touch

The ability of horses to give and receive information through touch is highly developed.

Touching with the muzzle plays a huge part in the daily life of a horse. Touching between animals (and humans) transmits messages and tastes/smells which identify and reinforce a sense of familiarity and security. Animals will also lick each other as an expression of affection. Touch also plays a large part in awareness of their environment. New objects and even food will be identified by the information relayed to the brain by the nerve endings at the base of each whisker and the surface of the skin, which have a high sensory capacity.

It is fascinating to watch a horse when a fly or leaf has landed on it. Even if it is out of reach of the tail to be swished away, the skin is able to twitch in precisely the correct location to remove the object of annoyance. Again, it is the simple fact of being a prey animal that has led to this characteristic – it is vital in the survival stakes to utilize all the senses to give advance warning of danger.

Although they may not have the same "fingertip" sensation as we do, horses, like many other animals, have the ability to pick up the slightest ground vibrations warning them of the movements of other animals, humans, and vehicles. The vibrations travel through the hoof wall, sole, and frog, are transmitted through the limb bones to the skull, and are registered by the internal and middle ear. Hard ground amplifies the vibrations, whereas these signals are partially absorbed and will not be so evident on soft ground.

Although not particularly dexterous when compared to human hands, the hooves and forelimbs are often used to examine or expose

objects on the gound. This is common in animals where there is a fear of the unknown and it would be unwise to lower the head and explore the object further with the muzzle until any chance of the object biting or spitting (as a snake might) has been ruled out.

The Senses of Smell and Taste

The sense of smell is of vital importance from the moment a foal is born. In a natural herd situation, it may well be difficult for the foal to recognize which of the many mares is his mother. He will have to rely on his mother's instinct and sense of smell to enable her to recognize him. Quickly he will learn to recognize his mother and the other members of the herd from the pheromones (chemical secretions) that are transmitted through the skin and from the scent of individual droppings and urine. Horses often greet each

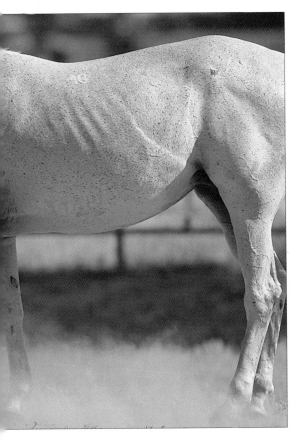

other by blowing and sniffing nostril to nostril, and they will also lick one another.

Any encounters with a new object or animal will be fully analyzed by smell to establish whether it poses a threat or not. Odors and flavors are actually minute particles that dissolve on the moist mucous membranes of the nasal passages and mouth and are translated into messages to the brain.

The ability to receive scent messages is further enhanced by the "Flehmen" response. This is when a horse raises his head to a horizontal position and curls back his top lip, which allows the Jacobson's organ (the vomeronasal organ) at the top of the nasal passage to assess the smell. Stallions frequently display this response during courtship when gauging a mare's willingness to mate. However, it is frequently seen being

> **It is fascinating to watch a horse when a fly or leaf has landed on it. Even if it is out of reach of the tail, the skin is able to twitch in precisely the correct location to remove the object of annoyance.**

Left: *When faced with a strange object, the action of pawing it with a foreleg allows the animal initially to keep a safe distance before investigating further.*

Left: *Horses often greet each other by blowing or sniffing nostrils. Information gained from the odor and flavor droplets they exchange in this way is transmitted to the brain.*

Above: *The "Flehmen" response allows for deeper intake of scent particles and is usually a reaction to an unfamiliar smell. Stallions assess the readiness of mares to mate in this way.*

FAVORITE GROOMING SITES

These are the areas most frequently groomed by other horses. It is mainly youngsters who nibble on one another's hocks.

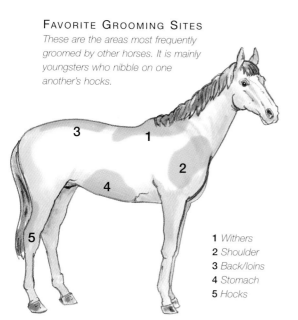

1 *Withers*
2 *Shoulder*
3 *Back/loins*
4 *Stomach*
5 *Hocks*

Above right: *Grooming plays a huge part in the well-being of horses. Make a point of allowing them this daily ritual – remove their rugs if necessary. Most horses enjoy being groomed by humans too!*

Below: *Rolling is a good measure of a contented and healthy animal as equines rarely roll unless they feel relaxed because they are vulnerable while on the ground. Rolling not only covers the hairs in a layer of dirt but also serves to remove "itchy" parasites and dead skin and to imprint the scent of the herd on the animal.*

used in a nonsexual way simply as a reaction to an unfamiliar or strong smell.

Marking territory is done by scent marking in the form of urinating or defecating. Some animals will actually cover up the smell of another by defecating or urinating over the top of the other horse's excrement.

Displays of Affection

Horses are very sociable animals and are happiest in a well-established herd with long-term friends. This applies to human friends as well and it is a shame that domestic horses tend to change hands so frequently, as this breaks their relationships and unsettles their way of life every few years.

Grooming This is performed between close members of the herd or pair-bond companions. It is usually the more dominant animal who will initiate the grooming session by positioning himself parallel to the other

> 66 **It is usually the more dominant animal who will initiate the grooming session by positioning himself parallel to the other horse and touching its shoulder or neck with his muzzle.** 99

horse and touching its shoulder or neck with his muzzle. They will then perform a kind of ritual using a combination of upper lip massages in a circular motion and gentle teeth nips. Working their way along the shoulder, withers, back, and sides, they will suddenly stop and walk backward or swing their necks over/under and reposition themselves to scratch the other side. It seems an excellent way of not only removing parasites, mud, and loose hair but also of cementing social relationships by allowing the other animal to share such a close space.

It gives me great pleasure to watch my horses grooming. In the winter when they are wearing rugs, I make a point of removing the rugs every couple of days for an hour or so (despite the cold) – within 30 seconds the horses are grooming each other. Sometimes, they are so keen that they start before I have even finished removing the rugs!

Nudging Horses and ponies are often seen nudging other horses' bodies with their heads or nudging their owners. From observation, it seems primarily to serve the purpose of a scratching post coupled with a show of affection or attention seeking. A horse's forehead is a very vulnerable area; it has little protective skin, and a vision blind spot exists between the eyes. By rubbing this area on a "soft" person or another horse/pony, they can be pretty certain that they will not encounter any dangerous unseen protrusions that may cause injury. This is also why you so often see horses rubbing their heads up and down on a soft haynet. Nudging can also be a type of dominant behavior.

Rolling Although this is often done to relieve an itch by dislodging a troublesome fly or as a dust bath after sweating, horses frequently roll in the same patch which serves to imprint the herd smell on them and any other animals that follow. Rolling also serves to fill the coat with dirt to protect the skin from insects and parasites.

Horses will usually only roll when they are fully relaxed and another animal is on guard as they feel vulnerable when not on their feet.

Playing All equines, from foals to veterans, indulge in play from time to time, although it is more common in younger animals. They may appear from a distance to be fighting by rearing up together and boxing and swinging around and bucking and kicking in the air, but most movements are not intended actually to make physical contact – they are merely an expression of high spirits. I have seen a very unlikely pair of domestic horses play fight, which was all the more amusing as one was a 16.2hh (hh means "hands high," a "hand" being 4 inches 10 cm) warmblood and one was a Shetland pony. The Shetland would assert his position and rear up confidently and the warmblood would kneel on one front leg from time to time to get down nearer to his playmate.

Teeth snapping Foals and youngstock curl

Above: Teeth snapping is a sign of submission, implying "I'll do as you wish" or "I'm worried."

Left: Play fighting is generally an expression of high spirits. Interaction in this way establishes relationships and releases mental and physical tension. Although the animals may not intend to make physical contact, injuries can unfortunately occur, especially with shod animals.

their lips back and make a snapping movement with their teeth. This is a signal of submission and is usually directed at their mother or another older member of the herd.

Displays of Aggression

Bullying Horses can form close friendships with any member of the herd, regardless of age or sex. However, in a herd situation, certain horses may be excluded if they are not fully accepted by the dominant members of the herd. Those favored by the herd leaders will take up superior positions, whereas others

may merely act as "hangers on." Repeated bullying will cause an animal a great deal of stress and, if attacked or deprived of food by the others, could lead to death.

In a domestic situation, if a dominant member of the herd has singled out one submissive animal, it may become an easy target for the others to bully or exclude from sources of food and water. Horses can be surprisingly aggressive to other herd members. You must observe their actions when turning them out in a group to ensure that an elderly or weaker animal is not being abused. If only two animals are kept together, this is less likely to happen, although one is certain to be dominant over the other.

Charging When horses charge and lunge with an outstretched neck at another animal, be it another horse or perhaps a dog, it is an obvious sign that they are trying to force the other animal back. This is an aggressive movement rather than one made in self-defense. It can be backed up with the baring of teeth while the ears

Pair-bonds affect herd status

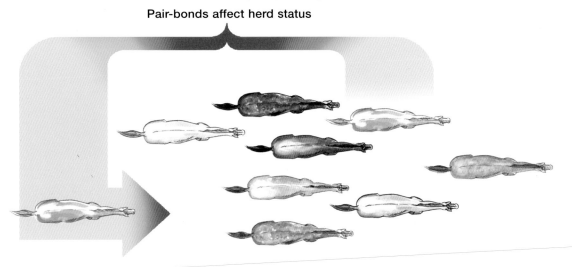

HERD HIERARCHY
A pair-bond established between these two horses will raise the status of the lower-ranking animal within the herd.

Right: Kicking out with a foreleg is generally intended to maintain personal space, whereas a "two-barreled" kick from behind is more likely to make actual contact.

> ❝ In a domestic situation, if a dominant member of the herd has singled out one submissive animal, it may become an easy target for the others to bully or exclude from sources of food and water. ❞

are pinned back. If this is ignored, the aggressor may actually bite the animal and strike out with a foreleg.

Stallions competing for status in a wild herd may sustain violent injuries with torn skin from bites or kicks. Their battles can last for hours, until one is finally too tired or weak to continue. Domestic horses tend only to "battle" for a couple of minutes if they are pressured into a corner or want to assert themselves and protect the space around them, especially if food is short.

Kicking Horses are conscious that kicking out from behind is a good defense against injury because only their rump is exposed to attack. By turning their head a fraction to one side, they have a good view of their aggressor. Most people don't notice the warning signs as the change in posture is so minimal, but it's no surprise to other horses. With ears back and sometimes tail raised, they warn their rivals. The timing of the strike is crucial as to whether it actually makes contact, but any horse that has sustained a full "two-barreled" kick in the chest is going to take care not to come up against it again.

Kicking out with the forelegs This is not usually an aggressive movement but more of an assertive warning action, usually when greeting a new animal.

Above: Charging or lunging is an aggressive action to drive away another animal. Fights are generally over status, mating, or food. However, as horses also rely on one another for safety, they rarely use more than a "warning" to provoke a desired response.

Understanding Facial Expressions and Body Language

The ears are a great signal of a horse's mood – combined with other facial expressions and body language, these signs communicate to us, and to other horses, pleasure, pain, fear, submission, intolerance, and aggression.

Picture 1 A relaxed, resting horse may well carry his ears splayed sideways or even backwards. His whole demeanor will be soft, with droopy eyelids and even a hanging lower lip. His tail will be down but still swinging loose to act as a flyswatter. He may well rest a hindleg and lock his front knee joints to enable him to rest fully while still upright. An unwell animal may well appear similar to this. Howerver, unlike a healthy animal who would quickly show an interest in sudden activity or a feed treat being offered, an animal in pain would show little interest in any stimulation.

Picture 2 Relaxed animals with a loose, swinging gait, low tail carriage and soft facial expressions. Although calm, they are still aware of their surroundings and their ears are listening for sounds. They are ready for action in a split second.

Picture 3 An alert ridden animal, showing a higher tail carriage and an altogether more compact, "higher" movement, with hocks underneath him and neck and head carried "on the bit." His ears show he is concentrating on both the direction of going and the rider on his back. His jaw muscles and eyes are more active as he is concentrating on the job in hand.

Picture 4 A startled or frightened horse. His whole body is inclined backward, away from the source of fear. His muscles are tense. He is likely to spin around and try to run away. His ears are locked onto the object

Picture 1 (above) A relaxed horse will have "soft" ears, muzzle, and nostrils. His facial muscles may be so relaxed that his lip droops.

Picture 2 (below) This contented pair move with a free, swinging pace but are still very aware of their surroundings and any threats.

Picture 4 (above) Some horses are inherently nervous, whereas others have a more laid-back nature. This horse is "on his toes" and will probably snort at the offending object before spinning round to flee.

> **The ears are a great signal of a horse's mood – combined with other facial expressions and body language, these signs communicate to us, and to other horses, pleasure, pain, fear, submission, intolerance, and aggression.** ""

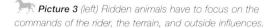

Picture 3 (left) Ridden animals have to focus on the commands of the rider, the terrain, and outside influences.

causing the anxiety, his nostrils are flared, and we can see the whites of his eyes.

Picture 5 An angry or unhappy facial expression with ears pinned back, hard eyes, and clenched jaw. His tail will also be clamped down, showing displeasure or swishing violently. This is a warning and, if ignored, may be reinforced by more aggressive behavior.

Picture 6 An aggressive stance showing ears pinned back, nostrils and upper lip curled back, and teeth bared. As well as serving as a warning, this prevents his protruding ears from being bitten or torn by his opponent. The lunging neck is "pushing" the opponent away, and he may well charge at him. If this display is

Picture 5 (above) Think carefully before approaching this horse! His facial expression is not welcoming. He is warning you to stay away – perhaps he has seen his tack!

*Picture 6 (left) This is certainly **not** mutual grooming. With a hard eye, flattened ears, and curled lip, his victim is about to lose some hair!*

ignored, it is likely to be followed up by a sharp bite. Swinging around to kick the animal is usually used as the last resort.

Picture 7 This high-spirited horse is showing off and displaying his physical prowess. He may just be happy to be out on new pasture, or a new horse or pony may have been introduced to the herd. This playful behavior can be recognized by his high neck

Picture 7 (above) The magnificence of the horse is most evident in displays of exuberance and high spirits. Taut muscles, elevated paces, and high tail carriage show how beautifully athletic horses are. Transitions from a gallop to a standstill and back again are easy.

Below: *"Don't leave me!" – a neigh travels over long distances and can be a desperate cry of "Where are you?" in the hope that a familiar reply will identify the location of a companion.*

Foot of page: *Playful animals often squeal with excitement when a familiar horse or person approaches.*

carriage, raised tail, and elevated strides, which may even culminate in an exuberant rear or a buck. Although not being in the slightest aggressive, it is unwise to get too close or block the path of such a highly charged animal. In a domestic herd situation, all the animals may well stampede around the perimeter of the field, suddenly coming to an abrupt stop and setting off again in a different direction. Once one animal decides to calm down, the rest follow quickly and the display ends.

Understanding Vocal Signals

Vocal communication between equines is generally secondary to the information picked up from visual signals and the subtle physical movements of their companions. It does, however, enable communication over greater distances where a horse's sensitive hearing can pick up far more information than can be derived from any long-range visual signals. Vocal calls are also used to broadcast obvious greeting messages to other equines, as well as warnings or displays of apprehension or excitement.

Whinny A loud high-pitched call made with the mouth open, usually used to signal to horses that are out of sight and to greet approaching friends. It enables horses to make others aware of their presence and to establish the location of those that are replying, if they are out of sight.

Neigh A loud, lower-pitched call which can travel over long distances. Insecure animals whose companions are taken away will often neigh incessantly in a frantic attempt to get a reply to enable them to locate their companion. This is usually a deeper, longer, more desperate sounding neigh than the higher-pitched shorter "hello" whinny.

Nicker A wonderful low-pitched, soft, staccato sound made with the mouth closed and used to display pleasure and to welcome friends in close proximity. It is used by stallions to display appreciation of a mare, by dams as a maternal call to a foal, and by all equines to greet a close companion (equine or human) or as a display of pleasure in domestic horses at the sight of food bowls being offered.

Snort A forceful expulsion of air through the nostrils heard from horses expressing alarm. In a herd situation it will alert other members to potential danger. When encountering a strange object or animal, horses often stand tall and snort loudly. The flared nostrils pick up the strange scent and the snort itself can signify alarm or fear as well as merely excitement.

Squeal A shrill, high-pitched shriek which can be heard during play to signify excitement and delight. However, it which is most commonly used as a protest signal when another animal is too close or to signify that its presence is unwelcome. This is often voiced by mares when a stallion (or gelding) chooses to introduce himself to her and is often

accompanied by a swift striking out of a foreleg to warn him to keep his distance.

Roar As its name suggests, a fierce scream generally only used by rival stallions showing extreme aggression when battling over status in the herd.

Blow A soft blowing through the nostrils, used not only to clear the airways but often also as a sign of contentment.

Grunt/groan These have no real meanings in terms of conversation, but are expressions of exertion or pain, for example, during foaling, getting up from rolling, or due to colic pain.

The Natural Rhythms of Sleep

Horses generally sleep for about four hours out of a 24-hour period. These naps are taken in short periods of 20–30 minutes at a time. This is because, as a prey animal, horses need to be constantly alert to potential danger. The time it takes to wake and get up from their lying position can make them vulnerable to attack. Their need to feel secure before lying down and the manner in which the herd takes

turns to rest and watch over the other members has not changed in centuries of domestication – despite there being very few lions lurking in fields these days!

Most sleep tends to be taken in the early hours of the morning between 2 A.M. and 4 A.M. and also in the early afternoon, although horses may lie down at any time if they feel safe and relaxed.

Horses can also rest for long periods of time in a standing position, thanks to their ability to "lock" the joints and ligaments in their elbows and stifles. They can doze in this position but have to lie down flat in order to dream and experience a deep sleep.

A domestic horse that feels stressed or insecure, or feels uneasy about lying down in the confined space of his stable, will be hampered physically and mentally if he is deprived of deep sleep. Horses will generally choose a dry spot to lie down and a field-kept horse may only get snatches of sleep if weather conditions are constantly wet and blustery with no shelter provided.

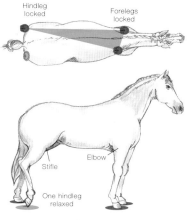

Above: *Horses seldom lie down unless they feel safe, so horses in groups are generally more likely to lie down in exposed areas than solitary animals.*

LOCKING MECHANISM
Horses have the ability to lock the joints and ligaments in their elbows and stifles to enable them to sleep standing upright without falling over.

CHAPTER 2

Your Relationship With Your Horse

Being in the company of any horse or pony should be a pleasure for you both. People who are accustomed to equines often find it amusing to watch nervous or novice riders approaching horses as they often show a very real fear of the animals. Worried about which end will "attack" them first, they tiptoe around the horse, jumping back in panic when he decides to rest a hind leg, or swing his head around to ward off an irritating fly! This may seem funny, but in reality most horses do not suffer fools gladly and humans can put themselves in very real danger if they do not understand the language of horses.

When handling equines, even small ponies, safety should be taken very seriously at all times – with body weights averaging between 770–1,760 pounds (350–800 kg), there is a very real potential risk of being hurt.

Above: Humans look like a predator but act like a friend – very confusing!
Right: *Pat Parelli is a true master of horses – he takes their instincts into account.*

COMMUNICATION

*Expert horse people advise that you **discuss** things with a stallion, **ask** a mare, and **tell** a gelding. This may be a generalization, but it often holds true.*

How many of us have been (very embarrassingly) dragged along when leading only a yearling or small pony. If we had actually thought what their natural instinct is (i.e., following the other ponies) and reacted accordingly, we would have avoided nose-diving into the mud and the telltale rope burns on our hands.

By understanding our animals, ideally to the degree of anticipating most of their actions before they occur, we can not only remain safe but also develop the relationship we share beyond that of simply a rider and mount partnership. By improving communication and trust, it naturally follows that both ease of handling from the ground and our mounted performance will benefit greatly.

> 66 ...most horses do not suffer fools gladly and humans can put themselves in very real danger if they do not understand the language of horses. 99

I believe that most people fall into the category of either being a good *rider* or a good *caretaker*. It is the lucky few who are more than simply utility riders and yet can devote time and energy into seeking a stimulating and rewarding partnership when off their mounts.

Sadly, people too often treat horses as a "pet" to be confined to their stables and pampered and petted as an expensive toy that can be shown off to friends. Others see their equines as a machine, bought and paid for to accumulate prizes or money rather than a creature with a nervous system and brain. They can lose the simple joy of relating to their horses as living beings, merely viewing their horses as something to be mastered in their quest for improved technique.

Above: *Horses are not living machines, nor are they purely pets. The most rewarding partnerships are those that combine love, respect, fun, and challenges. You don't have to win prizes to have a rewarding relationship. Just spending time together should give you real pleasure.*

Right: *Children often have an affinity with horses and ponies. Their innocence allows them to enjoy their animals without the barriers of fear or preconceived ideas.*

Getting the balance right between the two attitudes should be our goal. Horses do actually want "friends" (human and equine) plus mental and physical stimulation and play. We can give them what they want in the forms of both exercising at liberty and having a job to do under our guidance.

The Importance of Compatibility

When choosing horses, most people use only the physical appearance of the horse by which to judge its suitability. Any insights into temperament and character that we do manage to glean from the previous owner are

Above: People forget horses have different personalities and aptitudes. Just because you may like schooling every day, your horse may not be so keen. So don't abuse their tolerance and **be fair** – horses have off days too!

equally valuable as it is this two-way understanding between horse and rider that holds the key to a happy and successful partnership.

We may also have a tendency to prefer mares to geldings, or vice versa, judging by our past experiences and the level of understanding we have achieved with the respective sexes. I have always considered myself as a "mare" person, thriving on their sensitivity and enjoying their intelligent and

complex natures. Recently, I have come to appreciate the more forgiving and affectionate personality that many geldings possess. So all I can recommend is that you should treat each animal as an individual and hope that you will find your soulmate!

Above: You may think you have the upper hand but never underestimate a horse. Horses are **big** – take safety seriously!

For the average owner who cannot spend 24 hours a day keeping their horse well exercised, mentally stimulated, properly fed and cared for, a sharer is of great benefit to both you and your horse.

One of my horses, Harry, is ridden regularly by two people other than myself. He is an active and inquisitive type. Although he is kept out in the field with company, I feel he would like more of a "job" to do to keep his mind occupied. It is obvious to me that he enjoys being taken out for rides by these ladies, and loves the extra attention they give him – not to mention the extra tidbits! We all exchange stories of how he has bolted or bucked out of sheer exuberance or behaved impeccably when faced with a challenge, and I do not feel jealous that they are riding "my" horse. Quite the contrary, I am grateful for their input into Harry's life.

Above: Horses are versatile creatures and cope amazingly well with different riders and different types of work. Cross training is both enjoyable and beneficial as a good way of keeping a horse interested in work.

Right: Sharing your horse can be rewarding to all parties. The input from another person can add so much in terms of positive encouragement – not to mention practical and financial assistance!

Accept Your Limitations

Just as we have our fortcs and our weaknesses, one horse cannot be "all things to all men." We tend to expect that, with training, our horses should be able to do anything. We rarely make allowances for conformation and certainly not for inclination or aptitude. I believe that cross-training is very important. However, we should be aware of the forms of work that each horse enjoys and excels at, and not force our animals through particular types of training when there is an obvious failing or resistance. Bear in mind that horses have off days too!

Why Not Share Your Horse or Pony?

If you believe that you alone are the best person to ride your horse, then you are probably being arrogant. Unless you and your horse work together every day and have established a superb partnership, you should not ignore the potential benefits of allowing another person to have contact with him.

> 66 If you believe that you alone are the best person to ride your horse, then you are probably being arrogant. 99

It is necessary to establish that anyone caring for or riding your horse will be responsible and is sufficiently experienced in riding and handling horses that safety will not be compromised. Many people worry that it will confuse the horse to be ridden by several people as their aids may well be slightly different, but I have found that horses soon learn exactly who is riding them and act accordingly. It is not only the subtle aids that may change, but the weight of each rider may well be very different too. You may actually find that your horse improves as a result of the schooling sessions from a "detached" person who may well be fitter and more focused than you are. Alternatively, your horse may benefit from relaxed lazy hacking with this other person as a form of mental and physical release from the competition work you do with him.

Moving a Horse or Pony to a New Home

Horses in their natural state in a herd environment quickly establish their rank or position of importance. Horses may die and new ones may join the herd, but there is relative stability there. Their universal language and social skills are learned very early on in life and these equip them for most situations.

Therefore, if you acquire a new horse or pony, take the time and trouble to make his move to your surroundings a little less traumatic. First, do not immediately change his name. If it is so bad that it must be changed, try to use a phonetically similar sounding name. Ensure that you change any feeding patterns slowly and continue to use familiar smelling objects, e.g., his feed bowl, rugs, and a bale of his hay. These can be changed in due course, but it helps to have continuity during the transition period. Establish a friendship with just one of the other horses or ponies before turning him out with the rest of the group.

If he is to be turned out full time, the best period to make the move is in the afternoon, at least an hour before dusk. In this way he has time to explore the new field boundaries in the daylight. He will be occupied enjoying the new pasture and so be less likely to worry about having missed his old routine of, perhaps, a 4 P.M. curfew to come in. After spending the first night out, he will soon settle into the new routine.

Making Friends With You

Horses are naturally gregarious animals who, in the words of Pat Parelli, "desire love, language, and leadership." We should be thankful they are so easily pleased – most of us are a lot more demanding! Horses are less complicated than humans – it is far harder, if not impossible, to "offend" a horse, although it

> **❝** Horses are less complicated than humans – it is far harder, if not impossible, to "offend" a horse, although it is probably a great deal easier to confuse one. **❞**

Above: *Horses desire "love, language, and leadership." It can take years to establish a deep understanding of an individual animal. However, by appreciating simple achievements rather than any material winnings, the rewards are unlimited. Don't be complacent and assume that "I can ride horses, therefore I am a good horse person" – I think many horses would disagree!*

DON'T GET DRAGGED

If your horse is pulling away from you – you're unlikely to pull him back. You could lose control.

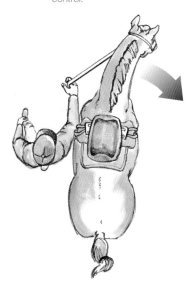

Instead, by pushing his quarters away, his forehand will swing back toward you.

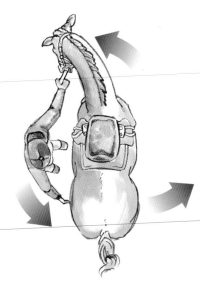

By swinging around and poking his ribs, you are mimicking the actions of a "biting" horse, and he should swing back around to face you and come back under your control.

🐎 **Left:** *Rushing or lunging at another horse usually has the aim of propelling the other animal in a certain direction. If the horse wants you out of the way – you had better either act **big** or move **fast**!*

is probably a great deal easier to confuse one.

This is where using a language that they understand will save a lot of unnecessary stress all around. It can take years to build up a true understanding of an individual animal. I have only one horse that I feel I truly know inside out. Having owned her for over 20 years, this is hardly surprising but, nevertheless, it is the most fantastic feeling in the world.

Having said this, a great deal can be achieved by "speaking" the horse's own language by mimicking movements and mannerisms used by horses themselves in a bid to achieve a closer partnership.

Mimicking Horse Language To Avert Dangerous Situations

If you have watched horses together in a group, you will have seen how subtle body language is all that is needed to communicate displeasure or to channel the motion of another animal in a specific direction. For example, if your horses are crowding around you in the field or bullying one of the others at

mealtimes, you need to take charge to avoid a dangerous situation. Although you may be small, in horse language you need to assert yourself by acting "big" by adopting an aggressive stance with eyes focused on the offending horse and shoulders and arms raised. This alone may not push them away, but by "rushing" toward them while taking big purposeful strides, you can "push" them away without physical contact, as they would push another horse.

Another example is an animal that tries to pin you against the stable wall. This can

🐎 **Above:** *Ignore a horse's body language at your own peril! This horse is showing distinct signs of displeasure and if this warning is not heeded, a less subtle aggressive nip may well be the next reaction.*

potentially be extremely dangerous and trying to push the animal away physically will achieve nothing – the horse will actually lean into you even more. The horse has, in effect, invaded

your space and a horse in that position would threaten to bite or kick their oppressor to force it to back off. An aggressive stance again is needed, but you will have no room to rush at the horse. You want his quarters to move away from you and by mimicking a "bite" with a sharp pinch to his side or using your toe to tap him on the quarters, you should, in theory, bring his head around to you.

If you are leading an animal from the left-hand side who is beginning to take hold and pull away from you, rather than tugging against him relentlessly, swing your upper body around in an counterclockwise direction, as if you were another horse lunging to bite his rear end and poke him with a finger behind his

ribs. This should result in him swinging his quarters away from you and thereby focusing his attention on you again.

Unfortunately, we do not have the ability to express ourselves with our ears, but signs of our displeasure or pleasure are soon picked up by equines. If you are consistent and always use these clear responses to unacceptable behavior, horses soon learn to take note of more subtle warnings.

When Communication Breaks Down

Sometimes, sadly, communication breaks down between horse and owner. You may not have actually done anything wrong. It may be that a sequence of events has worked against you or confused communication. Sometimes a change is the only answer – to change the location of the animal and start afresh. I recommend changing the location because sometimes, when all else has failed, simply changing the elements of the surroundings and daily routine has a dramatic effect. It is the easiest way to get the horse to become open to relearning or to changing his attitude. The horse is not confident in the new surroundings and looks for leadership and guidance. This is often the reason when animals (dogs as well as horses) can behave remarkably differently when re-homed with a new owner or when taken to a different location for training, even by the present owner.

Many apparently disobedient or dangerous animals are simply misunderstood, fearful, or in pain. Reestablishing trust begins with communication. We can learn a great deal from experienced horse people such as Monty Roberts and Pat Parelli, who are happy to share their "horse-whispering" secrets with us in order to improve our understanding of these animals and to promote equine welfare. The remainder of this chapter incorporates extensive quotations from *The Partnership Program*, Part 1 of Pat Parelli's Savvy System as an aid to helping us get inside the mind of a horse.

Above: *We can learn a great deal from horse people like Pat Parelli, who promote better welfare and understanding of equines.*

Far left: *A blasé or inexperienced rider may miss the warning signal of a swishing tail or flattened ears. Some horses (like people) are more bad tempered than others, and it only takes a second to get bitten!*

ATTITUDES

We often talk about difficult horses, but what about difficult owners? Some people are far more demanding and narrow-minded than any horses I know!

Safety 40%	Comfort 30%
Food 15%	Play 15%

A Horse's Needs

Understanding the basic things that are important to a horse will help us to make better sense of its actions.

Below: A prey animal will choose to run from danger provided there is space to run, like these Mustangs fleeing some perceived threat.

Understanding Equine Psychology...

"Put yourself in the horse's shoes. You are a prey animal. Your whole life is spent trying to avoid ending up as somebody's lunch. Your eyes are set on the side of your head so you have almost 360° vision... ."

Horses don't think like people. That's why so many people have problems with horses. To get along with horses, be safer, and achieve personal excellence, we need to learn to think like a horse.

As a horse, you can see potential predators approaching from just about any direction, and you are always on the alert for them. You also have acute hearing. Any rustle or unusual noise could signal the approach of a predator (things like rustling plastic can sound just like this!). For a prey animal like you, one second's hesitation could mean the difference between life and death.

You, the horse, are the supreme athlete. With your primary means of survival being escape, the first thought is always going to be to run. You make sure you are never in a confined or narrow space where one or more of your escape routes might be blocked. Your speed is all you've got, but if you are cornered

> 66 Horses don't think like people. That's why so many people have problems with horses. To get along with horses, be safer, and achieve personal excellence, we need to learn to think like a horse. 99

you have one other option: fight for your life. You have lightning-quick reflexes; can strike, wheel, and kick in almost a single move. You are not usually aggressive and will choose flight rather than fight, but if you have no option you will do whatever it takes to defend yourself.

Predators (humans) are easy to identify. Predators have eyes at the front of their head, and walk boldly and directly straight up to things they want. They smell like what they eat (meat). They focus hard on you when they're trying to catch and kill you, but most of them can't run very fast. It's only when they catch you by surprise or gang up on you that you haven't a chance.

🐎 *Below:* Domestic horses generally fight over supremacy or food. They dislike confrontations but in a confined area their freedom is compromised. The choice of "flight" is often taken away from them, so aggression is frequently the only recourse.

🐎 *Right:* The complex nature of horses is exaggerated by their heightened senses. Inside every domestic horse is a wild horse, always alert to danger. In their eyes, even we are predators.

The Basis of Equine Psychology

To understand the psychology of the horse, you need to understand his perspective on survival. Almost every reaction is based on this need to survive. So to put things into simple terms, there are only four things that are important to horses: **1. safety, 2. comfort, 3. play, and 4. food.**

Once a horse knows he is safe, he will put effort into staying comfortable. If he feels both safe and comfortable, then he will play. Horses are extremely playful, social animals. The final part is food. All of this I'm describing is especially related to the horse's life in humansville. It might help you understand

 **Above:** *Safety in numbers. Horses are most comfortable in a herd situation. Here they are at ease – lots of eyes and ears to keep them safe.*

> 66 **You can't force a horse to like you. You must convince him that you are his friend, his leader, and a part of his herd, even though you look like a predator.** 99

situations like why trying to entice a horse into a metal cave on wheels (a horse trailer) using carrots doesn't usually work too well! He's more concerned with protecting himself!

Inside every wild horse is a gentle horse. And inside every gentle or domesticated horse is a wild horse. Never, ever, forget this. You can't change millions of years of nature's programming. You can't force a horse to like you. You have to convince him that you are his friend, his leader, and a part of his herd, even though you look like a predator.

If the horse is skeptical or afraid, he is telling you that he still thinks of you as a predator. What you have to do is prove to him that even though you look and smell like a predator, you wouldn't hurt him even if you could. When horses are afraid, they're not afraid of being hurt, they're afraid of being killed.

Comfort and Discomfort

After safety, comfort and discomfort are what motivate and shape horse behavior. Discomfort is what motivates horses to find comfort. We can take comfort away in increments until the horse is motivated to respond in order to find comfort again. As soon as he does the right thing, the discomfort is released. He learns what he did in order to get that release, and next time does it again for the same result. Every communication with a horse involves affecting his comfort in some way, and the timing of the release is a critical factor.

Day-to-day activities – such as asking the horse to move sideways away from you in the stable or to be sensitive to the aids when mounted – can benefit if you are consistent in the manner in which you "ask" your horse to do anything. It can be compared to a progression from whispering a request to someone politely (and being ignored), then asking again in a normal tone (and being ignored), then demanding abruptly (and still being ignored), to shouting your request forcefully at the top of your voice. Ideally, our aids should only ever need to be at the "whisper" or "normal tone" level as the horse will soon learn to avoid being "shouted" at in terms of our aids. Many horses become hard mouthed or dead to the leg due to their riders asking at "full volume" rather than quietly in the first instance.

Pat explains, "A process that I call 'Four Phases of Friendly Firmness' helps you communicate more effectively. It helps soft people become more assertive and aggressive people to get firm without getting mean or mad. By taking a horse's comfort away in phases, you allow the horse time to think about his response, and ultimately to choose to respond at Phase 1 or 2. He learns that he can avoid the higher phases."

Phase 1 = minimal stimulus; Phase 2 = double that; Phase 3 = double that (without getting mean or mad!); Phase 4 = double that (until you get a response). By quitting what you are doing at the very moment the horse

responds, you teach him that he is right. The more he learns that there is always comfort and release as his reward, he get smarter about looking for the right response to your request at Phase 1.

Be Consistent

A word about punishment: Horses do not respond to punishment. They don't understand anything that happens later than the instant they acted, and will become fearful of emotionally based actions from a predator.

Reinforcement is the key. Let's say the horse is leaning against a cactus: the instant he moves away from the pressure, he finds comfort. As long as he keeps making the wrong move (leaning against it), the pressure gets worse. Reinforcement has to happen in the moment. The difference between punishment and reinforcement, therefore, is attitude and timing.

Above: *To begin with, keep body language clear and consistent. We can easily confuse horses with unclear requests. In time the level of command may only need to be minimal to achieve the desired response.*

COMMUNICATION

"I think horses do pretty well trying to guess what we want them to do. Horse language is pretty much universal between equines, but human/equine language must seem like Double Dutch to them!"

Left: *Pat uses a system of Seven Games beginning with the Friendly Game to show the horse that we are a friend and mentor, rather than an object of fear.*

> **❝ Learning to use the "Schwiegermutter" look to drive a horse back, or use a smile to invite him forward is very important. ❞**

🐎 **Left:** *Compare the picture of Pat adopting his "Schwiegermutter" look with that of the pony below – there are many similarities! Facial expressions alone can be powerful enough to drive a horse away (e.g., a hard, direct stare) or to encourage a horse to stand or approach you (eyes down, soft expression).*

Punishment is an aggressive act, a predatorial act, and often involves anger. Reinforcement is without emotion, is delivered as if the horse did it to himself (like running into your elbow when he tries to bite you!), and it is instant. It happens as a consequence of the horse's action rather than at our discretion. Punishment is delivered too late. Unless the reinforcement is instant, the horse will find it hard to associate it with his actions. As long as the human punishes a horse, shows anger or aggression, the horse will always perceive him as a predator, not to be trusted. It will affect the relationship.

Timing is critical to obtaining good results. The better the timing of release, the quicker the horse learns.

Your body language, learning to use the "Schwiegermutter" look (that means mother-in-law in German!) to drive a horse back, or use a smile to invite him forward is very important. Similarly, being able to relax your body when the horse is right – both on the ground and on his back – will offer the horse comfort.

BODY LANGUAGE

A horse's body language can tell you a lot about how it is feeling and how it will behave. In the same way, a horse will "read" our body language and respond to our visual signals.

1 *Hard eye*

2 *Flared nostrils*

3 *Ears flattened*

4 *Tense jaw*

5 *Outstretched "prodding" neck*

6 *Purposeful choppy gait*

7 *Tense muscles*

8 *Thrashing tail*

Below: Try to observe how horses naturally behave toward one another. Their action are often quite the reverse of a human's. Striding cheerfully toward your horse to give it a hug could be misinterpreted as a threat.

Right: Frontal attacks involve the risk of exposing the vulnerable areas of the underbody (see diagram below right) to counterattack, whereas "cow-kicking" behind only exposes the less vulnerable rump.

Horses use body language extensively in the form of a hard eye, ears back, nose wrinkled, mouth open to bite, a lifted leg to kick, and a switching tail. They use very little voice except to express greetings, squeal in their games, or as a threat. By not automatically using your voice, it will help you tune in to your body language more and to be effective with it. The voice also tends to make you express fear, frustration, or anger. Keep it inside and smile. You'll learn to override it.

How To Not Act Like A Predator

It's simple, just do the opposite of what you think you should do! Use reverse psychology. For example, in trying to catch a horse, we tend to approach and approach and approach, and the horse just puts more effort into running away. Something as simple as turning your back or stopping and smiling every time the horse looks at you, and walking backward if he approaches you, can make a big difference. He may even walk up to you in curiosity.

One time I was asked about a horse that was extremely hard to catch, and the gentleman said he'd tried everything except lying down! I answered that maybe that's exactly what he should have done! The reason it would work is because lying down is exactly the opposite of what a predator would do.

Horses are constantly on guard against being caught or trapped. The best thing you can do is teach them to come to you instead of chasing them down.

Approach and retreat As we've just mentioned, humans have a tendency to go directly for what they want, yet horses need you to approach and retreat until they feel safe.

For example, an ear-shy horse won't let a human touch his ear, even get near it, yet will happily rub it on another horse or on a fence! The ear is not the problem, the predator is.

Horses are particularly defensive of their most vulnerable areas – around the head, behind the ears, the flanks, under the belly, below the knees and hocks, the hamstring area, and under the tail. They know that one swipe of a powerful set of claws in any of these unprotected areas threatens their survival.

VULNERABLE AREAS

The areas highlighted in green are vulnerable spots on the horse's body – injuries here can be life threatening.

Right: *The most important elements in life for a horse are safety, comfort, and having someone to play with. What we provide for our horses may be very different!*

Above and top: *Weaving and crib biting are symptoms of stress or boredom. Installing an antiweave grill only removes the symptom and not the cause. The key to curing stable vices is keeping the horse interested and occupied.*

Rather than doggedly trying to grab the ear of an ear-shy horse, do the opposite. Pretend you aren't interested in the ear, don't even look at it.

Work first to gain the horse's trust and respect. Then, using approach and retreat, you can rub toward his ear and retreat before he gets bothered. Approach again, all the while keeping a smile on your face and rhythm in your movement. Look everywhere except at the ear! Pretty soon, you can rub around the ear and the horse will be totally relaxed. You just can't rush it.

Approach and retreat are important keys, but only after you've created a good relationship.

What's important to people is not necessarily important to horses.

People tend to like clean, well-groomed horses that are stabled and blanketed. They keep them away from other horses so they won't get bitten or kicked.

Horses love dirt, and hate stables. Being clean isn't important (in fact, they use dirt to keep the bugs off).

What is important to horses is being safe, comfortable, and having someone to play with. Getting bitten and kicked is all part of herd life and socialization, and for young horses it is a part of growing up.

Think of it from the horse's point of view. What would you prefer: 10,000 acres (4,050 ha) to roam and feed on, a herd for safety and recreation, or to be kept in a small space, in solitary confinement, worked daily or ridden now and then?

Many horses kept in confinement and isolation develop mental and emotional problems. So-called "vices" such as cribbing (wind sucking), weaving, self-mutilation, aggressive behavior, kicking at walls, popping lips, and other repetitive motions like nodding the head or pawing relentlessly are indications of mental torment brought on by deprivation of freedom and social interaction.

Horses kept in confinement and isolation often emerge full of pent-up energy and excitement. If not able to play dominance games with other horses, they'll want to play them with you! Striking, kicking, bumping, and shouldering are not meant to hurt, it's just how horses play. Don't be surprised if your horse wants to play rough, he doesn't know how fragile humans are. Instead of punishing him for it, learn how to channel it constructively by learning to play with him.

In looking after horses, we have a responsibility for their mental and emotional health as much as their physical, so:

1. Give your horse as much space as you can.
2. Allow him to socialize, or at least be in contact with other horses in some way.
3. Give him mental, emotional, and physical stimulation.
4. Put more emphasis on his internal well-being than his external appearance.

This doesn't mean you neglect the external, it means you don't put the external horse before the internal horse. We have bought or inherited horses that have had behavioral problems, socialization problems, and were even aggressive toward people. By turning them out with a herd on acreage, this behavior reduced dramatically or even disappeared altogether in just a few weeks. It was just a

> 66 **Think of it from the horse's point of view. What would you prefer: 10,000 acres to roam and feed on, a herd for safety and recreation, or to be kept in a small space, in solitary confinement, worked daily or ridden now and then?** 99

matter of allowing the horse to fulfill his basic needs.

Stable vices are often treated like behavioral problems and horses are punished for them or made to wear elaborate contraptions. Some of them can be quite cruel, having spikes in them for instance. The reason horses in confinement develop repetitive behaviors like cribbing, weaving, lip-popping, etc., is because they are trying to stimulate the release of endorphins. The endorphins produce a natural high or numbness that helps relieve the horse's misery. It's like self-induced drugs, which can become highly addictive because they represent some kind of solution for the horse.

Recent studies have shown that it's not so much the confinement as the isolation that produces these behaviors. Horses that live in tie-stalls where they are beside other horses don't develop these behaviors.

Horses are wild prey animals that have been domesticated by man. Whenever their basic needs are not cared for, it can affect them mentally and emotionally and this part is least

Above: A life with plenty of freedom makes for a happy, well-adjusted horse without mental hang-ups.

Below: Don't worry if your horse is muddy – the horse certainly doesn't care! Horses **love** to be dirty.

Right: *Rearing is one example of the Opposition Reflex – an action of self-preservation or intolerance stemming from fear, pain, anger, confusion, misunderstanding, or disrespect. Before reprimanding such actions, try to understand why the horse has reacted in this way.*

visible to us. It is our responsibility to learn how to look after these needs in the horse to ensure his total well-being while in our care.

Think Like A Horse

There are two terms I like to use to describe the thinking condition of a horse: left brain and right brain. When horses are left brain, they are using the thinking side of their brain. They are calm, in a learning frame of mind, and can think their way through situations and requests.

When they are right brain, they are not thinking, they are reacting on instinct. They are usually in the flight or fight survival mode where there is no time to think. A horse can run forward and stay right brained, which is why lunging is not very effective in calming horses down. But to go sideways or backward,

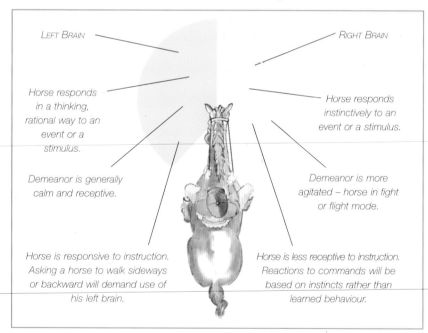

LEFT BRAIN

RIGHT BRAIN

Horse responds in a thinking, rational way to an event or a stimulus.

Horse responds instinctively to an event or a stimulus.

Demeanor is generally calm and receptive.

Demeanor is more agitated – horse in fight or flight mode.

Horse is responsive to instruction. Asking a horse to walk sideways or backward will demand use of his left brain.

Horse is less receptive to instruction. Reactions to commands will be based on instincts rather than learned behaviour.

LEFT/RIGHT BRAIN
Pat Parelli identifies two basic ways in which a horse will respond mentally to a situation – left-brain reactions are rational and thoughtful, right-brain responses are intuitive.

a horse has to think about it otherwise his legs get tangled or he runs into things. Just calmly persist until he makes the shift from right to left brain. When he does this, he will often lick his lips or "chew." (He'll also do this when he learns a new thing you've taught him.)

Horses in a herd, whether wild or domestic, will establish their status and influence over others by carrying out various patterns of movements which communicate the boundaries of their personal space and affect the behavior of others. Horses are not mind readers. Controlling a large animal can be very dangerous — almost all horse owners have been trodden on or dragged about by a horse or pony. By mimicking the language and the patterns of movements that horses understand, we can communicate with them without force that we wish them to be light and less "bargy" and therefore lead them without tugging or hauling the rope.

Pat Parelli has developed a system which includes "The Seven Games." These mimic the games that horses play with each other in a herd environment, for example, bonding, circling, driving away, etc., and these are practiced from the ground *in sequence*. The translation of human requests into "games" the horse understands improves communication between horse and rider which results in more "instant" cooperation from the horse with very little force having to be exerted.

The Herd Instinct

"Don't be surprised by a horse's need to stick with the herd or his desire to gravitate towards other horses. The herd represents safety and if a horse feels at all insecure he will always keep track of where the herd is or try to get back to it. He'll do the same with the barn or the pasture because he has learned to feel safe there. He'll want to return to it whenever he feels unsafe, uncomfortable, or stressed.

The more respect a horse has for you and your leadership, the less herd bound or barn 'sweet' he will become. If you represent safety, he'll stay with you and not seek the herd."

Opposition Reflex

Opposition Reflex is an instinct horses have that causes them to do the opposite of what a predator wants. It's a reaction of self-defense. A horse will have Opposition Reflex under the following circumstances: fear, pain, anger, confusion, misunderstanding, and out of disrespect.

Examples of Opposition Reflex include biting, kicking, rearing, bolting, bucking, pulling back, striking, opposing the bit, swishing the tail, grinding the teeth, laying ears back, refusing to move, pulling right when you try to go left, etc. Most people tend to think these are vices or signs of disobedience, but they're actually more related to the prey-predator relationship.

Learning about Opposition Reflex is critical to learning how to read a horse as well as

> **66** The more respect a horse has for you and your leadership, the less herd bound or barn "sweet" he will become. If you represent safety, he'll stay with you and not seek the herd. **99**

Below: *Pat Parelli is skilled at working with the horse to overcome Opposition Reflex. Averting eye contact, he uses movements to gain its attention.*

Below: Prey animals react in many ways to fear or pain, either aggressively or defensively. If their movements are restricted (i.e., when being ridden), their reactions may be less evident and their physical objections limited to a tense jaw or swishing tail.

understanding why he is reacting. Yes, it does involve a lack of respect, but this is due to a lack of trust and esteem for the human.

People have Opposition Reflex too! They get tight in the mind, tight in the body, and dig in with all their "claws." They grab or jerk on the reins, and cling and clutch with their legs (which scares the horse!). Fear, frustration, and anger are the main triggers.

Prey Animal Reactions

When prey animals get scared, confused, mad, frustrated, or hurt, the "hole under the tail" gets tight and they feel compelled to move their feet. If they can't move their feet, they'll move their tail, jaw, lips, etc. This is known as displaced behavior.

Specific reactions are: pulling back, kicking, striking, biting, nipping, laying ears back, spooking, violent behavior, rearing, bucking,

tugging on the reins, flipping the bit, chewing on the bit, tossing their head, jigging on the trail, prancing, not moving, being sluggish, nonresponsive, overreactive, not trailer loading, rushing off the trailer, cranking their tail, resisting lateral flexion, resisting vertical flexion, bracing their neck, not stopping, not going, not standing still, cold backed, cinch bound, pawing while tied, defecating; laying down, not opening mouth to bridle, hard to paste worm, hard to doctor, clamping tail, difficult to catch, whinnying to other horses, barn sour (actually barn sweet), herd bound, bolting, ear shy, hard mouthed, can't, won't, don't and yeah-but spots, overflexing, behind the bit, etc...

Predator Reactions

When predators get scared, confused, mad, frustrated, or hurt, the "hole under the tail"

Above and left: A horse may not treat his owner any differently to the way he treats another horse. A kick means "Keep Away" and you'd have to be very thick-skinned to ignore this warning – but why are you so unpopular?

gets tight, the feet do not move, they dig in, they freeze and all the "claws" go in.

Specific reactions (in horse people) are: the hands close quickly and lock onto the reins, the legs clamp to the horse's sides, the belly tightens, the seat tightens, breathing shuts down, they don't blink because they can't think, they take on the fight or defensive response (fetal position), they shout, growl, hit, kick, pull, jerk, yank, and their compete to win or "dominance reflexes" come into play.

Zone-ology

This is Pat Parelli's concept of copying horses' natural behavior and positioning our hands, legs, and other natural and artificial aids to cause forward, backward, or lateral movement. Just as one horse can influence the direction another horse will travel by tipping or lunging with his neck toward his opponent's head or flanks, etc., by learning how to position ourselves and our aids, we can control movement more accurately. As he explains:

"This is my system for finding the right position to be in when asking your horse to do something. It will help you to be systematic and find zones that your horse is defensive about.

A knowledge of zones also allows you to thoroughly teach a horse to yield to pressure. For example, you lead Zone 1, and drive Zone 1 to send the horse away from you, then lead Zone 1 and drive Zone 4 to disengage the hindquarters and bring him back to you.

There are five active zones on a horse and one delicate one (see diagram). The front legs fall into Zone 3 and the hind legs into Zone 4. The horse's hindquarters, including under the tail are in Zone 4. Zones 1, 4 and the Delicate Zone also have an inside: inside the mouth, the nose, the ears, and inside the 'hole under the tail.' (Then there is the seventh zone, the horse's personal space.)"

Most people never ask very much of their horse, or they pretty much do what the horse wants just to keep the peace. They may even have become so used to the horse's disrespectful behavior that they now accept it as normal. The goal is to change all that. You should become more conscious of how

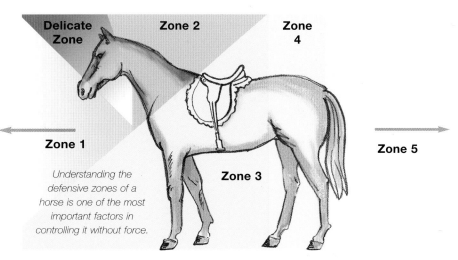

Understanding the defensive zones of a horse is one of the most important factors in controlling it without force.

your horse does or does not respond. You'll learn how to teach him to respond within a relationship based on love, language, and respect.

Natural Riding Dynamics

To ride like a natural you need to let go of many of the things you may have already been taught to do: heels down, hands down, push, push, push.

The stiffness of "educated" riding will be replaced by a more natural ease, grace, and feel, and by a connection and flowingness with the horse. This is about turning loose so your horse can teach you to get into harmony with his motion. The first steps for learning to become part of your horse... .

Don't just saddle up and get on! Learning to become a part of your horse starts on the ground, making sure your horse is in the mood and that he's in tune with you mentally, emotionally, and physically. Learn how to check your horse out to make sure he is safe to get on, like pilots using a preflight check before they fly a plane.

THE SIX ZONES
The drawing shows the six zones that govern a horse's responses.

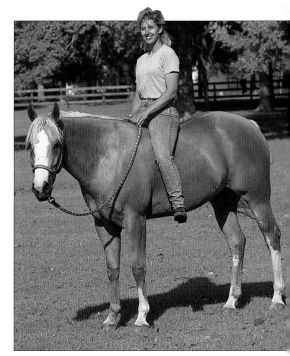

*Above: Riding is not about simply controlling your horse but about working as a natural partnership. Real success is making a horse **want** to perform with you.*

Check General Health and Demeanor

Is he alert, attentive, and pleased to see you? — **NO** | **YES**

Is there any discharge from his muzzle, or does he have dull, weepy eyes? — **NO** | **YES**

Are his eyes bright and clear? — **NO** | **YES**

Does he seem sullen and disinterested or bad-tempered toward you? — **NO** | **YES**

Are the mucous membranes around his eyes, nostrils, and gums a salmon pink color? — **NO** | **YES**

Does he seem agitated, uncomfortable, or distressed? — **NO** | **YES**

Does his posture indicate he is sound? — **NO** | **YES**

Is he shifting his weight, resting his legs, head shaking, or generally looking unsettled or uncomfortable? — **NO** | **YES**

■ **Do not think of riding until you have investigated the cause of the problem.**

■ **He appears to be healthy and happy, so continue.**

❏ **Check body visually** Check body and limbs for cuts, puncture wounds, bites, sores, girth galls, overreach grazes, mud fever, etc. Check that legs are not puffy or swollen. Pick hooves, and check for excessive heat in them.

❏ **Check tack** Check the fit of all tack and its positioning. Make sure all surfaces in contact with the skin are free of grease and mud, which could cause chafing.

❏ **Tighten girth straps gradually and check bit** Check positioning of bit in the mouth. Does the horse seem comfortable with it, or could there be a problem? Check for sores or cuts in the mouth.

❏ **Flex the horse before mounting** Stretch out forelegs to eliminate pinching from the girth. Lead the horse in a small circle, to the left and to the right, to allow him to feel the tack and loosen up.

❏ **Mount slowly** Ideally, mount from a mounting block and lower your weight gently into the saddle.

❏ **Warm up slowly** Begin riding at a walk for a minimum of five minutes. Start on a loose rein to allow him to stretch out. He should be happy and interested in his work.

A horse that is calm and thinking is going to be much safer to ride than a horse that is full of pent-up energy or is tense, hyped up, or afraid.

By learning his language and mentality you'll learn how to redirect pent-up energy, and get your horse thinking and calm again without stopping him from doing what he has to do. Think about it...if you'd spent the whole day in a stall and then finally got out, you'd want to buck and run and stretch and play. This horse doesn't need discipline, as it will just cause him to fight for his freedom. He needs something constructive to do with his energy.

The tense, scared, flighty horse is a bomb waiting to go off. You don't have to get on – you shouldn't get on – until this horse is calm and attentive. Some horses take longer than others to get in the right mood, and sometimes this depends on your skill level. In any case, take the time it takes so it takes less time. You and you horse will both survive and enjoy the experience!

Let Go of Old Habits

Riding the natural way will mean letting go of old habits like kicking to go and pulling on the reins to stop and turn. Sometimes, the best way to break a habit is to dissolve a pattern. If you are used to riding with two reins, whenever you have two reins in your hands you'll do what you always do – pull back on them! So, in their first lessons, we teach people to ride with just one rein, and in a halter! (Don't be alarmed, we prepare them fully beforehand, and safety is never compromised.)

I can tell you about hundreds of people who used to ride their horses in big bits and tie-downs and had all kinds of control issues. They have found themselves having calmer horses and no more control problems in a very short period of time...just by reevaluating their old riding methods.

Horses that won't stop or that get out of control are not dumb and insensitive, they are confused. They don't understand what you

❝ The tense, scared, flighty horse is a bomb waiting to go off. You don't have to get on – you shouldn't get on – until this horse is calm and attentive. ❞

Above and left: To watch Pat Parelli perform advanced riding patterns with only a neck strap is truly awesome. He shows the importance of learning how to "go with the flow" of an individual animal.

want. They are acting like prey animals, are defensive and trying to escape. You can change all this. With a little psychology, a lot of preparation, changing patterns, and learning to relax your own emotions and muscles, you'll have a different horse – because he'll have a different human.

Bruce Lee said that in learning to master yourself, you don't need to train your muscles, you need to train your mind. There is as much mental and emotional development to be learned here as there is physical.

Relearning to ride in a more natural way, you notice that very little resembles normal riding lessons! You need to learn how to be a good passenger before you ever try to guide your horse. When you do start guiding, ride with your whole body, with focus, without depending on the reins for balance and control. You'll learn the most natural ways to cause your horse to go forward, backward, sideways, and turn right and left.

The objective is to learn to become a part of your horse.

In Conclusion

Horses, in general, avoid confrontation and will often tolerate a great deal of discomfort or aggravation without retaliation. It is their willingness to follow, rather than lead, that has made them so trainable. But it is this subservience that leaves them open to abuse – surely it is far more rewarding to produce excellent manners and performance from a horse working willingly with you, rather than through brute force.

STAY COOL

Never attempt to school a horse if you are feeling stressed or short-tempered. Impatience will only lead to frustration. Go out for a hack instead and you can both let off steam.

CHAPTER 3

Stabling From Your Horse's Point of View

The most important question that you should ask yourself when you first think of getting a horse is "Where will I keep it?" The ambition of most of us is to have our own land and stables close to our home. We also have the choice of using boarding stables, which offer options from do-it-yourself to full board, plus various alternatives in between to suit our busy lifestyles. There is also the possibility of renting/leasing a barn or land for grazing.

Above: "How long until I am let out?" There has got to be more to a horse's life than hours spent in a stable.
Right: *Communal barn stabling is a superb system providing shelter and security in a sociable environment. This method of housing ought to be adopted by more establishments.*

Most owners assume that they will need a stable and in many situations such accommodation is useful – for example, in dreadful weather, for stall rest during recovery from injury or illness, or simply to keep the animal clean and give it that extra "edge" just before an event.

But is stabling essential? In my opinion stables should only be used infrequently, for reasons such as those listed above, but they should not be regarded as the normal "home" for the horse.

better than an equally well-run barn with older tatty stables, old pasture fenced by hedgerow and plain wire, complete with farm cats or perhaps an old goat wandering around the barn.

As discussed in earlier chapters, horses evolved to thrive outdoors. They are happiest when they have the freedom to roam over vast expanses of land, to search out a variety of foodstuffs, and when they have emotional stability and stimulation from living among well-known companions.

Why Do We Stable Horses For So Long?

We have stabled horses for centuries. Horses used for transportation, daily hauling work,

🐎 **Above top:** *Many people get upset seeing zoo animals confined in small cages, but amazingly few worry about stabled horses.*

🐎 **Above:** *Horses tolerate confinement, but it would never be their actual choice. Suppressing natural desires is not conducive to optimum health or performance.*

It is very pleasing to us to arrive at a boarding stable to see spotless stables, hanging baskets, swept barns, and tidy muck heaps while the turnout resembles manicured lawns with immaculate post and rail fencing. Horses' heads hanging over their doors ready to be petted complete the idyllic picture.

This is regarded by the majority of owners as representing the epitome of a good, well-run barn. It will be judged by most people to be

army duties, or sport and pleasure were stabled so that they would be available, clean, and ready for action whenever required. This is still the case for some horses used in competition or for sports. Thankfully, they

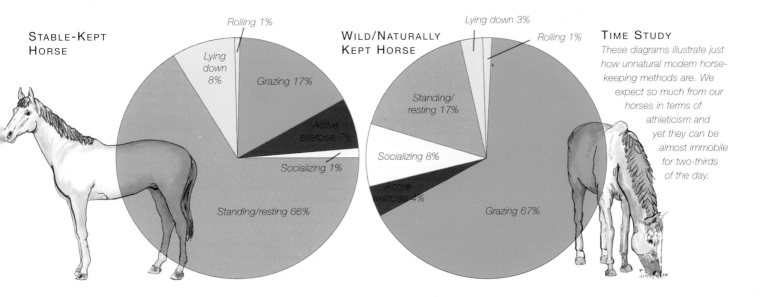

STABLE-KEPT HORSE

- Rolling 1%
- Lying down 8%
- Grazing 17%
- Active exercise 7%
- Socializing 1%
- Standing/resting 66%

WILD/NATURALLY KEPT HORSE

- Lying down 3%
- Rolling 1%
- Standing/resting 17%
- Socializing 8%
- Active exercise 4%
- Grazing 67%

TIME STUDY

These diagrams illustrate just how unnatural modern horse-keeping methods are. We expect so much from our horses in terms of athleticism and yet they can be almost immobile for two-thirds of the day.

> **Stables should only be used infrequently, they should not be regarded as the normal "home" for the horse.**

also generally get some turnout or, in the case of point-to-pointers and polo ponies, even several months off as some recompense for this lifestyle.

Accepting stabling as the "norm" has been ingrained into our mentality as being part of the correct method of horse care. Being seen to have an immaculately clean horse in a pristine stable with top-quality rugs and matching feed bowls seems to be many people's yardstick for proving themselves better owners than others.

We must look beyond what is simply aesthetically pleasing to ourselves. At the very

Above: Having smart facilities is a bonus, but it does not mean that the stables are better from the horse's point of view. When looking at accommodations, think in terms of equine comfort – what facilities does it offer your horse for work, rest, and play?

Left: These stables may be slightly tatty, but this is of little consequence to their occupants, who have the benefit of dual-aspect views from each stable.

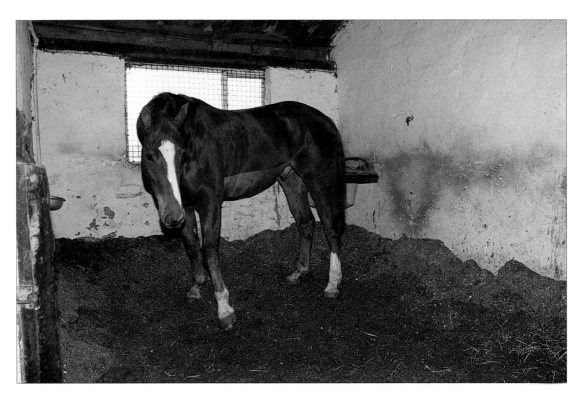

66 If your local barn does not offer daily turnout and you cannot guarantee that your horse will be given varied daily activities, either through being ridden or turned out in a communal barn, etc., then quite simply change barns. **99**

Right: *Every stable is, by definition, a "cage" and it is totally unacceptable at any time – other than because of injury or illness – effectively to imprison a horse in a stable for 24 hours a day.*

Opposite page: *This picture speaks for itself. Keeping your horse mentally happy will pay dividends in terms of performance, temperament, and health.*

CONFINED

The argument that horses have been domesticated and so are happy with their contrived lifestyles does not stand up – would you ever consider keeping your dog or cat in a cage the size of a fridge?

least, assess the requirements for the period of stable confinement in terms of our horse's needs, and not our own or our friends' image of what is "correct."

First, a horse would *never, ever* choose to be stabled for more than a few hours a day. It is *totally unacceptable* at any time other than through injury/illness to confine a horse in a stable for 24 hours a day. If your local barn does not offer daily turnout and you cannot guarantee that your horse will be given varied daily activities, either through being ridden or turned out in a communal barn, etc., then quite simply change barns. Daily turnout or activities means daily, Monday through to Sunday. So if you ride at 12 noon on Mondays and Wednesdays for an hour but on Tuesdays have a day off, your stabled horse would be standing in his "prison" for a total of 35 hours! He then may have to wait three more days until the weekend until he is let out again. Many a "respectable" owner of a pleasure horse manages his or her horse in this way.

To get an idea of just how dreadful this normal practice is for the horse, try staying in one room for, say, 24 hours and deprive yourself of TV or any reading material. Eat and sleep in this one room on your own with only the windows as your means of seeing other people's movements. Bear in mind that, unlike our horse, we may spend eight hours of this 24-hour period in a deep sleep!

But my horse is desperate to come in. Although horses are often seen waiting anxiously at the gate, and seem keen to be let into their stables, this is normally because they associate the stables with food or as a preliminary to riding or other activity. Once they have had some food or returned from their ride, they would far rather return outside to graze and to socialize with other horses than be confined to their stables.

I know from experience when my horses have been kept in overnight that I feel enormous guilt if I sleep late or get delayed going to the stables in the morning. I know

WEAVING

Weaving is when a horse shifts his weight from side to side and weaves with his head and neck, usually across the doorway opening. It acts as a therapeutic release from a stressful situation.

they will be impatient to get out or at least be topped up with hay. An extra hour or two makes no difference for horses who can *turn themselves out* in the field as and when they choose. If food is also on tap 24 hours a day, your life is made far easier.

If your horses are stabled because of their high workload and in order to keep them in pristine condition, they can become stale and begin to dread their work. They are always half-expecting to be ridden at any moment, so they never fully "switch off" and rest. This can often be remedied if they are given a *regular* day off where they are simply turned out for the whole day and not touched, not even groomed, until they are brought back in at the end of the day. This gives them the opportunity to "be a horse" again rather than

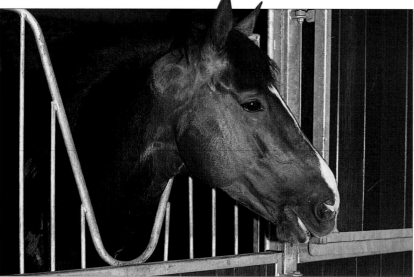

Above: *Installing anti-weave grills addresses the symptom but not the cause. Poor management is really the stable "vice" here.*

Above right: *Cribbing releases natural endorphins and once established is a hard habit to break. Turnout and company is a better way to make the horse feel good.*

our commodity. "Time out" may not be viable every week but somehow you should make some kind of change in the routine so that the horse is aware that he will not be hauled in to be ridden/lunged/groomed for that entire day. For example, if he normally wears a halter, turn him out without a halter on or perhaps in a different field. In this way, his routine is changed. He can fully relax and mingle with members of his own species.

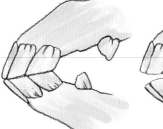

NORMAL TEETH   UNNATURAL WEAR

THE TEETH OF A CRIB-BITER

A crib-biter's incisors wear unnaturally, which may cause problems later on. Wind sucking is an extension of this habit.

Stable Vices

Horses kept in for long periods often develop stable vices like cribbing, weaving and stall walking. This often leads to stress or depression. Even horses which show no outward signs of intolerance to this artificial lifestyle may well have a tendency to blood composition disorders, circulatory problems, or respiratory conditions, which will adversely affect their health and performance.

If your horse has to stay in for long periods of time and unfortunately develops vices such as weaving or cribbing, try to avoid the easy "solution" of installing antiweave bars or such like. I know of an owner who put up these bars. Within a very short time, her animal had developed a way of weaving with just its head as moving the rest of its body was impossible. The owner then totally barred the door opening so the animal could not put its head out at all. This, in turn, led to stall walking. In short, this "remedy" merely disguises the symptoms without solving the cause – and the cause is very simply *boredom*. There are limits as to how much we can suppress the inborn needs of these free-roaming, space-loving animals.

What we may class as irritating behavior may simply be our horse's way of communicating his frustration or eagerness to us; for example, by banging on the stable door as soon as he hears the feeds being made up or head shaking in a desperate attempt to be chosen as the next horse to be turned out.

As in humans, exercise releases endorphins (naturally occurring substances in the body) that lift the spirits. In contrast, stressful situations such as frustration, boredom, or fear can suppress the release of the neurotransmitter serotonin in the brain, resulting in depression. Unfortunately, once behavioral problems have become established, they are often difficult to reverse.

You want your stable to be a palace and not a prison. So imagine how your horse feels locked in a 12 foot × 12 foot (3.6m × 3.6m) box. If this were you, you would certainly want the comforts of a soft, warm bed, plenty of food in the fridge, and something good to watch on the TV! So apart from his bedding and hay/feed, give your horse a room with a view to watch other animals or people. Failing this, if your barn is deathly quiet, turn on the radio to improve the atmosphere! There are now toys on the market to keep horses occupied while stabled. The ones that encourage the horse to forage for the food inside them are a good idea, if a little expensive. A good alternative is to hang a root vegetable like a rutabaga from one of the rafters or hide carrots in the bedding. Collect soft willow branches, which horses love to strip and chew (with the added benefit that willow has a calming, soothing effect).

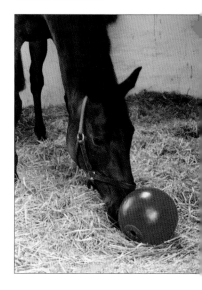

Below: *Nothing can take the place of equine or human company, but stable toys certainly provide short-term mental stimulation in the form of a task and a treat.*

> 66 What we may class as irritating behavior may simply be our horse's way of communicating his frustration or eagerness to us. 99

Left: *Horses are intelligent and inquisitive. This horse is certainly enjoying this treat/toy combination. Try also hiding carrots in clean bedding as a low-calorie nutritious treat for him to search for – but watch out for of rodents!*

Seven Steps To Alleviate Boredom and Keep Your Horse Mentally Happy and Healthy

Below: Horses hate lack of equine company. These stables have been designed to allow some contact between neighbors.

Above: Horses enjoy the company of other animals for interaction and entertainment. Last winter, a pair of wild pheasants decided horse food was delicious, and my horses were happy sharing their feed bowls with them!

1 Provide a view. Movement and activity in your horse's field of vision will help to stimulate his mind. It can be human, animal, or even farm machinery working in the next field.

2 Provide equine contact. If your horse is kept out in a field, make sure that he has company that he can touch. If this is not possible, turn him out somewhere that has horses in neighboring fields so they can communicate and smell each other. Stabled horses should be able to see other horses. However, this is not as rewarding as being able to groom and socialize freely. So make sure that they are turned out frequently with at least one other animal, and allow them to build friendships.

3 Provide long-lasting forage. Horses' digestive systems were designed to take in small amounts of food throughout the day by constant grazing rather than having one or two large meals a day as we do. A small-holed haybale and several small feedings a day will be easier for the horse's gut to digest and will keep him occupied for longer while he enjoys his food.

4 Provide a task. Horses are intelligent and have to search for food in the wild. To stimulate stabled horses, leave treats hidden under clean straw to be found later or hang a rutabaga on a rope from the rafters, which will take time to eat. There are toys on the market which incorporate licks and others that the horse must roll on the ground to release pony nuts or treats hidden inside. It all helps to keep him mentally stimulated.

5 Provide entertainment. You can use a horse toy to distract a solitary animal, but other animals can help to provide entertainment in the form of something to watch and even play with. A stable cat can act as companion and rat catcher combined!

6 Provide atmosphere. A lone horse in a quiet atmosphere will retreat into itself, so provide an atmosphere if there is nothing else to stimulate the horse. Horses enjoy music, so leave a radio on for an hour or two on a suitable station. If you have no power at the stables, radios are now on the market which need no electricity or batteries – they run off solar power or by being wound up.

7 Provide comfort. Apart from food and water, a stabled horse needs suitable bedding to help support his weight on his legs or to allow him to lie down or roll safely. Remember that horses are not designed to stay in one place for hours on end. So unless injury dictates otherwise, they must be allowed to exercise freely to prevent fluid retention, swelling in the legs, and general stiffness.

Above: Suitable music from a radio is an excellent way to alleviate monotony. Soft music can be both soothing and uplifting, but the volume should not be so loud as to mask other sounds or the horse may not feel secure.

Discourage cribbing using natural ingredients. A "hot" effective paste can be made from mixing mustard powder and vinegar together and applying it to affected areas of the stable.

So how should we assess the facilities offered to our stabled horses if the criteria for judgment are not simply the provision of shelter, food and water, and bedding?

Design and Location

Typical stablebarns are designed to be human friendly rather than horse friendly. However, if we understand the horse's behavioral needs, we can endeavor to make his stabled time as stress free as possible.

Ideally, your horse will be able to see other animals from his stable. This does not mean two horses on a hill miles away but animals close enough for him to be able to smell them and communicate with them. You may feel that because your animal grazes with others during the day, he will find solitude no problem at nigh. However, horses are herd animals and live by the code of safety in numbers. Just being able to hear a neighboring horse or donkey moving about will help to ensure that he can more fully relax.

In an ideal world, a stable would lead directly into a field, paddock, or at least some kind of courtyard. This would enable the stable door to be left open most of the time so that the horse could choose when to go in and rest and when to come out for some fresh air and sun (or rain) on his back. This may mean erecting or moving a fence to enclose the courtyard or keeping the gates to your site closed when horses are loose. This is a simple remedy which will reap great rewards.

We often worry and dash back to bring our horses in before a shower. Quite often, they find this very refreshing, especially followed by a roll in the resultant mud! At least this way our animals have the choice.

Above: Ideally, the stables should lead directly into the barn and paddock. Many barns are designed this way. Unfortunately, few owners leave the doors open.

Above: The desire to be "part of a herd" never leaves socialized equines. Having familiar animals in close proximity goes a long way to making the animals feel settled and safe.

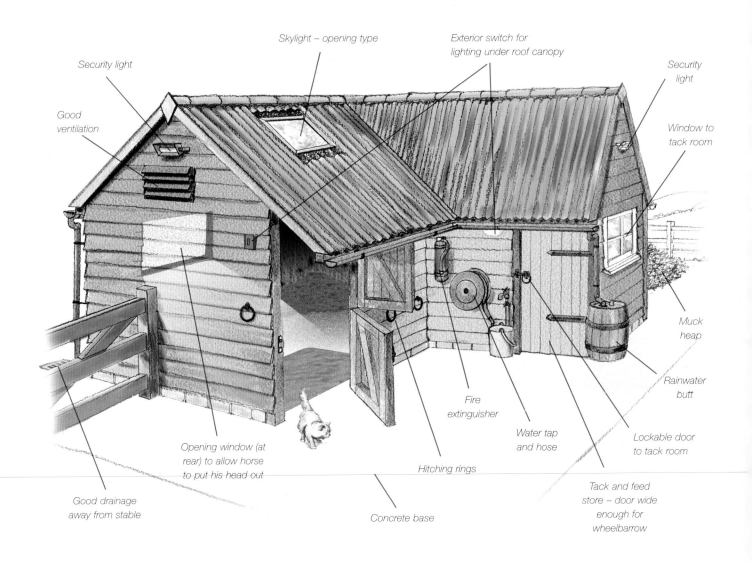

Skylight – opening type

Exterior switch for
lighting under roof canopy

Security light

Security
light

Good
ventilation

Window to
tack room

Muck
heap

Rainwater
butt

Opening window (at
rear) to allow horse
to put his head out

Fire
extinguisher

Water tap
and hose

Lockable door
to tack room

Hitching rings

Good drainage
away from stable

Concrete base

Tack and feed
store – door wide
enough for
wheelbarrow

Above: *If you are
fortunate to be able to design
and build your own stables,
taking this opportunity to
combine factors of **safety**,
convenience, and **benefit to
the horse** will make your barn
a cut above the rest. Location
is of crucial importance –
stables should be adjacent to a
turnout area which will give you
the option of allowing free
access rather than "turning
horses out" and "bringing
them in."*

Riding Arena Footing

The type and quality of riding arena footing you choose is critical to your horse's long-term soundness. While wet, muddy, or frozen ground is obviously unsafe for riding, poor footing can become dangerously slippery even when dry. An arena surface that is too hard provides little or no shock absorption for each hoof as it strikes the ground. This can cause concussive injuries to the horse's feet, legs, and joints. A too-soft or too-deep surface can put added stress and strain onto the tendons and ligaments.

Carrying a rider is not really natural to horses. They did not evolve specifically for this purpose. A rider's extra weight only adds more stress to the work we ask of them. Therefore, to minimize stress and injury, we need to provide appropriate footing in the schooling arena for maximum safety and comfort. Arena maintenance is one of the most neglected aspects of horse care. However, a little research, knowledge, and planning can ensure that your horse has a safe surface to work on.

Grass isn't used for footing in riding arenas because, aside from being slippery when too wet or too dry, grass is difficult to keep level, as horses create divots in the soft earth where their feet grip the ground. Without constant upkeep, the turf becomes uneven and pocked with bare spots and mud holes. Like lawns, grass arenas must be regularly mowed, fertilized, thatched, weeded, and watered. Maintenance is therefore much more time consuming than the cultivating and watering that generally suffices for other footings.

You can enjoy the natural aesthetics of grass footing while you're trail riding. However, for everyday schooling, your horse needs a level, well-cushioned surface with good traction.

Do research before you make a selection; you want a surface that is long lasting, easy to maintain, and doesn't cost a fortune. Ask horse professionals what they prefer. Also, your specific riding discipline – whether you ride jumpers, barrel racers, gaited, or dressage horses, for example – may demand that your footing be heavier or lighter. Building an arena from scratch is a major investment. So you don't want to waste money by making the wrong choices.

The arena site needs to be on high, level ground with a slight slope to encourage good drainage for rainwater. Footing that tends to puddle in wet weather will become slippery and dangerous for riding. Installing a drainage system around the outside of the arena to improve drainage may be necessary.

The arena base, typically clay, stone dust, or fine gravel, acts as a protective layer. It keeps rocks, roots, and other debris from working their way into the surface footing that tops it. The base needs to be packed down hard with heavy machinery, and made smooth and level.

The layer over the base can be a mixture of materials, such as sand, topsoil, sawdust, wood chips, and rubber or fiber additives. This surface layer needs to be laid down several inches deep (2–3 inches [5–8 cm] or deeper, depending on the demands of your riding discipline) so that it provides suitable cushioning and traction for the horse's feet. You will need to replenish or replace this layer from time to time as it packs and wears down.

If you have an existing arena that needs to be refurbished, consider having a sample of the current footing evaluated by a soil-testing laboratory. The analysis may help you decide whether removing what is there and starting over is better or if simply adding fresh footing is.

Common footing faults: Dust is the most common complaint about footings. Regular watering with a hose or sprinkler system is the most common remedy. Dust-control additives available in the form of water-absorbing crystals, salts, or environmentally friendly oils can be mixed with the surface material. However, most are expensive and have to be reapplied.

Salts can also be used to help prevent footing from freezing, but they are corrosive and drying to your horse's hooves. If you use salt additives, be diligent about hosing off your horse's feet and legs after every ride, and apply a commercial hoof dressing routinely.

Because of the dust factor, indoor arenas must have good ventilation. Even after sprinkling the surface, an even air flow is necessary to help dissipate the fine particles of sand and soil churned up by the horse's hooves. Otherwise, arena dust could cause respiratory problems for both horse and rider.

If your footing is too hard, you can usually correct it by regular cultivating and watering or by adding new footing. Sometimes adding wood shavings or rubber additives (made from recycled tires) to the surface layer can put a little spring back into the mixture.

To cure too-deep footing, removing some of it is often best. Because this is a lot more trouble than adding footing, in the beginning, building up the surface gradually by putting down only a couple of inches of footing at a time is better.

> **The location of the muck heap can be a contentious issue and is frequently the cause of complaints.**

Above: Take advice if you are planning to build new stables or change the use of existing buildings to accommodate horses. You are likely to run up against local planning regulations. If you ignore the rules, the consequences can be dire.

GOOD DESIGN

*For a few hours per day, a stable **can** be a safe haven, providing peace from mithering companions as well as food on tap. Important considerations for stable design should be adequate space to move and lie down, soft flooring to mitigate the ill effects of standing still, and allowing a view of or contact with the horse's close companions while stabled.*

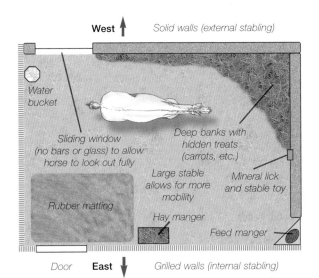

West

Solid walls (external stabling)

Water bucket

Sliding window (no bars or glass) to allow horse to look out fully

Deep banks with hidden treats (carrots, etc.)

Large stable allows for more mobility

Mineral lick and stable toy

Rubber matting

Hay manger

Feed manger

Door East Grilled walls (internal stabling)

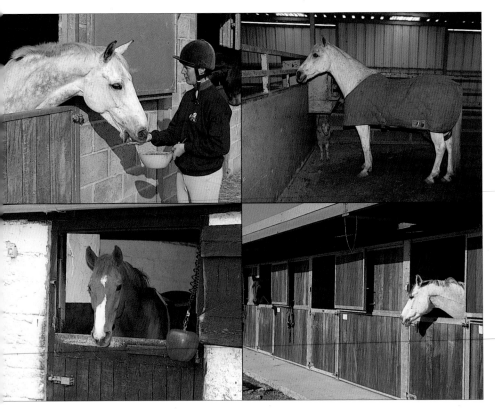

Above group: Stabling is usually made of materials such as wood, concrete block, brick or metal grills, or sheeting. Take into account climate and the insulation and ventilation that each provides.

Guidelines on the Structure

Stabling can be made from wood, concrete block, brick, or even metal sheeting. Metal needs to be lined and strengthened with wooden kickboards or rubber sheeting for insulation and to prevent injury to the horses.

Good ventilation is crucial as it allows fresh air to circulate and stale air to be expelled, so apex roofs are desirable with ventilation gaps under the eaves. Most stables tend to have door and window openings on the same side. Ideally, another opening, such as a sliding window or half-door opening at the horse's chest/head height on a side or back wall, helps to create better air movement and a lighter environment. Additionally, it offers an extra view, giving the horse twice as many sights and sounds to keep him amused. As a prey animal, a horse needs to see all around the horizon to feel secure, so several viewpoints are beneficial.

The standard size recommended for a stable is usually 12 feet × 12 feet (3.6 m × 3.6 m) to cover all but the largest of horses or foaling stalls. Recent veterinary guidelines have suggested that this size is adequate only for a 12.2hh pony! Horses need a lot of room just to lie down and get up safely (let alone to roll). Horses may be put off lying down altogether, or risk getting cast, if they choose to roll in a stable. It certainly does not allow them adequate space to move about. My 15.2hh cob takes up 7.5 feet (2.3 m) in length of a 12-foot (3.6 m) stable. To appreciate how cramped this is, it is like you or I standing in a 4-foot (1.2 m) square box, able only to shuffle two steps forward or backward or to turn round. This is not an acceptable way to keep such an athletic and powerful animal and does not promote health or fitness.

Think about doubling the size of your stable by incorporating sliding grilled walls (or even just slip rails) as an "extension" over part of your barn area, providing an outdoor play area with the existing enclosed walls and bedding at the back section to give security – a similar arrangement to a dog pen and run. With this method, it is also possible to open the gate/slip rail between two adjoining stables, allowing both horses access to one another's areas and doubling the size yet again. The animals have

Left: *This internal stabling has good ventilation with fans to keep the air circulating. Often it is beneficial in hot weather to shade horses from the heat of the sun during the day and to turn them out at night instead.*

> 66 **As a prey animal, a horse needs to see all around the horizon to feel secure, so several viewpoints are beneficial.** 99

Above: *Generally, horses need to see all around them to feel secure enough to lie down. It is dangerous for horses to roll in confined spaces in case they get injured on feed mangers or become cast and cannot right themselves again.*

the choice to socialize or to stay apart from each other. This arrangement can be used to extend existing stables or as a design for internal barn stabling. I favor loose housing in communal barns, simply incorporating a couple of stalls with slip-rails to segregate animals when necessary.

If your budget is limited or you do not own the buildings, traditional stables can still be modified to give their occupants the choice of whether to be "in" or "out." Sectioning off parts of the barn with temporary fencing or

SPACE TO MOVE

A 15.2hh horse can take up 7.5 feet (2.3m) of floor space. It is not right that we expect horses to be fit, flexible, and athletic when we often allow them little freedom of movement in a conventional stable.

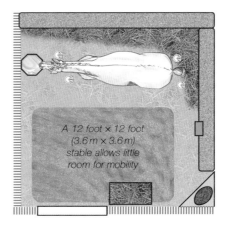

A 12 foot × 12 foot (3.6m × 3.6m) stable allows little room for mobility

Above: *When building internal stables, try to maintain an airy feel with good light and ventilation. Internal stabling is ideal for a rotational release system as the "free" animal can wander along the corridor of horses, providing companionship for all.*

Release System

A more practical approach, perhaps in a boarding stable or events barn where horses need to be worked frequently but where you do not want to have to "catch" your horse from among the rest of the herd, would be for alternate "release" days or nights on a rotation system.

In this approach, the majority of horses are stabled or in stalls as usual. The barn door is closed or the yard rails pulled across. One or two animals (probably owned by the same person) are left with their stable doors open, allowing them access to roam around the barn.

In this way, they can not only socialize and have free exercise, but they also provide entertainment and distraction for the other horses still in their stalls. Depending on the number of horses in the barn, this might mean

🐎 **Above:** *Metal grilled walls allow horses to groom one another over the bars. Make sure all neighbors are friends, however, as trying to kick through bars can cause injury.*

even just a square outside the stable door will more than double the 12-foot × 12-foot (3.6 m × 3.6 m) stall in which you had previously confined them, as well as improving viewpoints, air quality, and sunlight therapy!

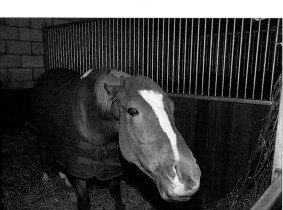

to stable them next to one another. Partitions between the stalls up to chest height still prevent injury due to possible kicks but they allow horses to groom one another. Grills between stables at least enable the animals to touch and smell.

Bear in mind that not all horses are "good company." A horse that bullies others in the field or is aggressively possessive when hay or feed is around is potentially an unsuitable neighbor who could cause anxiety to others. He should be placed into a nonconfrontational position in the barn.

Study their personalities. For example, a confident, forward-going, heavyweight hunter with a tendency to barge and nudge people and a desire to be involved in all the action would probably enjoy being at the hub of the yard. However, a more nervous type who finds it difficult to settle and is easily distracted may do better in a quieter area with just one neighbor who is likely to be on the scene for some time.

that your animal has one night out every week or ten days and is "entertained" on the remaining nights.

Equine Neighbors

Take into account your horse's neighbors. In the wild, your horse would be able to choose his companions and would have ample space around him to avoid close contact with those who harassed him. If you know your horse or pony enjoys the company of another, then try

Below: A rotational release system is simple. One horse is allowed the freedom to wander in and out of his stable and this provides entertainment and contact for the stabled horses.

Top left: These two horses are trying to touch and smell one another. A half wall between the stables or a grilled segregation wall would make it less of a stretch!

Lower left: Not all horses get along. Stabling incompatible animals next door to one another can cause anxiety, a poor appetite, or restlessness, as the intimidated animal is unable to get away or fight.

FOOD FOR A STABLED HORSE

Food or, more accurately, forage is required not only in terms of sustaining dietary needs but to keep the gut functioning correctly and for the horse's mental well-being. Horses evolved as "trickle feeders" who had to search for food, and they grazed more or less constantly on a large variety of plants of different nutritional values. This satisfied both the horse's intellectual need to be occupied and his physical needs in terms of keeping the intestines functioning well as small amounts of food were digested throughout the day.

If a horse or pony is stabled for most of the day, his access to daylight is limited and so he may be deficient in the "sunshine vitamin," vitamin D. While we can rectify this by adding a vitamin supplement or oil to the diet which contains adequate amounts of vitamin D, we all know how good it feels to have the sunshine beating down on our backs. So on bright winter days, even if it is still cold, take off your horse's rug when he is tied up in the barn or for some of the time if turned out. This gives him the opportunity to soak up the Sun's rays and for all the horses to groom each other. You will be amazed at how this "feel good" sunshine factor really works.

The positioning of feed mangers and hayracks is very important. I knew one Thoroughbred mare who was unhappy when confined to her dark stable and refused to eat anything unless it was put in a hook-over manger on the stable door or hung in a hay net at the door, so that she could look around her while she was eating.

As a general rule, I would encourage feeding forage off the floor as this mimics a horse's natural grazing position and assists the respiratory system, mucus drainage, saliva glands, and general musculoskeletal posture.

Left: Horses evolved as trickle feeders, covering many miles in search of sufficient food. Naturally kept horses rarely succumb to the many illnesses associated with stabling.

Many horses naturally want to look around them as they eat. This is easy when they are grazing in the field. When enclosed by solid walls, it means they have to take a mouthful then raise their necks to look over the stable door. This emphasizes the unsuitability of most stables because they prevent the animal from looking in all directions so that they can reassure themselves that they are "safe." By using hay nets or racks at an appropriate height (level with their muzzles to avoid dust falling into their eyes) and positioning these adjacent to the door opening or, perhaps, on a grilled separating side wall, they can look around and watch their neighbors while eating and so relax more fully.

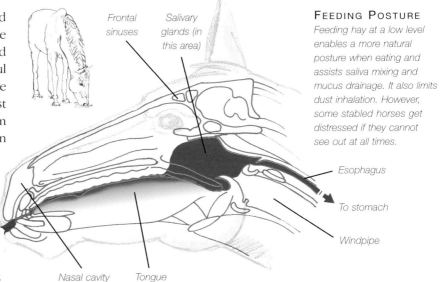

Frontal sinuses

Salivary glands (in this area)

Esophagus

To stomach

Windpipe

Nasal cavity

Tongue

FEEDING POSTURE
Feeding hay at a low level enables a more natural posture when eating and assists saliva mixing and mucus drainage. It also limits dust inhalation. However, some stabled horses get distressed if they cannot see out at all times.

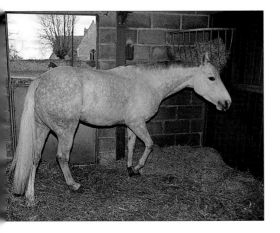

Left and far left: Put the hayrack somewhere with an interesting view. Providing a constant supply of forage in an effort to reduce boredom will not have the desired effect if the horse is expected to face a blank wall for hours on end!

As a general rule, we normally offer our animals two meals a day with hay given in between, which is a pretty good compromise. The lack of variety and the fact that often processed foods are used is not wholly satisfactory. There are a vast quantity of excellent quality feeds on the market, specially developed for different "types" of horses and ponies. For most horses and ponies kept outside, they provide a convenient way of ensuring energy levels, as well as vitamins and minerals, are "topped up."

❝ If a horse or pony is stabled for most of the day, his access to daylight is limited and so he may be deficient in the "sunshine vitamin," vitamin D. ❞

Stabled animals do not use much energy keeping warm or move around much searching for food. So they should not be offered food constantly through-out the day simply to alleviate boredom, because of the risk that they will get too fat. However, I feel that offering two meals a day of "quality" feed plus hay to a stabled horse prevents the animal from enjoying a more regular supply of natural-type feeds.

We concern ourselves with the quality of hay too much. Although it is an important

Above: Not only is the location of any hay net important, but the height is too. If it is hung too high, grass seeds and dust may fall into the horse's eyes or be inhaled. If hung too low, it may get caught by rug straps or wrapped round legs. Muzzle height is a good guide.

DIETING

An overweight horse has more fun eating its calories in the form of a bucket full of chaff with a few pony nuts rather than a handful of a higher nutritional feed.

consideration, supplying top-quality hay may not actually be the best solution for some animals. For horses or ponies requiring large quantities of fiber and bulk, it is often advantageous to substitute thrashed grass or straw as part of the diet, provided it is free of poisonous plants and mold. This adds interest to the diet and keeps the gut working, which in turn will make the animal feel full and content without too much weight gain.

Succulents are *so* important too. As they consist of predominantly water and fiber, they can be fed to "fatties," and they add moisture and interest to the diet. One thing I would stress is *do not cut them up, at all.* Whatever they are, carrots, apples, cauliflower leaves, or tree branches, leave them whole so your horse or pony can bite and nibble at them as he wishes. Why people cut up food is beyond me. Horses are quite capable of biting off suitably sized mouthfuls. This is also far more satisfying to them. It also helps to exercise the horse's jaw and teeth more than eating already chopped-up "baby food"!

The subject of feeding is covered in detail in Chapter 7, but I include an example of how to create a more natural diet for a stabled horse here. First a word of warning: In practice, this timetable would be very difficult to achieve unless you were at the barn almost all day. It would probably still result in an overweight animal as the horse has expended no effort in the search for the food offered. However, it is included here as food for thought:

❏ **7a.m.** Very small feed of quality mix + fiber in the form of chaff or alfalfa depending on dietary needs

❏ **8a.m.** One section of hay in hay net or from the floor – good quality, fine hay

❏ **9a.m.** Large branch of willow tree/bunch of blackberry brambles/branch of rose hips/bunch of cow parsley/bunch of cleavers

❏ **10a.m.** Thrashed grass hay or hay/straw blend offered in hay net or off the floor

❏ **12p.m.** Very small feed of economy-type pony nuts with chaff/alfalfa, etc.

❏ **1p.m.** Fresh grass, horse either led out to eat this for ½–1 hour or grass picked and offered to the horse (very time consuming!)

❏ **2p.m.** Haylage or dried grass in small-holed hay net

❏ **4p.m.** Very small feed of economy-type pony nuts with chaff/alfalfa, etc.

❏ **5p.m.** Thrashed grass hay or hay/straw blend offered in hay net or from the floor

❏ **7p.m.** Very small feed of quality mix + fiber in the form of chaff or alfalfa, depending on dietary needs

❏ **9p.m.** Bucket of carrots or other fresh root vegetables

🐎 *Above and top: There are many types of grass hays, straws, and legume hays. Don't simply look for one that offers high nutritional value, but assess your horse's needs. Stabled horses may benefit from three hay nets of a nutritionally lower-fiber source rather than one section of top-quality forage to maintain condition. Succulents can be fed in large quantities.*

❏ **10p.m.** Thrashed grass hay or hay/straw blend offered in hay net or from the floor to last through the night plus some kind of trickle-feed feeding toy

Left: Stabled horses often suffer from respiratory problems as well as poor function of the digestive and lymphatic systems.

Below left: Sharing jobs with other people at the barn means the horses receive more attention than would otherwise be possible.

Below: Field-kept horses have many choices: when to eat, where to eat, what to eat, and who to eat with!

Of course, this is a very impractical way of feeding. It still does not allow for dietary variation during the nine hours between 10 P.M. and 7 A.M. It is rather intended to highlight just how inadequate are the "normal" methods of feeding a stabled horse in terms of its mental and physical well-being. In the wild, food is often scarce. So while animals would not be eating constantly, they would be actively occupied looking for food or water.

Standing still for hours on end is detrimental to all the main life-supporting systems in the horse's body, including the blood, lymphatic, respiratory, and digestive systems. By using small-holed hay nets and by

putting several small hay nets or piles of hay/straw/carrots, etc. at different corners of the stable or yard, you guarantee that your horse will have to move around to get its food, aiding digestion and helping to disperse gas and avoid colic. It is also a lot more mentally stimulating to find food. This plays a small but significant part in making our horses' lives more stimulating.

It may be possible to share jobs with other people at a barn. This means that there are people on hand at different times to distribute feeds or turn out horses (or lead out in hand to graze) at as many opportunities as possible.

> ❝ For horses or ponies requiring large quantities of fiber and bulk, it is often advantageous to substitute thrashed grass or straw as part of the diet, provided it is free of poisonous plants and mold. ❞

🐎 **Below:** *Change the water in buckets completely rather than just topping them off. Once it has become stale, it will not be palatable.*

🐎 **Bottom:** *Automatic waterers provide a constant supply of fresh water and cannot be tipped over. The only drawback is that you cannot gauge the amount your horse is drinking, and the time the bowl takes to fill can frustrate a thirsty horse.*

WATER

Water should be available 24 hours a day. In the wild, horses do not have water on tap wherever they may be, but they never stray far from a water source. Water is drunk from lakes, streams, and canyons. Domestic horses often favor flood surface water, or other natural water sources, in preference to the tap water we offer them.

Automatic waterers Although convenient, these do not allow you to check how much your horse or pony is drinking, and an early

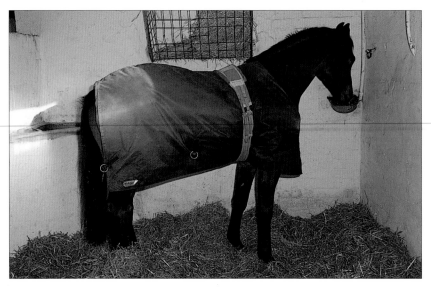

symptom of illness could be missed. Waterers with small drinking bowls may be slow to refill and therefore frustrating for a thirsty horse. They do, however, maintain a constant fresh supply which is unlikely to become stale or contaminated.

Buckets These are preferable to the horse as they allow it to take a full quaff of water in one go to quench its thirst. A disadvantage is that they can be knocked over or not filled

🐎 **Left:** Horses often drink from sources that we may deem unsuitable, e.g., a muddy puddle or a tub full of rainwater. This may be purely for convenience, but it may also be that the mineral content of natural rain or river water differs from water that comes from a tap.

WATER INTAKE

Fresh grass contains up to 80 percent water, whereas hay and cereals average 15 percent water. Hard work and hot weather mean water intake will increase – 5.5–15 gallons (25–70 l) of water derived from fluid and food sources will be needed per day.

❝ Horses often favor flood surface water, or other natural water sources, in preference to the tap water we offer them. ❞

regularly enough, leaving the animal without water. Buckets can be hooked or mounted onto the wall of the stall to prevent them being tipped over.

Water in stables can become stale or contaminated with dust, droppings, or old food, making it unappetizing or not drunk at all. When refilling buckets, do not simply just top off with clean water but, at least every other day, renew the water completely.

Rainwater can be collected from gutters along the stable roof and channeled into water butts with taps from which you can fill buckets. This allows your horse the benefits of natural soft water without the fluoride, chlorine, and other chemicals which are often added to our water supply. Make sure the water butts are fitted with grills to stop leaves or other debris from collecting in them and contaminating the water as they rot.

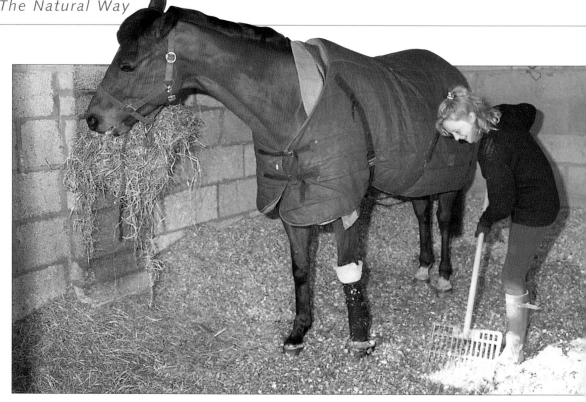

Right: *If you have ever stood for a long time on a "designer" quarry-tiled floor and been racked with backache for the rest of the day, you will appreciate how some form of cushioning underfoot places less strain on the joints and tendons. For a horse it is essential.*

66 Horses, even those who live out, love to come into a stable with a new, deep bed and will often dig it up, snort at it, circle, and almost immediately roll in it with great delight. 99

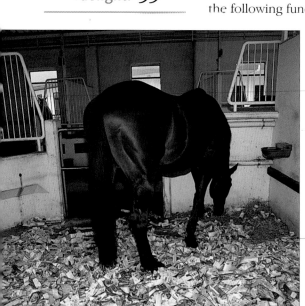

Above: *Paper bedding is highly absorbent and can be homemade by using a shredder machine.*

BEDDING

From the horse's point of view, bedding has the following functions: it

❑ provides somewhere comfortable for them to lie down,

❑ allows them to stale without splashing their feet and legs,

❑ provides insulation and creates a nondrafty warm/cool atmosphere,

❑ enables them to dig, forage, or pursue another natural activity that a floor of concrete does not allow. The choice of bedding available to us is excellent, and nearly all materials satisfy the various needs listed above.

Winter bedding My personal choice for winter would be baled long-stem straw or, if this is impractical, chopped straw, flax, or hemp. Make a deep bed to cut out drafts and to keep legs warm even when horses are standing. A deep bed with banks helps to prevent injury from getting cast when rolling or lying down, e.g., capped hocks. It also has a cushioning effect to help alleviate joint strain. Straw very rarely causes a problem if eaten and gives the horse another source of dietary fiber and foraging activity. Some chopped straw-type beddings are processed with chemicals including denatonium benzoate to discourage eating if this is what you require. A deep litter system can be used provided the ventilation is good and plenty of new bedding is added so that the ammonia from the urine does not become overpowering, leading to respiratory and skin complaints.

Summer bedding For summer use, my preference is for using wood shavings as these form a good, soft bed without creating too much heat in warm weather. Even their light-colored appearance seems to impart a cooling image to a stable. Added to this, they are quicker to clean and, in turn, make a smaller muck heap, which has to be good news for any owner.

Although even better in terms of minimal waste material and speed of muck removal, rubber matting without bedding or with only a sprinkling to soak up urine is not ideal from the horse's point of view. First, many horses are put off urinating as they dislike their legs getting splashed. Second, some can be reluctant to lie down. Yes, horses frequently roll and lie down outside on hard ground and rubber matting offers far more cushioning than this. However, if you offer your horse the choice of two stables, one with a deep bed and one just with rubber matting with/without a sprinkling of bedding, it is likely that he will choose the deep bed. (Note: If you try this experiment, be sure to use two totally new stables as a horse will instinctively go into its usual stable out of habit.)

Horses, even those who live out, love to come into a stable with a new, deep bed and will often dig it up, snort at it, circle, and almost immediately roll in it with great delight.

Rubber matting is, however, useful as a base under all bedding to insulate against the cold of a concrete floor. It is especially effective as a cushion used where their forelegs stand, just behind the stable door where there would be little or no bedding. It is also useful in shelters in the field which cannot be bedded down daily.

COMPANY WHEN STABLED

Being stabled does not have to mean the same as being secluded.

Communal barns catering for between two and 20 horses, depending on the size, can be used. Indeed, when you consider how successful this method is for dairy herds of 100+ cows, it is amazing that it is not used more widely. I would strongly advise that you keep the numbers to below ten animals, however. Unless horses, ponies, and donkeys with compatible temperaments are chosen as companions, you may learn the hard way that equines are far more aggressive toward one another in a confined area than cows are!

This is a simple method which requires little time and effort in maintenance as the barn can be bedded in a deep litter system which can be mucked out by a tractor every

Above: *Communal barns may be the way forward for many establishments. The horses enjoy social contact, and daily maintenance is far less time consuming.*

FEEDING TIME

Horses kept in barns can be fed their forage in long troughs (like cattle) and fed concentrates in well-spaced hook-over mangers.

Left: *A horse will be more comfortable when lying down, rolling (and urinating) on some form of thick bedding, or even a sand/dirt bed, rather than on rubber matting alone.*

Above: We should aim to provide more freedom of choice for our horses. We spend far too much time and energy working against nature instead of with it, and we still expect our horses to be fit and happy. Horses want freedom, friends, and food.

Right: Horses **love** to be dirty. Generally, we **hate** them being dirty. If they are happy, we should be happy! Remember: you can still ride a muddy horse.

few weeks. It may have a similar surface to a manège and be skipped out as necessary.

If looking at stabling from a *horse's* point of view has not persuaded you that it is a bad idea to keep your horse in for long periods of time, perhaps the many advantages of not keeping your horse stabled from a *human* point of view will.

❏ Less mucking out

❏ It is much cheaper – little or no bedding is required.

❏ You will have a lot more free time to enjoy your animal rather than just cleaning up after it, changing hay nets, water, etc.

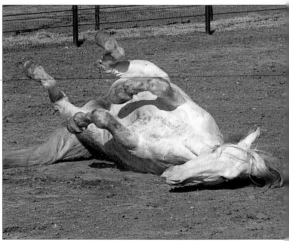

❏ Sleep late in the morning! No more getting up early every day just to let your horse out – a field-kept horse or even one in a yard is free to come and go as he likes.

STABLE CARE FROM THE HORSE'S POINT OF VIEW

Horses do not "fit" with our picture-postcard image of them. We love them to be clean, they love to be dirty. Naturally they will roll in mud to coat the hair as a form of insulation against the wind or lie down in marshy plains to cool and refresh themselves. Dust "baths" are used to remove flies and loose hairs. All forms of rolling (in healthy horses) are a sign of contentment and indicate that they feel secure and happy in the environment around them. Unfortunately, this pleasurable pastime for the horse is a positive nuisance for us as owners. However, the time spent in "rectifying" the results of rolling, and returning the horse to our desired "clean" image by copious grooming, is time well spent.

Grooming develops a social bond between you and your horse or pony. It stimulates blood flow to the skin's surface and often produces a calming effect on the horse, lowering his heart rate. It also allows you to examine the animal's body for scratches and swellings that could easily be missed from a distance. It should be enjoyable for both parties, but always bear in mind the following points.

❏ Groom outside the stable, otherwise you and your horse will inhale dust and particles of mud. Hair and dust will be dispersed into the bedding or water in the stable.

❏ A wet or muddy horse can still be ridden. If time is short, just clean (and dry off with a towel) the areas where the saddle, bridle, and girth will lie.

❏ Don't worry about having a muddy horse – the horse does not care!

Stabled horses, especially those with rugs on, should ideally be groomed daily as they will not have the benefit of rubbing against scratching posts or enjoying the attention of an equine friend to relieve any itches. They will greatly appreciate this attention.

I groom my loose-housed horses fully only once a week, other than when they are shedding. They actually seem happier being dusty or muddy. This is proven by the fact they don't stay clean for very long after a thorough grooming!

 **Above:** *Grooming your horse develops a bond between you. Some horses even try reciprocal grooming to their owners' surprise!*

❝ **Horses do not "fit" with our picture-postcard image of them. We love them to be clean, they love to be dirty.** ❞

Left: *Always try to groom **outside** the stable. Inside, the dust and hairs are more likely to be inhaled by both of you and particles may fall into the water container.*

> ❝ Water is good for the hooves, better than any hoof oil on the market ❞

Below: Wild horses encounter many types of terrain, and their hooves still remain surprisingly sound.

Looking After Hooves

Most people insist on picking out their horse's hooves immediately after the animal has been turned out in the field or ridden and before returning him to his stable. Could this actually be detrimental?

Wild horses encounter all types of terrain, from dry and stony to muddy and marshy. While they may become lame from time to time with bruised soles or puncture wounds,

constant. Moisture can transfer through the tissues of the frog, which contain about 40 percent moisture, to the sole and hoof wall, which have a moisture content of about 15 percent.

Nowadays, it is common practice to bring a horse in from a saturated muddy field where he may have been standing for hours, pick out his feet and then stand him on a bed of spongelike wood shavings! Much of the moisture held in

Above right: Trying to maintain a constant moisture content in the hooves is difficult in a domestic situation. Hoof oil can help to lock in moisture after a hoof has been hosed with water.

THE UNDERSIDE OF THE HOOF

Many breeds of wild horses utilize the horn, sole, bulbs, and frog for weight bearing. The frog is often wider and flatter than in domestic shod horses, who carry most of their weight on the hoof wall (horn) alone.

they rarely have the hoof problems that we so frequently experience today, such as dry and splitting hooves or thrush.

Climate conditions change *slowly*. This means that the balance of moisture contained in the hoof wall, sole, and frog stays fairly

the hoof is then rapidly absorbed, drying out and contracting the hoof tissues and causing cracks and splitting. We may then return the horse to damp conditions the following day, where the tissues will expand again in the moisture, and then back into dry bedding again, exacerbating the problem each time.

The problem here is simply the sudden change in conditions. By not picking out the feet and leaving the mud in situ (other than removing any large stones embedded in it), we are maintaining a stable hoof environment for longer. The bedding will dry out the encased mud rather than the sole of the foot.

The frog should be slightly longer than the hoof walls to allow it to make contact with the ground. This promotes blood flow to keep it healthy. Sudden changes in temperature and moisture content cause the thrush bacteria to thrive. Any dried-out dead flesh which would

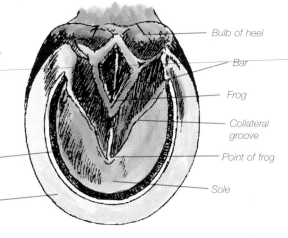

Bulb of heel

Bar

Frog

Collateral groove

Point of frog

Sole

White line (junction between horn and sole)

Wall (horn)

harbor these bacteria should be carefully trimmed off by the farrier to maintain a healthy frog.

Be brave! We must try to balance the use of what we have been taught as "correct" horse care with its potential detrimental effects. I have been living by this system for two decades now, and the horses in my care have *never* had problems with weak or brittle hooves. I only pick out the hooves fully just before riding.

Above: If you are bringing in a horse from a wet environment onto dry, absorbent bedding, it is actually better *not* to pick out his hooves (except for stones). Leaving the mud in place will stop the hooves from drying out so rapidly.

Water is good for the hooves, better than any hoof oil on the market, although oils can help "lock in" moisture if it is applied after the hooves have been hosed with water.

"But My Horse Is Too Delicate To Be Living Out"

At the time of writing, it is 36°F (2°C) daytime temperature, falling to 23°F (−5°C) at night. Unfortunately, I have recently had to move to a barn where the stables are situated away from the field. Every evening, I allow my horses to choose where they would like to spend the night. Two of them are kept overnight in the barn with their stable doors left open to wander in and out as they wish, but my Thoroughbred chooses to stay out in the field. In the last three weeks of bad weather, she has decided to come in only twice. She is rugged and does not miss out on her feed. This is simply given to her in the field, and a hay net is tied to the fence to avoid the hay freezing on the ground in these low temperatures. She is free to choose her place for the night, and her choice surely shows that horses naturally like an outdoor life.

Above: Any breed of horse can thrive living out, but I encourage the use of rugs when necessary. Although not "natural," it avoids some of the harsh realities of living out in bad weather, including rain scald or loss of body weight through shivering.

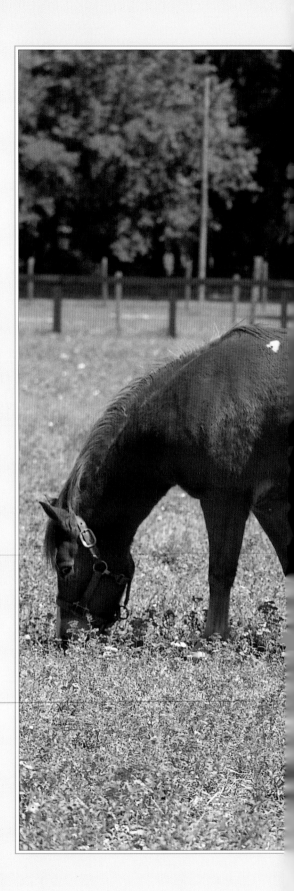

CHAPTER 4

Field and Grazing Requirements

From Your Horse's Point of View

Despite thousands of years of domestication, the behavior of horses has changed very little from that displayed by their free-roaming relatives. Even if they are restricted to small paddocks rather than huge expanses of changing scenery, they will still attempt to use the available space in a similar manner, using the same areas for dunging time and time again and returning to other areas for rolling or shelter. They may also have favorite scratching posts, whether natural or manmade.

Above: A horse's lips are surprisingly dextrous when selecting and sorting herbage or grains. The touch and smell of plants helps identify which are palatable and which are poisonous.
Right: Free grazing provides the most natural diet and assists better digestion and circulatory function in the form of gentle exercise.

Below: *All horses need to be turned out to graze – the trick is to select the type of grazing to suit the individual animal. A pony may be healthier on unfertilized permanent pasture, whereas a performance horse may need highly managed three-year leys to thrive.*

Many of us do not have the benefit of our own unlimited grazing. At some time during the year, it is almost a foregone conclusion that we will have some kind of problem – either too little or no grass available or grass growing too readily for the type of animals we are feeding.

We tend to simplify and generalize our requirements and assess suitable fields by asking the following questions:

❏ Is the grass of high nutritional quality; does it resemble a beautiful lawn?
❏ Is the fencing how we would like it, e.g., post and rail?
❏ Is there a barn nearby into which the horses can be brought?
❏ Is the field relatively flat to allow lunging/riding in it?
❏ Can the field be sectioned off into several smaller paddocks?

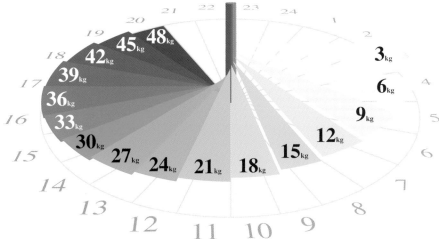

❏ Is there a field rotation system, and how are worms controlled?

Horses need a diet made up predominantly of fiber, topped off with any vitamins or minerals that may be lacking. They have a psychological need to chew and can eat up to as much as eight percent of their body weight in grass. They can eat around 6.6 pounds (3 kg) of grass per hour and generally eat for about 16 hours out of a 24-hour period. By a simple calculation, we can see that they get through an enormous amount of fiber in a day – 106 pounds (48 kg) approximately.

To summarize, horses want *freedom, forage,* and *friends.*

DIETARY INTAKE

Horses have a prodigious appetite for grass – up to 6.6 pounds (3 kg) an hour for 16 hours a day. They are capable of eating from early in the morning until around about midnight.

Opposite and below:
Horses evolved as free-roaming animals. In most cases, it is healthier and more natural to allow them more – in terms of grazing time, land area, and intake – on poorer grazing or scrub rather than a couple of hours on a postage stamp of highly nutritious grass.

Conversely, we should be aiming to match the requirements of our animals as individuals to the type of field(s) we are going to use and take into account possible climatic changes throughout the seasons. Therefore we *should* be asking the following questions:

❏ Is the blend of grass of a suitable nutritional quality for our horse/pony?

❏ Is the fencing safe and suitable for our type of horse/pony?

❏ Is the size of field(s) adequate to last the entire year or, if not, are there alternative areas for turnout?

❏ Is the grazing *too good* and, if so, are there alternative areas for turnout?

❏ Will the horse have company, at least for most of the time?

❏ Is there adequate shelter in each field?

❏ Is there good drainage in the field, either natural or manmade?

❝ **Horses have a psychological need to chew and can eat up to as much as eight percent of their body weight in grass.** ❞

GRAZING

Poor doers require highly nutritious grass to thrive. Good doers and laminitics require the grazing to be consistently lower in starch, sugar, and fructans.

Grass Quality

Grass is the best diet we can provide, and the cheapest. It is our most useful asset, so we must preserve it as best we can. One common misconception is that horses and ponies need top-quality grass, almost to the standard of a putting green on a golf course! Feral horses travel between lush lower plains with an abundance of · nutritious vegetation to inhospitable dry mountainous areas where food is scarce. Their weight and condition fluctuate greatly throughout the seasons as they are forced to live off fat reserves in times of cruel weather or lack of sustenance. Fortunately, we are able to control the provisions for our domestic horses and relieve the stresses and physical problems caused in the wild by food and water shortages and adverse climatic conditions.

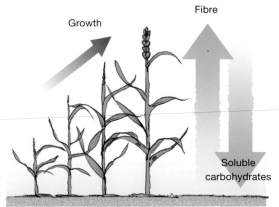

THE GROWTH STAGES OF GRASS
Regularly topped or young, leafy grass is higher in soluble carbohydrates but lower in fiber than grass allowed to go to seed, which has a higher fiber-to-carbohydrate ratio.

 ***Above:*** *Wild horses and ponies are able to graze without constraint. Although their weight fluctuates greatly from midwinter to high summer, they seldom suffer the problems (laminitis, colic, etc.) that our domestic horses seem predisposed to.*

What nondomestic equines do show us is that horses' physical makeup has changed very little despite mans' intervention. Many horses and ponies can still thrive on poorer-quality grazing. In fact, it is the pampered lifestyle of living on overrich grazing and over-compensated concentrated feeds, and not having to expend energy in searching out food,

that is one of the reasons why domestic horses seem to have an inherent predisposition to the common problems we face today, such as laminitis, obesity, and hoof problems. These rarely affected their feral relatives.

Horses are designed to eat plants other than just grass. Wild horses encounter barren landscapes with very little grass. Their diet may

more or less common practice to restrict the grazing of obese or laminitic ponies to a couple of hours in a small paddock of good grass (or, alternatively a starvation-type paddock which may contain grass high in fructans due to its stressed growth). Both of these methods can cause problems. By lowering the nutritional value in the grass generally by year-round grazing and increasing the area in which the animal has to move in order to find food, a large field of even four or more hectares (10+ acres), which would previously have been out of bounds, can be grazed by more animals for more of the time. The digestive systems of animals like these which are kept out *all year-round* on these pastures will actually become more tolerant of chemical and nutritional changes in the grass.

consist of mainly gorse, brush, or even twigs for several months. Even when grass becomes readily available, they will still supplement their diet with tree leaves, hawthorn berries, wild rose hips, and other vegetation to gain vitamins and add variety to their feed.

When you view a potential field for grazing your horse, always take into account the nutritional requirements of the individual animal. Is it a poor doer – one that is hard to keep weight on? If this is the case, a long season of highly nutritious grazing is desirable, which can be supplemented when the nutritional levels in the grass fall. You may find that several paddocks of lush grass, which are rested in turn to allow the growth to replenish, are the most suitable grazing for this type of animal.

On the other hand, a good doer or an easy keeper, such as a warmblood who still requires bulk and fiber to satisfy his grazing instincts, could be turned out on old pasture which may have areas of lawns and roughs or even rocky or sandy areas containing longer grass that has dried out or gone to seed. Nowadays, it is

Left: *Stabling ponies who may then gorge on rich grazing causes problems. Many ponies are directly related to feral ponies of the same breed (e.g., Welsh, Dartmoor, New Forest, etc.) who consistently live on a diet of grass but they do not get problems like laminitis. We overmanage domestic ponies – it is **our** fault!*

Below: *Horses relish the choice to eat plants other than grass alone. What we perceive as unpalatable is often beneficial to them. Horses often enjoy the new growth on prickly plants such as thistles, gorse, and even pine needles.*

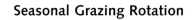

To prevent vitamin deficiencies in animals relying on a diet solely consisting of grass, vitamin/mineral blocks can be put out for them. Check every animal *daily* for signs of injury or illness, and monitor their weight and condition carefully.

In most cases, quantity is more important that quality.

I appreciate that it may be difficult to find adequate grazing, but this should be your priority at the start. In the longer term five into two does not go – five horses into 2 acres (0.8 ha) that is, so you must think quantity as well as quality.

A larger area of grazing or turnout allows you to section it off into small parcels of lush grass on a rotational system or to use large areas as rough grazing for a less cultivated diet.

In the wild, horses migrate around chosen grazing grounds, following seasonal growth and climatic changes to enjoy optimum food and water sources and shelter. Although their

Above: *Horses at grass should have free access to a vitamin/mineral block to balance any deficiencies that may occur. I prefer those without molasses.*

Left: *Rotation of fields extends the grazing season and allows the sward to recover from overgrazing and trampling.*

Seasonal Grazing Rotation

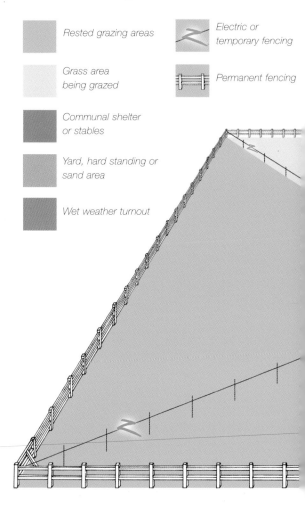

Rested grazing areas	Electric or temporary fencing
Grass area being grazed	Permanent fencing
Communal shelter or stables	
Yard, hard standing or sand area	
Wet weather turnout	

> 66 In a small way, by using a rotation system, we are mimicking nature by allowing our animals to move on to a fresh area. The delight they display when a gate is opened to new pasture is all too apparent. 99

Left: *It is easier to remove droppings from smaller areas. Strip grazing is a good system to preserve grass if space is limited, although not as equine friendly as grazing a large field.*

territory may extend over many hundreds of miles, they tend to return to the same areas year after year.

In a small way, by using a rotation system, we are mimicking nature by allowing our animals to move on to a fresh area. The delight they display when a gate is opened to new pasture is all too apparent. I suggest dividing up the land into three patches and grazing each for about four to six weeks before worming the horses and moving them on to the next area. This gives each field between eight and 12 weeks to reestablish a strong sward.

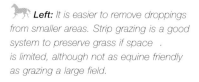

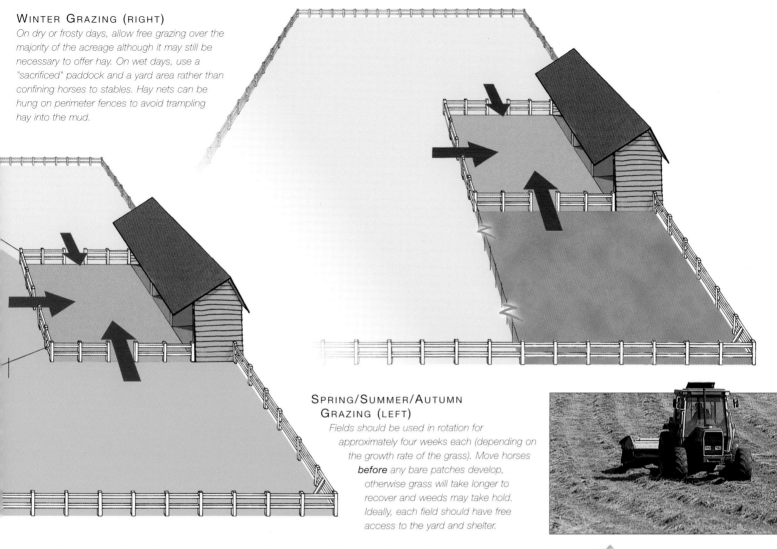

WINTER GRAZING (RIGHT)

On dry or frosty days, allow free grazing over the majority of the acreage although it may still be necessary to offer hay. On wet days, use a "sacrificed" paddock and a yard area rather than confining horses to stables. Hay nets can be hung on perimeter fences to avoid trampling hay into the mud.

SPRING/SUMMER/AUTUMN GRAZING (LEFT)

*Fields should be used in rotation for approximately four weeks each (depending on the growth rate of the grass). Move horses **before** any bare patches develop, otherwise grass will take longer to recover and weeds may take hold. Ideally, each field should have free access to the yard and shelter.*

In the winter, when the growing season has finished and the grass is virtually dormant, any dividing fences can be removed and the animals allowed to graze on the full expanse for several months until just before the start of the growing season in the spring. In this way, the animals benefit from the extra freedom and can use this extra space to keep active and warm, and to mooch about and find additional sources of vegetation as the season progresses. There is likely to be a wider choice of shelter available. Because old pasture is better able to withstand hoof damage than newer sward, the larger area offered should help with problems of poaching in wet weather. Contingency plans should be made to cope with this if necessary. Perhaps a small area can be given up as allocated turnout during the wettest periods.

There is also the potential for making your own hay from any excess grass allowed to grow in the idle area. The animals only have to be kept off the fields in the growing season for a total of about four months. Although the timing of harvesting hay is a tricky business with the risk of the whole crop being lost if it does not dry out quickly, any crop you do obtain will be from a known and trusted source.

Above: If you are fortunate to have excess grassland, it is possible to take a crop of hay or haylage. It's good to know that you can be confident of its quality and source.

SOIL TESTING
Identifying the pH of your soil will assist you with identifying ways to improve its quality. The factors of soil fertility, temperature, and rainfall combine to convert energy from the Sun into plant growth.

9.0 pH	Alkalinity too high for horses
8.5 pH	Alkaline
7.5 pH	Progressively alkaline
7.0 pH	Neutral
6.5 pH	Progressively acid
6.0 pH	**IDEAL FOR HORSES**
5.5 pH	Acidic
4.5 pH	High acidity

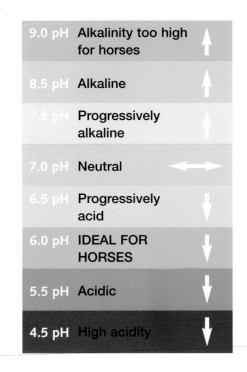

🐎 **Above:** *Conservation and pasture management can go hand in hand. Established permanent pasture naturally has an abundance of wild herbs, grasses, and flowers.*

IMPROVING POOR PASTURE

If the number or type of horses or ponies being grazed on the land dictates that better pasture is needed, or the land has been overgrazed and taken over by weed infestations, you may need to take action to preserve your asset.

Step 1 Analyze Your Soil

Before anything can be done, you need to assess how fertile the soil is. The quality and speed of plant growth, including grass, is dictated by the nutrients present in the soil. Deficiencies or imbalances in your soil are what cause the weak growth or invasion of weeds, such as buttercups or nettles. It may be that your soil has compacted, restricting root development. An aerator will then be needed to lighten the soil and improve drainage.

It is usually possible to work out where the problem lies, be it a mineral deficiency caused by soil that is overacidic or over-alkaline, or simply that drought or water logging has damaged the root system of the sward. Acidic soil is obvious by the prevalent growth of buttercups and may weed, while alkaline soil is most commonly associated with chalky or limy areas. It is, however, far better and more accurate to test your soil using a kit available from farm and garden centers or have it analyzed by an agronomist.

Soil testing is equally important whether you are improving your existing pasture or seeding agricultural land to create new pasture. The pH required for grazing equines is

> 66 **The pH required for grazing equines is about 6 – horses grazed on pasture designed for dairy cattle, with a pH of up to 9, can have serious problems.** 99

about 6 – horses grazed on pasture designed for dairy cattle, with a pH of up to 9, can have serious problems.

If you are planting land with new seed, the soil should be balanced beforehand. For example, add lime or seaweed to neutralize an acid soil, or sand to lighten heavy clay soil. However, the vast amount of sand required for this purpose often makes it an uneconomical option. In this situation, regular surface dressings will need to be applied.

Step 2 Choose Your Grass Seed Carefully

Modern farming methods favor quantity and speed of growth rather than being concerned with the diversity of meadow species that were prevalent years ago. It is a shame that the limited range of herbage available in most paddocks may actually be contributing to dietary imbalances in our animals when such a wealth of beneficial grasses and herbs can so easily be included when planting land to pasture or oversowing existing pasture.

There are many grass varieties, and when choosing seed, it is advisable to select a mixture of species to enable you to benefit from the different qualities they offer. Some, such as timothy, fescues, and bents, produce a low sward of tender leaves with a high nutritional content, but they are slower growing and less resilient to frost or hoof damage. Others, such as ryegrass, are faster growing but have tougher leaves and may require more fertilizer. Clovers put nitrogen back into the soil, which will reduce the amount of fertilizer needed on the pasture. White clover is more beneficial in equine pasture, as it is thought that red clover may have a possible link to grass sickness in horses.

Including clover, alfalfa, and trefoils in your mix of herbage will enhance its nutritional value. A combination of all these

Left: *Acidic soil is obvious by the prevalent growth of buttercups. Horses manage admirably to eat around them, but they are poisonous if consumed in large quantities.*

Below: *Organic dressings of minerals or seaweed can be used as well as organic foliar sprays, which feed plants through their leaves*

together will form a dense sward to fight off invasive weeds, such as docks and ragwort.

If you are reseeding small bare patches in a field, it may be possible to do this by hand. Otherwise, it is best to seek assistance from a specialist contractor. Reseeding should take place in the spring or autumn.

Step 3 Apply Fertilizers

If you have a pony or horse susceptible to laminitis, it is wise to avoid chemical fertilizers completely as the changes in the structure of the grass and the increased soluble carbohydrates that they encourage can actually trigger an attack.

However, if your agronomist (or agricultural extension office) has advised on the deficiencies existing in the soil and a boost in your crop of grass is required, spring and autumn are the times when a surface dressing of fertilizer can be applied. Most of these contain a mixture of the three major nutrients required by the soil – nitrogen, phosphates, and potash – with sulphur, sodium, zinc, and other trace elements added in varying ratios.

Nitrogen is responsible for "kick starting" and promoting the growth. However, the maximum amount recommended for horse pastures (as opposed to those for dairy or beef cattle) is 27–36 pounds per acre (30–40 kg/ha). Nitrogen cannot, however, be used on its own. For every unit of nitrogen used to promote growth, equal amounts of phosphates and potash are needed to replenish and balance soil nutrients in the longer term.

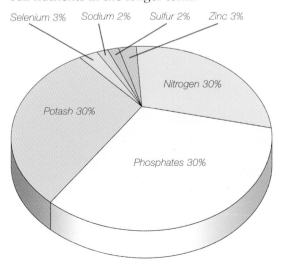

Selenium 3% Sodium 2% Sulfur 2% Zinc 3%
Nitrogen 30%
Potash 30%
Phosphates 30%

THE COMPONENTS IN FERTILIZER
Although not "organic," these components are present in all living cells. However, excessive fertilizer use may only help in the short term. Caution is advised as sudden changes in grass structure can trigger an attack of laminitis.

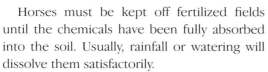

> **Horses must be kept off fertilized fields until the chemicals have been fully absorbed into the soil.**

Below: *Grass is a valuable asset. Although methods of management will be dictated by the types of horses or ponies grazing, all horses benefit from year-round palatable grass, so you should strive to provide it.*

Right: *Farmyard manure and muck spread on rested fields provides beneficial organic fertilizer which may not be as "instant" as artificial types but is unlikely to eradicate weeds (good and bad) or pollute water sources. Chain harrowing is useful not only to spread manure but also to remove dead grass and moss (perhaps after the field is topped) and to allow more light and air to get to the new shoots.*

Horses must be kept off fertilized fields until the chemicals have been fully absorbed into the soil. Usually, rainfall or watering will dissolve them satisfactorily.

I am in favor of being natural and organic. It is possible to achieve good results by using organic dressings or organic foliar sprays which replenish the plant through the leaves rather than via the roots in the soil. Natural minerals, such as limestone and rock phosphate, can be added as well as calcified seaweed to condition the soil. Well-rotted farm manure or horse manure (minus the bedding) can be spread by machine on rested fields or spread on *larger* fields rather than poo-picking. Regular chain cultivating of the muck over the fields in hot, dry weather will help to kill off any worm burden. This manure will subsequently be broken down by heavy rain and insect and worm action into an excellent fertilizer. The muck *must* be spread or cultivated over the grass to make it an effective fertilizer – leaving it in piles has the opposite effect of actually killing the grass, making patches unpalatable and allowing weeds to thrive in its place.

Step 4 Manage the Grass

Although horses demand grass year-round, the pattern of grass growth is seasonal, resulting in either too much or too little grass at different times of year. The fast spurt in grass growth during the spring and summer may mean that your horses do not keep up with the rate at which it is growing. Tall, stemmy growth and patches of "old," bitter wasted grass will result. Although it may seem drastic, topping the field with a tractor mower or similar will encourage the swards to tiller (produce side shoots) and create a more even, denser crop of sweeter grass. About 3–4 inches (8–10 cm) is ideal. This "topping" may need to be carried out several times during the year.

It is a good idea to use an aerator once a year to improve the filtration of air and water through the soil if it has become compacted. You should also chain harrow the surface at least twice a year to remove any dead grass or moss and so increase light and air flow to the new shoots. You may be able to acquire a set of chain harrows and either hitch them to a four-wheel-drive motor or tractor, or perhaps use the traditional method of horsepower to drag them around the field!

Make it a habit to pick up droppings on small paddocks. Leaving them for more than 24 hours causes tainted and unpalatable burned patches of grass, making an already

Above: *Rutting caused by water logged fields in winter could cause severe lameness and even broken limbs when the ground dries hard and is disguised by a flush of grass growth. Make sure these areas are rolled flat in spring.*

Below: *Droppings can usually be left on larger areas of winter grazing as they are soon washed into the soil by rain. Remove them daily from summer grazing, otherwise they taint the grass and exacerbate worm problems.*

small field even smaller in terms of the available grass. This is also the best way of ensuring that horses sharing a field are not constantly re-infected by the worms they pass.

If the field has become rutted or poached after a wet spell, it may be beneficial to roll the affected areas, taking care not to damage unaffected areas by using machinery on fragile, water logged soil.

Step 5 Dealing With Weeds

First, not all plants other than grass in a field are undesirable weeds. Nevertheless, do take time to identify all "rogue" plants and *remove* them immediately if poisonous.

In an effort to copy the horse's natural diet, it is beneficial to include in it various "weeds" as long as they are kept under control because weeds, by definition, are plants that invade and

Above: *Although humans prefer lawnlike weedless paddocks – **we are not the ones eating it!** Horses often select plants we would class as "weeds," and many have beneficial properties. We should value weeds, eliminate only those that are poisonous, and control those that are invasive.*

> 66 **Never chain harrow a field containing ragwort as this will spread the plant. Shoots will break off and dry out on the grass, where they may be eaten by the horses, leading to possible serious consequences.** 99

SELF-SERVICE
Herbs and natural remedies are becoming popular. Why not let horses choose their own!

suffocate other plants. Perhaps set aside a strip around the boundary where useful weeds, such as nettles, cleavers, dandelions, daisies, clovers, brambles, yarrow, chicory, burnet, etc. are allowed to remain, or even plant or grow some from seed for their beneficial qualities. By not allowing these to encroach beyond a certain point, you will have improved the choice of diet for your animals, adding interest to their grazing but still providing them with excellent grass. If the horses do not eat these weeds quickly enough to keep them in check, it may be necessary to use a mower or strimmer to curtail their growth.

Other intrusive plants, like docks, thistles, bracken, and especially ragwort, *must be removed,* probably by digging out by hand or by selective spraying. Use gloves if pulling up by hand, as some plants contain toxins which can cause severe allergic reactions. Also, *never chain harrow a field containing ragwort* as this will spread the plant. Shoots will break off and dry out on the grass, where they may be eaten by the horses, leading to possible serious consequences.

Step 6 Drainage and Climate

In Great Britain, we seldom experience a regular pattern of gentle rain and warm sunshine to help prolong grass growth. Prolonged dry spells will kill off all but the toughest species of grass, leaving more tolerant, undesirable weeds with a free rein to spread over these bare patches. Grass should not be grazed too short during droughts. If there are areas that can be reached with a hose then watering will help. (Note: Ideally, water in the early morning or the evening when the areas are not in full Sun.)

Heavy deluges of rain causing water logged bogs cut off the supply of oxygen to the grass, weaken the root system, and encourage moss growth to thrive in the damp conditions.

Sloping fields and lighter soil usually result in good drainage. However, if your patch resembles rice paddy fields in China, then the only recourse is to get digging and channel out ditches, either open or piped, to carry away the excess water. An open ditch can be an excellent drinking water source. You will find that your horses will probably choose to use this rather

BENEFICIAL PLANTS – NATURE'S LARDER
Learning to identify beneficial plants will open up a cheap and nutritious larder for your horse. I often take a bag when walking to collect plants, berries, hips, and branches to feed to my horses.

Blackberries

Beech

Left: *In places where fields are water logged for many months, grass quality will deteriorate, but turnout is still essential. Hay can be offered.*

Above: *Most horses will choose to drink from a natural source (muddy or not) rather than a water butt.*

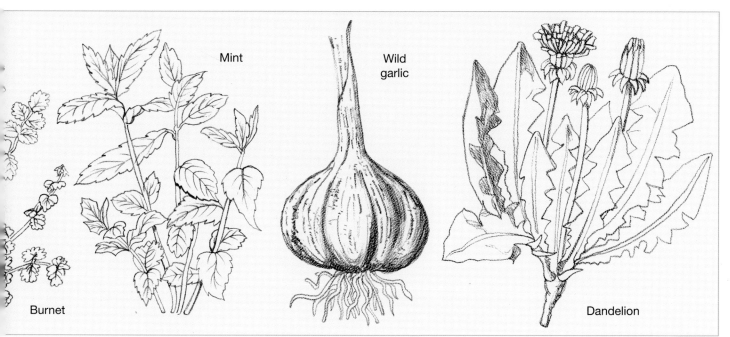

Mint

Wild garlic

Burnet

Dandelion

Above: *On frosty mornings, offer hay in a restricted area. This limits damage to the fragile, frozen grass and protects sensitive horses from having to eat it.*

SANDY SOIL

If you graze horses on sandy soil which may only have sparse areas of grass, it is essential to offer any feed or hay in raised troughs to mitigate sand ingestion.

than your water trough during the seasons when water is available there. (Note: Check blockages in the ditches regularly as hooves can very easily dislodge earth from the banks and droppings will pollute the fresh water supply.)

In prolonged wet weather, it is almost inevitable that gateways will become poached and cause problems for our four-legged friends, our vehicles, and ourselves when having to negotiate the wet, sticky mud. It is a waste of time to add anything, even stone chippings, to this mud while it is soft. It will simply be mixed into the mess. However, by taking action *before* the wet weather sets it while the land is still relatively hard, or by removing the saturated surface soil until you reach solid ground, you can improve these areas permanently.

After removing the surface layer of soil either:

❏ add a thick layer of lump chalk or road planings/crushed stone and compact it with a "whacker."

❏ lay down some mesh sheeting (metal or polypropylene examples are available) and fill with soil, chalk, or stone chip and compact as before, or

❏ fill with wood chips; these are cheap but need to be replenished from time to time.

On frosty mornings, try to keep your animals on a restricted area until the frost has lifted, and offer them hay as an alternative food. There is a slight chance that some equines may be intolerant to frozen grass and may display signs of colic, although this is unusual. Their hooves easily bruise the delicate structure of frost-covered leaves, so restricting them to a limited area of turnout will reduce any potential damage to the grass.

All this maintenance sounds like hard work. Remember, though, that your fields are a valuable asset and the gateway to letting your horses or ponies enjoy a more natural lifestyle.

> 66 **All this maintenance sounds like hard work. Remember, though, that your fields are a valuable asset and the "gateway" to letting your horses or ponies enjoy a more natural lifestyle.** 99

FENCING AND SHELTER

When choosing where to put your horse, try to think what the horse would want. Fine, so the yard looks smart and all the fields are post and rail fenced, but the horse does not have the same aesthetic considerations as we do. It is very pleasant to be in nice surroundings. The first concern must be to satisfy yourself that all the buildings and fencing are *safe*.

It does not matter whether the fencing is old or new as long as there are no dangling wires or weak or broken fence posts that will allow an animal to escape or potentially cause an injury. Do NOT use barbed wire around horses because of the added risk of it causing cuts and other injuries.

Think about whether the fencing is suitable for your animal. For example, many a heavy cob type has broken even the newest, professionally erected post and rail fencing, so electric fencing or wire would be better suited for him. You may feel that, although expensive, polycarbonate fencing would be especially suitable for Thoroughbreds and other thin-

Below left: Post and wire fencing is relatively cheap and smart to look at, but it is easy for horses to paw at the lower wire and get their hooves caught in the process.

Below right: PVC fencing looks smart and has no splinters on which horses might catch their skin. Remember, however, that it is a very expensive option.

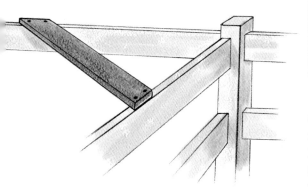

SAFE FENCING
Any sharp angles created by fencing should be squared off to avoid horses becoming trapped in corners in the dark or by being herded into them by other aggressive horses.

skinned or valuable animals for the peace of mind of having post and rails without the danger of jagged edges, splinters, or nails causing injury.

Strip grazing small areas may be fine for some animals that like (or need, because of injury) to be more or less static when feeding. In the wild, though, a horse will cover up to 20 miles (32 km) a day. If you have a lively animal who relishes the ability to expend energy, again this may not be the right choice for him.

All types of fencing have their merits, whether it be the permanence and smart appearance of wooden post and rail, the durability of polycarbonate fencing, the economy and versatility of post and wire, or the flexibility of both metal sectional hurdles or electric fencing. Choose whichever is right for you and your horse.

Above right: Post and rail can look very smart initially, but it soon becomes tatty after being chewed or leaned on. Larger horses tend simply to lean on it and break it.

Above left: Electric fencing can be temporary or semipermanent. It is a very cheap, adaptable, and effective option but can be blown down and requires energizers and batteries to be maintained.

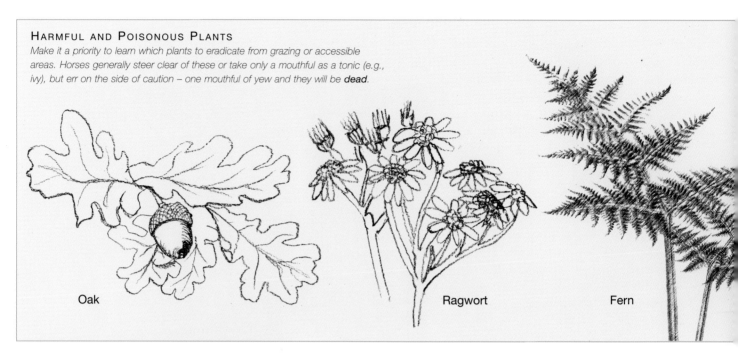

HARMFUL AND POISONOUS PLANTS

*Make it a priority to learn which plants to eradicate from grazing or accessible areas. Horses generally steer clear of these or take only a mouthful as a tonic (e.g., ivy), but err on the side of caution – one mouthful of yew and they will be **dead**.*

Oak

Ragwort

Fern

🐎 ***Above:*** *A field shelter provides protection from rain, wind, and sunshine. It allows horses far more freedom than a stable as they can choose to be in or out – a far more satisfying existence. Shelters need not be this basic; you can still have a deep bed and fit hayracks and feed mangers.*

It is also worth considering erecting a tethering bar or corral in the field where horses can be segregated or tied up to be fed or groomed without the danger of horse or owner being mithered by other animals.

Freedom of Choice

It is just as unfair to leave a horse for more than a few hours out in a field without any kind of shelter as it is to keep him out of the elements

POSITIONING YOUR FIELD SHELTER

When siting your field shelter, consider which direction the wind and rain generally come from. Position it so that the back bears the brunt of the bad weather. Allow enough room for the horse to move right around it without getting impeded.

in a stable for too long. Irritation from flies and the heat of the Sun or chills from wind or heavy rain can make outdoor animals miserable. Unfortunately, the majority of paddocks are designed this way.

Rhododendron   Ivy   Yew

The key to better welfare is *freedom of choice*. If shelter is provided in each field, either natural or man-made, then your animals will always have the choice of whether to be in or out of the elements. Ideally, design or alter the layout of your facilities to provide walkways leading from the turnout areas to the stable or barn. Not only will it benefit the animals, but it will also obviate the need to rush about getting horses in when the weather conditions are unkind.

If the grazing available to you is set away from any stabling and/or you do not want the effort or expense of trying to get planning permission and actually building the stable/shelter, the best investment is to purchase a portable field shelter. These are extremely well made and provide excellent shelter. They are available with interchangeable stable doors and partitions to enable you to segregate animals when feeding or keep them in overnight if necessary. Portable shelters are supplied with wheels or skids to enable them to be towed from field to field.

Natural Hedging

I think that a large field encompassed by brambles and bushes is preferable to a lawn surrounded by post and rail fencing. The dense vegetation provides shelter, scratching posts at different heights, and, more importantly, a variety of natural forage (all characteristics that wire or wooden fencing do not offer).

With the availability of such plants as blackberry brambles, hawthorn, crab apple, and perhaps rose hips, your horse or pony can benefit from the various trace elements and vitamins that they contain as well as enjoy a more natural way of life by foraging the hedgerow rather than simply acting as a lawn mower. As with the grasses, the bushes and trees will change throughout the season, adding variety to the horse's diet and stimulating his mind. Think of it as the garnish and sauces to accompany your daily meal – steak is greatly improved with béarnaise sauce and onion rings on the side!

Check for poisonous evergreens such as ivy, yew, and nightshade. Oak trees are

Above: *I cannot overstate the advantages of natural hedging as fencing. It is ecologically advantageous to many species of bird and animal, provides shade and branches to scratch on, as well as abundant vitamins and trace elements in the form of a natural "larder." Horses can browse happily as they wish.*

in winter when the lack of leafy foliage will make any escape routes all the more evident to your horse. Young shoots can be intertwined and trained to lie horizontally while they are still soft to strengthen the natural hedging.

The only drawback I have found with this type of fencing is that you may get a few more snagged and torn rugs. You may, on the odd occasion, find a purple-bottomed horse if he has decided to scratch in a blackberry bush!

In any field, however it is fenced, try to *include* rather than exclude any useful shrubs, herbs, or trees, and even plant them yourself. The young plants will need protecting until they are fully established. However, in years to come, the field will be enhanced in so many ways. To adopt the old cliché, "The grass is always greener on the other side," but you want to aim to create that "other side" where every horse dreams to be!

ALTERNATIVES TO GREEN PASTURE

It may be that it is just not possible to find adequate grazing, at least for part of the year, or your horse's health problems dictate that

Below: Feeding in small piles in various locations over the turnout area encourages the horse to search out his food and keeps him active rather than hanging about in one area.

Above: A manège can be used for free exercise. A few hours loose in the yard or even in a parking lot is better than confinement in a stable.

Above top: Any secure area can be used for turnout. Many horses only feel confident to roll when outside rather than in the confined space of a stable.

a common sight in fields. Although the tree itself provides excellent shelter, the acorns are very poisonous. It is rare for horses to eat poisonous plants unless they are totally desperate. It is better to err on the side of caution and either remove the plants completely or fence off these areas.

Maintenance is still important. Wire fencing will almost certainly be required to horse proof any gaps between shrubs and trees, especially grazing must be limited. Any safe, contained area (large or small) can be used as a turnout to allow your horse to socialize, mooch about, forage for food, and lie down or roll.

Indoor arenas are excellent. However, it is preferable to have at least some outdoor area so that horses can enjoy the benefits of fresh air, natural light, and sunshine and rain. Outdoor arenas, open barns, and even park lots can be used, as long as visitors are aware of this and gates are kept closed. Concrete areas should include a small area of grass, sand, soil, or other cushioning material to allow the animals a place to roll.

If your immediate landscape is mountainous, rocky, or sandy and contains very little grass, this can still be used as a turnout area (check first for holes or dangerous crevices that might cause injury). Exercise here will keep a horse mentally and physically active. Alternative forage rations should be offered in place of the grass he is lacking.

Instead of just offering one hay net per animal (or one hayrack if several are sharing), divide the ration into smaller nets or piles and spread it out over the entire area. Carrots and other succulent vegetables can also be hidden in several locations. Pony nuts and other food can be fed off dry ground in small piles. This encourages the animals to move around the whole area (rather than hanging about at the gate or next to their hay nets), helps prevent bullying, and satisfies their natural instinct to keep active and search out their food.

Note: The food offered "ad-lib" is just as a maintenance ration and can almost be regarded as a form of recreation. It is important to keep an eye on how much each horse is eating and, if necessary, to segregate animals at feeding time.

HERD MANAGEMENT

I have emphasized the importance of providing a physically suitable environment for our animals by offering them a degree of freedom and the ability to forage for food and water at will. In the same way, if we recognize the importance of catering for their mental needs as well, it can only improve their health and well-being.

It is certainly not a good idea to leave a field-kept horse or pony on its own. Wild horses' lives revolve around seeking mates and companions. Although a gelding will not have the same drive to find a mate as a stallion, all horses desire companionship. If we are forced to keep a solitary animal, we should compensate for the loss of companionship by spending as much time as possible with him. This is one situation in which an animal may be happier to be stabled, as the stable may well be close to his owner's house. The owner has to visit him regularly in order to muck out and feed. A solitary animal in a remote field may, more easily, be forgotten.

Herd behavior is dealt with more fully in Chapter 1. However, when choosing field companions, it is wise to take the following factors into account:

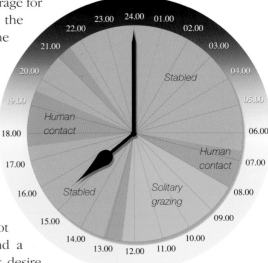

SPEND TIME TOGETHER

A horse or pony is likely to be miserable if left turned out without a companion and very little human contact. In this situation, it may be kinder to stable the animal for part of the time as this will compel you to spend longer with him.

Below: *A solitary animal in a remote field may be forgotten about and lead a miserable, purposeless existence as a consequence.*

Left: *Horses enjoy human company, and time spent with your horse (other than riding) helps create a satisfying bond between you.*

Right: *Although it is more natural to keep all animals in a herd, elderly or nervous animals often fare better when kept with just one other animal who will become their "pair-bond." They may otherwise be bullied or injured by dominant animals who are not reliant on them in the way that their pair-bond is.*

66 **Horses, as prey animals, have an inbred fear of being alone and instinctively are happiest in pairs or groups.** 99

Below: *You need to establish more than just a "working" relationship with your horse if you want him to enjoy being with you enough to leave the herd.*

❏ Do not overpopulate a field. Horses need space to feel safe, to feed happily without competition, and to flee from any perceived danger.

❏ Keep dominant or territorially aggressive animals away from weaker, elderly, or very young animals to avoid the risk of them being injured.

❏ Mares and geldings can be put together, but you may find that they have to be separated during the spring and summer to avoid competitive confrontations when the mares come into season.

❏ Elderly or nervous animals should be kept with other calmer animals, young or old, who will not pose a threat to them from bullying. Alternatively, they should be kept with just one other animal to create a "pair-bond."

❏ Try not to chop and change the animals which graze together. Instead, try to establish a stable group which will form its own hierarchy and long-term relationships.

DEALING WITH PROBLEMS

Not being able to catch a field-kept horse or pony There are many reasons why a horse or pony does not want to be caught. This is one of the most frustrating problems encountered by an owner. Possible excuses for the horse include the following:

❏ He is blissfully happy grazing and does not want to be taken away from this.

❏ He fears that being caught will mean leaving the field companions.

❏ He fears that being caught will mean being ridden or being confined to the stable.

❏ The owner has not established a good relationship with the horse who then sees the owner not as a friend but as a threat.

❏ He has been allowed to get his own way and has learned that evading the owner means being in control.

❏ He is being bullied and cannot walk through the rest of the herd to get to you or the gate.
❏ The horse simply sees it as a game.

It is a very difficult problem to break and will probably involve changing your routine to break the cycle. Horses are very social and inquisitive. Sometimes when we offer them the ultimate in care by giving them back unlimited freedom, forage, and friends, we become purposeless in their lives.

It can also be very dangerous, when you do finally catch the animal, if it suddenly pulls away and gallops back to the herd, possibly dragging you behind it. In this case, we need to rebuild the bond between horse and owner by spending more time together and perhaps using join-up or other horse language to strengthen communication (see Chapter 2). This may mean that for the short term, our mount has to spend more time stabled or turned out alone so he will associate *us* with providing of his companionship and feeding requirements. It seems cruel to deprive him of a more natural way of life, but it should quickly be evident that he now views the arrival of his owner with delight and anticipation rather than indifference or fear.

If this is not possible, just spending time in the field (poo-picking, weeding, or sun-bathing!) can stimulate the inquisitive nature of horses and ponies. They will often come over or follow you round rather than do their own thing. The addition of pony cubes or such as a reward serves to strengthen your image as a useful friend to them.

Make your horse's work fun by building in lots of variation in schooling and hacking in company if possible. Stabling can be made less of a bane by associating this with feeding times.

In short, give them reasons to want to be near you.

Dealing with a stressed animal who will not settle when his companion is taken out of the field Horses, as prey animals, have an inbred fear of being alone and instinctively are happiest in pairs or groups. Being alone is unnatural for them, but most cope well for short periods of time. Some, however, display dramatic insecure behavior when left alone, repeatedly calling, charging around the field, or even trying to jump out to find their companions.

Horses may be worse in unfamiliar surroundings where the slightest upset unsettles them. They usually improve over time, though, and once they have learned that their companion does return to them.

If the situation does not improve, you might try borrowing or acquiring another animal, such as another pony, donkey, sheep, or goat, which will provide a "permanent fixture" and an alternative companion to settle the animal. The problem with allowing a friend's pony to share your pasture is that you and your friend will probably want to ride out together, resulting in the anxious animal that cannot be ridden still being left alone at times.

*Above: Many horses exhibit stressed behavior if they are left alone, even for short periods. In time, they usually come to realize that their companions **do** return.*

Above: Sometimes, although not often, horses enjoy living out so much that we become purposeless in their lives. Other reasons for not wanting to be caught are fear of leaving the herd, fear of being ridden, or fear of being stabled. The instinctive reaction is to run away from their fears.

Above: Keeping horses with other animals which are "permanent fixtures" in the field helps them always to feel secure in their environment.

Below: Turnout provides exercise which strengthens muscles, promotes stamina, and improves circulation, respiration, and digestion – perfect for an athlete.

Another method is to use this period of solitude for the benefit of this animal. Perhaps it does not get a great deal of attention or has a struggle competing for food. If you bring the anxious animal in at the same time or just before the companion leaves, and perhaps groom it and leave it in the stable for the duration of your ride (with a feed or hay net), it may well be blissfully unaware that its partner has gone.

HORSES ARE ATHLETES

The skeletal and muscular frameworks of a horse make it ideally suited to the demands of an active life in the wild or as a performance animal. However, while any reasonable human athlete will maintain a consistent level of fitness and always warm up slowly and rest efficiently, horses are often expected to switch on and perform as soon as the stable door is opened. Confinement in a stable for long periods of time is certainly not conducive to building up stamina or strengthening muscles, tendons, or hooves.

Regular and gentle movement encourages the production of synovial fluid, which lubricates joints. The activity also keeps muscles warm and exercised, which greatly reduces the risk of lameness, such as pulled tendons and torn ligaments.

> 66 **Horses need to be able to stretch their frames fully, perhaps by galloping, bucking, or rearing.** 99

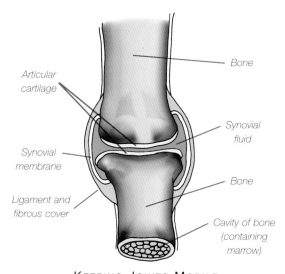

Bone

Articular cartilage

Synovial fluid

Synovial membrane

Bone

Ligament and fibrous cover

Cavity of bone (containing marrow)

KEEPING JOINTS MOBILE
Regular movement encourages the production of synovial fluid, which the body creates to lubricate the joints.

If a horse is turned out for most or all of the day, especially in a large area, the experience will strengthen limbs, improve circulation, and provide safe, gentle exercise. Not only will it maintain and enhance the fitness level developed through riding or lunging, etc., it will also curb the over-exuberance so often connected with a lively animal that has been confined to a stable.

Horses need to be able to stretch their frames fully, perhaps by galloping, bucking, or rearing. A stabled animal will have little room to move. His joints and muscles may be cold and stiff. Then he may be ridden and asked to move in a restricted outline, exacerbating any stiffness in the back and neck. Gentle exercise and even a good blast in the field will, among other things, help to loosen and soften his frame and actually benefit his work under saddle.

CAN ALL HORSES LIVE OUTSIDE VIRTUALLY FULL-TIME?

All horses and ponies benefit from daily turnout, but they cannot be expected to thrive in a field full-time if they are not accustomed to it. Changes to their management must be

performed gradually. Fortunately, our changing seasons and the gradual lengthening of daylight hours normally mean that horses and ponies are gradually turned out by their owners for longer periods of time as the summer months arrive. This means that in high summer, many horses are turned out for 24 hours each day. In hot regions, horses may be better off kept in during the day and turned out at night.

Unfortunately, seasons of temperate weather can be short. This means our horses may have very limited turnout for periods of up to nine months of the year, depending on where you live. This is not really satisfactory.

All horses and ponies living in temperate regions – be they coldbloods, warmbloods, Standardbreds, Thoroughbreds, Morgans, Shetlands, etc.; whether they are worth a few dollars or a fortune; or are used for general riding, racing, or ranch work – can live outside year-round provided they have adequate feed, water, and shelter.

It is, however, necessary to take the nature of the individual animal into account and tailor his care accordingly. The main aims are to

BREATHING CYCLE
During active exercise muscles require higher levels of oxygen to function efficiently. However, at a gallop respiration rate is "governed" and a horse can only inhale/exhale once per stride, breathing out each time a foreleg hits the gound as its guts swing forwards in the abdomen.

Inhale

Exhale

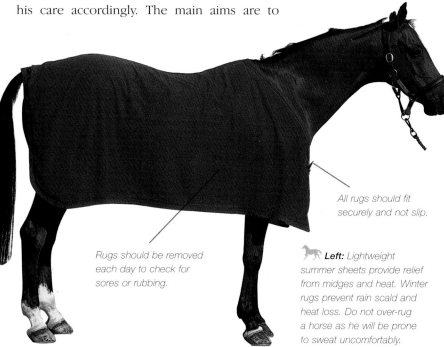

Rugs should be removed each day to check for sores or rubbing.

All rugs should fit securely and not slip.

Left: *Lightweight summer sheets provide relief from midges and heat. Winter rugs prevent rain scald and heat loss. Do not over-rug a horse as he will be prone to sweat uncomfortably.*

🐎 **Above:** *Most horses can live outside year-round provided they have adequate food and shelter. If they are clipped or unable to grow thick coats, rugs may be required to keep them warm.*

🐎 **Above:** *It is forage that provides the fuel for warmth and sustained energy as it takes longer to digest than concentrates.*

maintain a happy and healthy horse, ready and able to perform the type of work you want to do.

If your reasons for keeping him stabled for most of the time are to keep him clean and safe or to give him an "edge" to perform, think again! I do not think these are valid reasons unless applied only on infrequent occasions, such as just before an event. Performance horses can be kept clean and warm by the use of summer sheets and protective rugs. They will be safe if integrated slowly into the herd. The lively edge they may display from being stabled is short-lived. In fact, they are likely to perform better when allowed to pursue a more natural way of life.

Increasing turnout may not be possible or desired year-round. If this means that your horse lives outside 24 hours a day for most of the year but is stabled or in a barn for part of the day in times of bad weather, that is fine, provided it works for you and him.

People harp about routine being essential in good horse management. It is necessary for stable-kept horses who are relying on us for their next meal or stimulating activity. Horses in the wild, however, do what feels right at the time. They do not put themselves to bed at 6p.m. or eat meals at 7a.m. and 5.30p.m.! We need to "go with the flow" as they would do, and if weather conditions allow them to stay out for 24 hours one day but need them to be brought in overnight the next, then so be it.

How should we acclimatize animals to live outside on a more permanent basis?
It is very difficult and not advisable to try to turn out permanently a stable-kept animal halfway through the winter season as there is no time to "rough" him off and acclimatize him gradually to the change. Ideally, you should wait until the summer months when your horses will spend most, if not all, of the time outside anyway.

As the cold or wet weather gradually begins to set in, delay rugging the animals and allow them to grow full winter coats. You may find that if shelter and good forage are provided, they will be able to maintain a good weight and no rugs will be required at all. Other animals who may be prone to losing condition or who need to be clipped to keep them comfortable in work should be rugged to avoid depleting their resources just to keep warm.

Most animals in full work will be shod as normal. If the horses are being turned out for a "vacation," perhaps after a season of polo, their shoes should ideally be removed. This will allow the hooves a period without nails, which will help to strengthen them, and will also lessen any kicking injuries or loose shoes which may be overlooked if the horses are visited only once a day.

If any of the horses do need rugs, it is probably better to invest in just a couple of thinner outdoor, waterproof-type blankets that can be used together or taken off in milder weather. There is no point having non-waterproof underblankets as you will be constantly adding and removing them rather than just simply taking off an outer layer.

CARE OF THE FIELD-KEPT HORSE OR PONY

Even if they have plenty of grass, water, and shelter, all animals should be checked every day, whether they are being worked or not.

For horses relying on just their own coats for protection from the elements, grooming should be kept to a minimum – just remove the clods of mud and dust before riding. You may see some scurf in the coat, but the oil in the coat is required to make it waterproof. However, if you see excess scurf on a rugged animal (other than on the exposed areas), this may be a sign that he is too hot and has been sweating. To tell if your animals are warm enough, feel the very base of the ear or behind the elbow. These places should feel warm, whatever the weather, and the horse or pony should never be shivering.

Run your hands down each horse's limbs and examine their entire bodies for any small cuts or swellings which may be masked by mud.

Most working animals will still require additional forage in the form of hay, which can be put out in piles on the ground. Make sure there are more piles of hay than there are animals or bullying may occur. If short-feed is required to sustain energy levels, this can be fed in buckets off the floor or hook-over mangers on the fence. The ideal set-up, though is to have a field shelter or stables in the field. This allows the horses (and you) to enjoy the very best of both worlds – they can eat their short-feed in peace and, in bad weather, stay dry and warm in the shelter while they eat their hay. It is also far easier to check over or groom horses with this kind of setup than if you have to follow them around the field. In a shelter, or if the stable doors are left permanently open, they can then go out again whenever they want to.

Check water troughs daily. Clean them out regularly. Break any surface ice if necessary.

In the spring, when their coats begin to shed, your horses or ponies will probably need

You can get a good idea if your horse is warm by feeling the temperature around the base of its ear or behind its elbow

These areas should feel nicely warm to the touch

IS YOUR HORSE WARM ENOUGH?

The weather may be bitter, but you can tell if he is warm enough by feeling the base of his ear or behind his elbow. These areas should feel very warm. Horses are more likely to shiver in wet weather as the insulating properties of their coats do not function as well.

Above: Horses need to be checked daily. Running your hands down each limb should help detect any swellings or cuts that may be masked by a thicker coat or encrustations of mud.

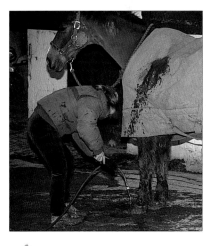

Above: Fine breeds can have mud hosed off their legs as they will be quick to dry. Mud on "feathered" breeds probably does not extend beneath the top layer of hair and is best left alone.

regular grooming to extract any shedding hair. They will appreciate a bath on a milder day to get rid of excess scurf.

By offering our horses more freedom of choice and a more active daily life, they will become happier, healthier, fitter, and so more willing and able to achieve their optimum performance.

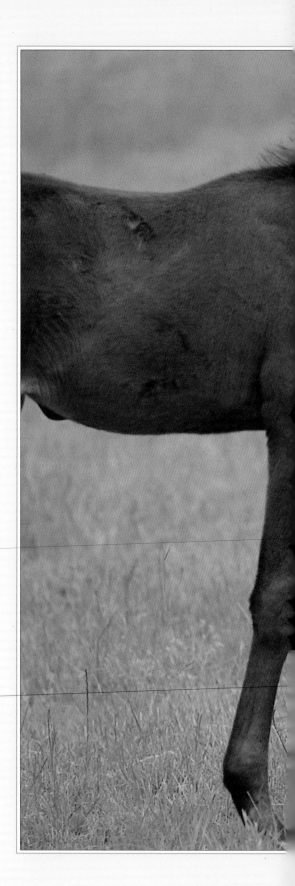

CHAPTER 5

Caring For Your Horse Throughout Its Life

Like humans, horses do not have a predetermined life span. One thing is for sure, however, a domestic animal has a far greater chance of living well into his twenties than his wild counterpart. Ponies tend to live longer than horses. However, a great deal is dictated by the care, nutrition, and workload experienced by the individual animal. Interestingly, while some breeds – like the Tarpan, which is similar in appearance to the Exmoor pony; the American Buckskin; or horses bred from wild Spanish mustang ancestors – remain virtually unaltered

Above: *Just as in the human world, the young learn from older horses, particularly their parents and siblings.*
Right: *Whether you own a horse from foalhood or for only a couple of years, you can enjoy and learn so much from one another.*

natural model. For the most part, there is a fairly consistent pattern in the development of an equine from foalhood to old age.

FROM BIRTH TO SIX MONTHS OLD

From the moment a foal is born, it faces demands simply to survive. In contrast to babies or puppies and kittens, which can be lifted to their mother's teats, horses and ponies generally need to stand within a couple of hours to take their first colostrum milk. Unlike other young offspring which can be carried away from danger by their mother, it is amazing to see how foals with their overly long legs can keep pace with their mares from day one. They are born with legs two-thirds of the adult length. This natural phenomenon has been one of the major factors that has allowed wild horses to do so well against their natural predators.

Before the age of six months (and perhaps for a while after in some cases) a foal will spend its time suckling, sleeping, and growing under the guidance of the mare. Apart from daily handling, we should not expect too much from such a young animal. Its growth rate is so rapid that it will have reached almost half its adult weight by the time it is seven months old. The protein requirements of a foal from

Above: *With such a long gestation period – 11 months – you do not want to miss the moment! A mare's breeding season normally spans from March-October with ovulation every 21 days although conception is only likely between the 18th and 23rd days of the cycle.*

from their "wild" profile, modern breeding has fundamentally changed the equine – lightening bone and increasing athleticism while dispensing with some of the hardy traits, such as resistance to bad weather and the ability to survive on poor-quality food. The rapid growth development of some breeds, for example the Thoroughbred, is quite unlike the

> 66 A foal's growth rate is so rapid that it will have reached almost half its adult weight by the time it is seven months old. 99

ADULT WEIGHT

Mature animal

Fully grown:
100%

Growing foal

6 months:
40%

At birth:
10%

ADULT HEIGHT

Fully grown:
100%

6 months:
80%

GROWTH PATTERNS

Prey animals generally grow rapidly as a survival tactic to enable them to flee from danger from an early age. Foals can stand within hours of being born. Their birth weight is approximately 10 percent of their adult weight. By six months of age, their weight is 40 percent of their mature weight and their height is 80 percent of their projected adult height. Therefore, a foal that has reached 13hh at six months of age can be expected to be just over 16hh at maturity.

two weeks to ten months are as much as 20 percent of its diet compared with about 12 percent for an adult horse. However, their fiber requirements are low – about six percent of the diet as opposed to 25 percent or more in a mature animal (see Chapter 7 for diet comparisons).

For the first few days after birth, the mare and foal should be allowed peace and quiet away from other animals to form a close bond and to allow the foal to gain in strength. The foal only has the antibodies that it has derived naturally from the mare. It takes several months to build up its own resistance to disease. Wild foals are susceptible to illness, and many are lost in this way. We are fortunate that we can vaccinate domestic foals against many diseases, like tetanus and equine influenza (see also page 181). It is also important to begin a worming regimen from the age of one month as foals are susceptible to worms picked up via their mother's milk and from grazing.

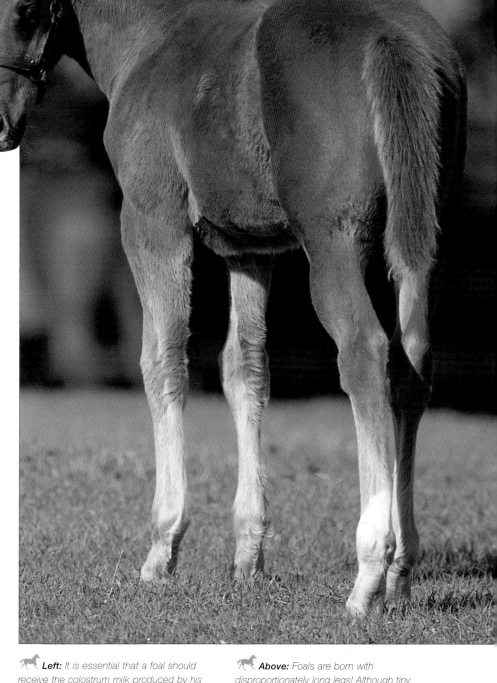

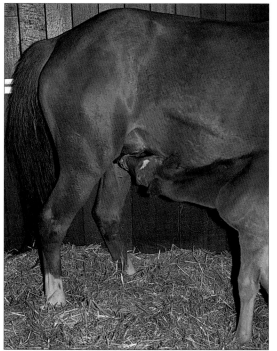

Left: It is essential that a foal should receive the colostrum milk produced by his mother in the first few days after birth. It contains valuable antibodies that help to protect the young animal from illness.

Above: Foals are born with disproportionately long legs! Although tiny overall, a foal's shoulder reaches about two-thirds of the way up his dam's legs. Growth is very rapid during the early months of life.

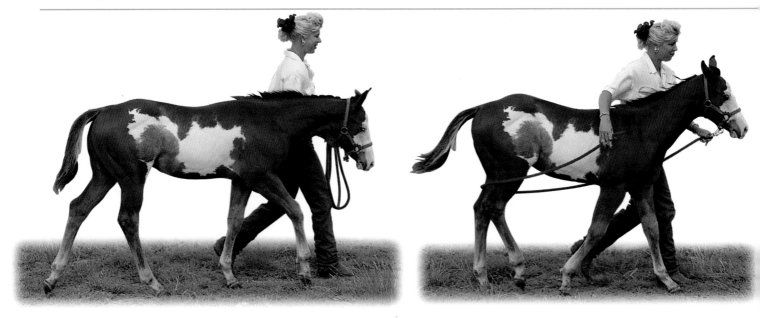

🐎 **Above:** *Leading out in a foal slip should be done for short periods with the dam in close proximity. The technique shown on the right makes the foal aware of his movement and accustoms him to pressure on sensitive areas.*

🐎 **Below:** *Checking hooves and limbs for correct formation is essential as growth spurts can cause deformities. Gentle manipulation should also get the foal used to handling.*

Early Learning

Although bred in a domestic situation, it is important for the foal's development to try to mimic the natural "herd" social system and, if possible, to have other "nanny" mares and horses/ponies around, as long as the animals get along well together and are free from disease. Other youngstock will be playmates. A calm veteran will act as a confidence giver and steadying influence when the foal is faced with new sights and challenges. Horses and ponies brought up with purely human companions from such an early age often exhibit dangerous behavior, such as biting and barging, as they have not learned the basis for bonding and subordination gained from a natural herd structure. They may also be unable to cope in a social group of other horses and inadvertently give the wrong signals, making them the subject of bullying.

All we should aim to achieve in the form of schooling is to be able to lead the animal about in a foal slip, tie it up calmly for a few minutes to be groomed, and lift up each leg without resistance. All this should be done with the mare in close proximity.

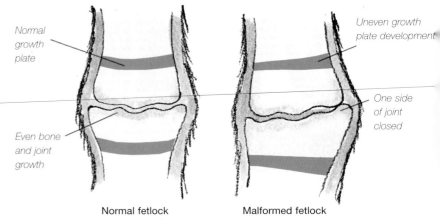

Normal growth plate

Uneven growth plate development

Even bone and joint growth

One side of joint closed

Normal fetlock — Malformed fetlock

ENSURING NORMAL JOINT DEVELOPMENT
Regular attention by a farrier will prevent the hooves from becoming unlevel, which causes unequal pressure on the limbs that could cause uneven growth plate development.

It is important to have limbs and hooves checked by a vet and farrier. Most of the bones in the limbs have growth plates containing cartilage positioned near the top (proximal) end and the bottom (distal) end of each bone. As the cartilage is soft, the limbs need to experience even pressure as they grow for correct limb alignment. The growth plates are soft to begin with and ossify over time, beginning from the hoof and working up the leg.

In the wild, any conformational deformities cannot be corrected. They would certainly handicap an animal in later life, if it managed to survive at all. Fortunately, with human intervention, slight misalignments can usually be corrected at this early stage in its development.

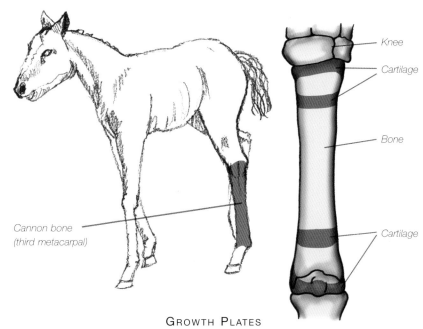

Cannon bone (third metacarpal)

Knee
Cartilage
Bone
Cartilage

GROWTH PLATES

The bones in young horses develop from areas of cartilage at the ends of the long limb bones that gradually turn to bone. Each of the long limb bones has two areas of growth plates at each end. During maturity, the cartilage cells swell and then ossify into living bone. Ossification begins in the lower bones and works upward as the horse matures to enable growth in height and weight to balance.

66 Horses and ponies brought up with purely human companions from such an early age often exhibit dangerous behavior as they have not learned the basis for bonding and subordination gained from a natural herd structure. 99

Above: *This young foal will need his halter adjusted frequently to avoid chafing as he grows. It is unwise to leave it on him unsupervised in case it gets entangled.*

SIX MONTHS TO TWO YEARS OLD

After about six months the foal should be a great deal more independent and we should continue to build up its confidence in people and other animals. In the wild the youngstock would learn from siblings and the older members of the herd, interacting with them and learning their role in the herd hierarchy. The domestic animal has got to become part of the human "herd" in the same way. We are fortunate that these young animals will be reliant on us for food and perhaps company, so the process of imprinting desired behaviour on them should not be too difficult as they look on us as both provider and friend.

GROWING UP

For healthy, straight limbs, the blood must provide all the essential nutrients to the bones. Dietary imbalances during these formative years and accelerating growth for showing purposes can cause erratic bone formation leading to deformities.

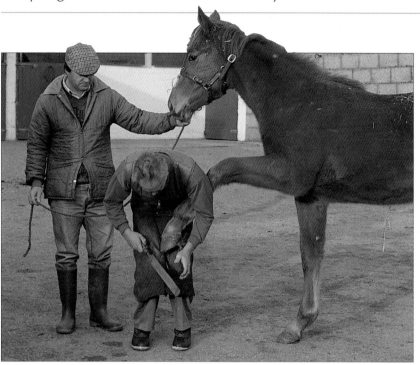

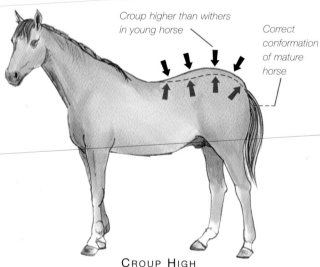

We must be aware that horses and ponies mature at different rates depending on their breeding. So while a Thoroughbred's genes determine that it will be more or less fully developed by the age of two years, it is certainly a risky business (and one that may have detrimental effects in the longer term) to overfeed a lanky two year old for the purpose of accelerating its growth for the showring. You must allow sufficient time for the muscles and bones which support the structure to mature.

As an owner, it is far better simply to give adequate forage and a hard feed designed to prevent deficiencies in youngstock and permit ad-lib grazing if at all possible. Turning the animal out to exercise itself is all that is necessary for muscle development. In this way, we are not trying to force the young animal to resemble and perform like an adult horse. Exercising an immature animal, by lunging for example, can put strain onto the joints and cause deformities such as splints.

The hooves should be regularly trimmed every six weeks by the farrier. This will probably minimize problems when fitting shoes becomes necessary.

Above: With the groundwork done, visits by the farrier will not be too traumatic. Hooves should be trimmed every six weeks.

Throughout the first two years, the bodies of these young colts or fillies will be growing tremendously quickly. It is important that we do not put too many extra strains on them, either physically or mentally, which could impair their natural development. As owners, we should be there to support their needs. By adopting a more natural system of care, we can help them in their development. By this I mean by providing equine (and human) companions to teach them their place in the herd and allowing them time to play and rest so they can both build up muscles and grow without putting too much strain onto their weak frames.

A weaned animal will not have the tailor-made natural diet it previously received from the mare. So it is important that adequate levels of calcium, minerals, and protein are included in the feed intake. The diet of youngstock is a contentious issue as overfeeding or an incorrect diet can lead to problems in later life.

Above: Companionship helps to keep youngsters emotionally and physically stable. Equine friends provide an outlet for play, which is difficult for humans to offer.

Croup higher than withers in young horse

Correct conformation of mature horse

CROUP HIGH

In the course of growing the hindquarters develop faster than the forehand causing the croup to be higher than the withers. Two-year-olds frequently have an unbalanced "gawky" appearance but the front end should catch up by the time they are three or four.

Understanding Learning Ability

Horses naturally learn to recognize connections between signals or events which dictate how they should respond. For example:

HOW PREY ANIMALS REACT TO STIMULI

Prey animals are programmed to respond rapidly to threat messages; as they learn through experience, their response times shorten.

| Rustling in bushes | predator jumps out | subject horse startles and shies/bolts from possible danger |

Response time is shortened to just the initial stimulus

| Rustling in bushes | subject horse startles and shies/bolts from possible danger |

| Dominant horse flattens ears and lunges with bared teeth toward subject horse | dominant horse bites subject horse | subject horse backs away |

Response time is shortened to just the initial stimulus

| Dominant horse flattens ears and swings extended neck toward subject horse | subject horse backs away |

Much of a horse's behavior is copied from other members of the herd. If one animal in the herd suddenly bolts in a certain direction, then the rest will almost certainly stampede after it, although they may not have been exposed to the stimulus. The purpose of learning is to ensure survival. Horses learn to react in a certain way to avoid an unpleasant consequence, to get a reward in the form of food, or to flee from a potential threat.

For our own benefit, in order to create a safe riding animal, it is necessary in the early training of horses and ponies to expose them regularly to stimuli such as barking dogs, noisy cars, etc. until they no longer react in such a dramatic way. We should aim to be as calm and impassive as possible when exposing the young animal to new experiences as they will be all too aware of any nervous tension that we might display.

❑ Have regular contact with your horse or pony throughout the day, but allow ample opportunity for real rest and quiet.

❑ Speak or make a recognizable noise before approaching or touching the animal.

❑ Always handle your horse in a calm but purposeful manner.

❑ Try to anticipate your horse's reactions to the unpredictable.

 Above: *A calm approach encourages confidence when a young horse faces new challenges.*

Right: *Leading out in hand and teaching via ground work are good ways of establishing leadership using body language and vocal commands. Horses and ponies, even when young, are powerful animals. If they are ignorant of manners or blind to our instructions, just something as simple as turning them out could lead to disaster.*

TWO TO FOUR YEARS OLD

Colts and fillies are now gaining in confidence and in the wild would be trying to establish themselves as potential dominant stallions or mares to replace others in the herd.

Physically, they are gaining muscle and may be almost fully grown. As owners, we need to be aware that their strength and hormonal activity can, in some cases, trigger aggressive and dangerous behavior. As their caretakers and the providers of food, humans should have established a superior status in their eyes. However, now is the time that we need to reinforce our position as herd leader.

Colts and stallions generally prove more of a problem than fillies and mares because of the powerful nature of their developing sexual urges. When this begins to cause a problem with handling and socializing, you will know it is time to consider having the animal gelded if it is not to be used for breeding.

Training should continue with regular handling and the imprinting of physical and vocal commands such as "over," "walk on," and "stand." Our body language is a significant factor here in communicating our clear intentions. It is very important to be ready to

> 66 **Humans should have established a superior status in horse's eyes. However, now is the time that we need to reinforce our position as herd leader.** 99

We can use these early years profitably to establish a secure background by introducing new sights, new sounds, and constructive exercises, including the use of voice commands and body language to reinforce actions. This is discussed in more detail in Chapter 2. Leading out in hand or off another animal and long reining are good forms of exercise to impart the action of moving forward in response to our contact and command.

By this form of training, we are already imprinting desired behavior such as remaining calm in traffic, being rugged up, walking through water, and even traveling in a trailer or truck. Good behavior should be reinforced and rewarded. Generally, life should be stress free for all parties!

praise and reward the good behavior that the horse has learned. Bitting the animal will assist with handling now that his strength may put us at a disadvantage. We must be aware that their teeth may be undergoing dramatic changes as milk teeth are replaced by permanent molars and incisors. Make sure that the use of any halter or bridle is not causing pressure on the cheeks or inducing pain in any way.

In the wild, unruly or aggressive behavior would be reprimanded by a senior herd member. Although we are unable to flatten our ears and lunge at or nip to reprimand this behavior, we can instead use stern vocal commands and a dominant stance with the addition of firm handling or, if necessary, a pinch to the skin to mimic a nip.

Above: Long reining teaches the animal to move forward and become accustomed to steering via two reins. It is excellent for improving suppleness and muscle tone without fear of putting too much strain on the limbs, which lunging in a small circle could do. Just make sure you are fit enough to keep up!

Far left: Leading off another animal is an excellent way of exercising any horse but is especially valuable in the training of youngsters as they gain confidence from the more experienced animal.

117

BACKING

Backing a horse in a familiar situation, standing next to a companion horse, is far less traumatic than sending your horse to a strange place where fear may overwhelm the occasion.

Far right: *Anyone assisting in backing a horse will need to be unflappable. It is not something that should be undertaken by a novice.*

Backing The Young Animal

By the time the animal is three to four years old, it should be sufficiently mature to cope with the physical strains of being backed. No two animals are alike. This can be as easy as feeding one a carrot or as difficult as stabling one with a lioness! I once owned a relaxed three-year-old gelding who allowed me to put on a saddle, mount him, and then walked, trotted, and cantered obediently around the field in the space of ten minutes. However, you could equally have to cope with a bucking bronco. Fortunately, most animals fall in the in-between category.

Again, the communication between you is vital. Think about your stance on the ground, where you stand in relation to the animal's field of vision. Allow him to approach and sniff the saddle before placing it onto his back. Beaware of your voice and body commands when you are finally on board. If you and the horse are speaking the same language, it should not be a stressful experience.

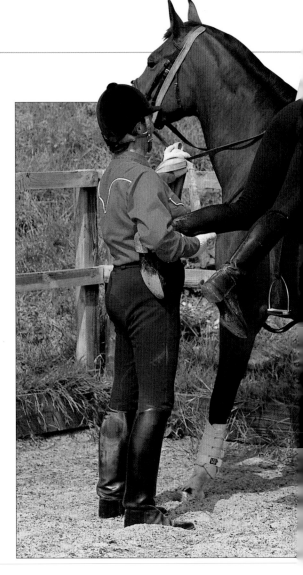

A three or four year old is still mentally, if not physically, immature. We must not expect any more than hacking or simple schooling in a long outline. This will allow the animal to learn to carry himself and become balanced in his paces with the added handicap of having a rider onboard! He is likely to be on the forehand. So be aware of your own center of gravity to assist the horse to carry your weight evenly over all four legs and to develop even muscle tone. Schooling sessions should be *short* and varied, as young animals, like children, have a brief attention span and can become bored easily. Some people like to back their youngster and then turn it away without riding it for another six months to allow it to mature further.

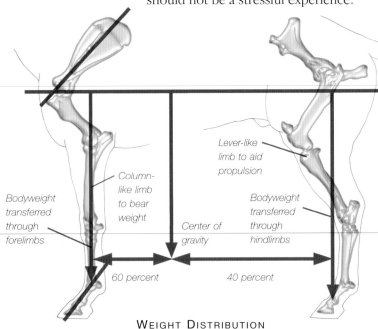

Bodyweight transferred through forelimbs

Column-like limb to bear weight

Center of gravity

Lever-like limb to aid propulsion

Bodyweight transferred through hindlimbs

60 percent   40 percent

WEIGHT DISTRIBUTION

Weight is carried 60 percent on the forehand and 40 percent to the rear. Be patient with youngsters who fidget when asked to stand with a rider on board. They lack muscle tone to support the added weight, and the back sinks when immobile.

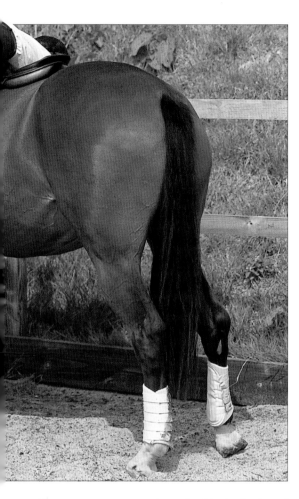

may cause some animals to develop signs of the foot condition called laminitis. You will have to redefine grazing arrangements to deal with this. If the condition is in remission, I prefer to continue turnout if possible but on poorer-quality grazing (with a muzzle if necessary) or in a yard or manège for part of the time. Two hours a day on good grazing followed by stabling is not ideal as food intake is not consistent. Lush grazing compromises the condition, while the subsequent periods without food are not good for the function of the stomach. On top of this, standing in a stable reduces blood flow to the limbs.

🐎 **Below:** *Schooling should be done in short bursts, using voice commands if this makes your intentions clearer. A gentle stroke on his neck will show him he is doing well, and if things are not going to plan – he is probably confused! Ride with long reins or a loose contact.*

🐎 **Below:** *Even at four years of age, horses are still very immature mentally. Their concentration span is brief and while some animals take new challenges in their stride, others cannot cope with too many demands placed on their performance. Playing relieves stress and improves coordination.*

If your youngster enjoys the kind of relaxed life I recommend, with plenty of turnout in company and no stresses related to food shortages or a harsh climate, your relationship with him should be such that backing and the first schooling lessons will be greeted with interest, as a challenge that stimulates the brain of such an intelligent animal.

Feeding Recommendations

As its growth rate has declined to a more gradual pace, the horse's diet will be based on forage. Additional feed should be allowed as build and individual temperament dictates, as in an adult horse.

Our "manmade" cultivated grazing, with the contributory effects of nitrate-rich fertilizer,

Below: Horses native to countries with a hot, temperate climate generally have hard, upright hooves to cope with the dry, abrasive terrain. Your farrier can advise whether or not shoeing is necessary.

HOOF SHAPES

In their natural environment, hotbloods tend to have more upright, narrow hooves with a hard wall, whereas coldbloods have wider, flatter hooves which distribute weight more onto their heels and frogs.

New Shoes

With the increased wear and tear on its hooves from being ridden, foot trimming may now need to be extended to the point where some or all of the hooves have shoes fitted. In their natural surroundings, wild horses can cover miles of country in search of food. Their constantly growing hooves are automatically trimmed by abrasion with the ground. Geographic location and diet also have a direct impact on the quality of the hoof. Horses native to hot countries naturally have upright hooves with a hard wall, whereas habitually water-logged ground creates softer, wider feet. Therefore the innate qualities that allow a purebred Exmoor pony to cope so well in its natural situation on the moors in England or permit an ancient breed such as the Arab (which dates back at least 3,000 years) to walk for miles in abrasive, moisture-free sand, will be challenged by a change in location and climate. The result is weaknesses in the hoof, which make shoeing necessary. If your young animal has become accustomed to the sight, smell, and sound of the farrier already, this should not present too much of a problem.

Above: Fifteen minutes of lunging will improve stamina and suppleness. Do not allow your horse to hang on the lunge line, but encourage bending by altering the size of the circle.

Below: Loose jumping improves confidence as there is no rider to restrict or affect movement. The horse should be properly warmed up, and the ground surface should be supportive but not too soft.

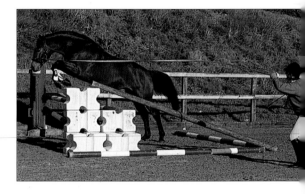

FIVE TO EIGHT YEARS OLD

Your horse is maturing and should be confident in most situations out hacking now. He should be accepting hand and leg aids and gaining balance in his gaits.

Schooling can now continue, asking for more complex transitions and turns. Pole work can be introduced, leading to training in jumping. Horses, by design, are generally good jumpers although the weight they carry on their forehand means that their forelimbs experience great force upon landing. It is important they are fully mature to withstand this concussive force. In the wild, they would

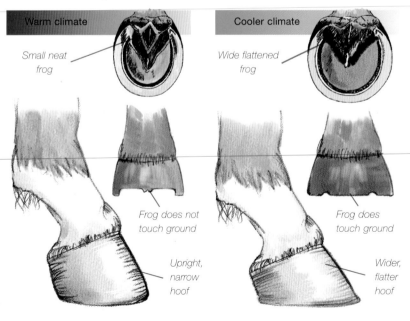

Warm climate	Cooler climate

Small neat frog

Wide flattened frog

Frog does not touch ground

Frog does touch ground

Upright, narrow hoof

Wider, flatter hoof

Comparative Training and Fitness Schedules

	Four Year Old All-Around Training		Eight Year Old All-Around Training	
MONDAY	**DAY OFF**		**DAY OFF**	
TUESDAY	15 min.	Lunging or loose schooling (walk, trot, canter on both reins)	2 hours	Hacking (including trotting and cantering up long hills)
	1 hour	Hack (mainly walk with short periods of trot or canter on soft ground)		
WEDNESDAY	15 min.	Lunging or loose schooling	1 hour	Schooling (including canter-walk-canter and trot-halt-trot transitions, circles and lengthening of stride)
	30 min.	Lesson or schooling (half halts, transitions, circles)	45 min.	Lesson or jumping practice (including upright fences up to 4 feet/1.2 m and also spread fences)
THURSDAY	60-90 min.	Hacking (mainly walk with canters on soft ground)	1-2 hours	Hacking
			1 hour **or** Event	Schooling including pole work **or** jumping grids **or** Evening show jumping competition
FRIDAY	**DAY OFF**		**DAY OFF**	
SATURDAY	45 min.	Lesson or schooling (including pole work and single jumps up to 2 feet/60 cm)	3 hours	Hacking, drag hunting, or team chasing **if not competing on Sunday**
			or 30 min. + 1 hour	Schooling – flatwork Hacking
SUNDAY	2 hours	At a show – 1× clear round jumping class + 1× showing class **or** 2× showing classes (timed close together) **or** 60–90 min. hack	Event	One day event or combined training **or** Hire of cross-country course

rarely be forced to jump anything more than a fallen tree. Many of our domestic animals, though, have been bred to enhance the jumping talent that they innately possess.

Free from the burden of further growth, these are the beginning of the prime years – when a horse is able to cope with greater physical demands. As long as he is sound, you

Below: *Every animal, from highly charged event horse to family pony, will benefit from the relaxation and low-level exercise derived from grazing.*

can take on anything from showing and dressage to show jumping, eventing, polo, or competitive trail or endurance riding. You can build up the horse's experience and skill in any fields that suit you both best. An increase in the workload should be introduced gradually to build up muscles and avoid "overfacing" the animal, which risks a loss of confidence.

Make the most of this time to build up your rapport with your horse. Enjoy working together, and stretch both your capabilities to reach maximum potential. In the wild, horses face daily challenges such as finding food, crossing awkward terrain, and sorting out inter-herd squabbles. A fit and healthy animal with a job to do will derive more satisfaction from life than a sluggish, bored animal with no purpose.

Feeding Recommendations

In the prime of his life, without the demands that growth or old age bring, your animals should have optimum gut function to convert good-quality forage to sustain their well-being. Now fully grown, the animals' diet should be based on their condition and the levels of energy required. Horses should be allowed as much time as possible at grass because the act

STARTING OVER

Horses do remember positive or negative incidents. There are many ways to reach a common goal. Sometimes restarting training in a different place and in a different way will help overcome problems.

DIGESTIVE SYSTEM

The horse's digestive system is designed to receive food "little and often." The food consists predominantly of forage which is broken down in the hind gut. Grazing horses receive this naturally. For hard-working animals, concentrates of cereals need to be added to this to provide higher levels of energy and maintain stamina.

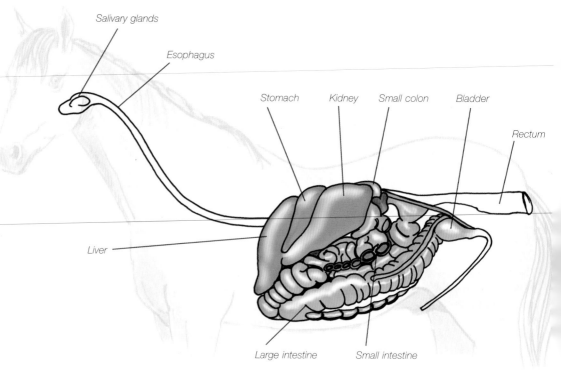

Salivary glands

Esophagus

Stomach   Kidney   Small colon   Bladder

Rectum

Liver

Large intestine   Small intestine

of grazing, as well as supplying food, also provides a low-level exercise to maintain loose joints and fitness levels.

Forages are broken down slowly in the hind gut, producing a slow-release energy adequate for light work. During winter, and for more demanding levels of work, cereals/grains and oils can be added, depending on the individual animal's requirements. The food should be balanced with the work being done and the amount of weight the horse is able to maintain. All straights or mixes added to the diet should be balanced for its needs. Be careful not to feed high levels of starch or sugars, which can bring on attacks of azoturia (stiffening of the muscles of the back and hindquarters) in animals suddenly brought into hard work.

An animal making the transition into full work will change shape dramatically as muscle tone forms, so it is important to check that the tack is suitable and fits well. As for bits, a lot of experimentation may be needed in your quest for lightness and control.

NINE TO 15 YEARS OLD

Horses and ponies in this age group have now reached their peak. They have a vast wealth of experience and, rather than needing more instruction, are usually able to teach their riders a thing or two!

Throughout these years, a competition horse will probably be at the summit of its success. By the age of 15, he may be coming to the end of competing at the highest levels in terms of consistently maintaining the stamina and physical strength necessary for regular top-level competition in disciplines such as eventing. Horses in a dressage or cattle-roping career may well continue to learn and improve far beyond these years. Former competition and dressage horses of this age are much sought after.

Again, the type or breed of the animal will play a big part. In terms of ease of handling, a pony of this age is far more likely to be

a suitable mount for a child than a younger animal. A fine-bred show pony or Arab may begin to look aged and be less suitable for showing than a native type, which tends to age physically at a slower rate. However, all should be very capable of all pony club or 4-H type of activities.

16 TO 24 YEARS OLD

A valuable asset to any owner, animals of this age are normally relatively cheap to acquire but still have a lot to offer. For nervous children or adults learning to ride or those who are happy with just gentle

Below: Barrel racing demands speed, power, and agility. If the horse is not fit, you could encounter injuries such as back problems or overreaching.

Right: Experienced horses are worth their weight in gold. They know their job inside out. In their teens they have more common sense and sanity.

TOOTH GROWTH

After the baby teeth are shed, the permanent teeth continue to grow. On some fine-bred young horses and ponies, you can actually feel the outline of the roots projecting down along the length of the lower jaw. After about the age of seven, the growth stops and the teeth erupt upward into the mouth to replace the surfaces that have been worn away. Once the teeth have erupted to their full extent (25-35), the teeth may be totally worn down or come loose, making eating extremely difficult.

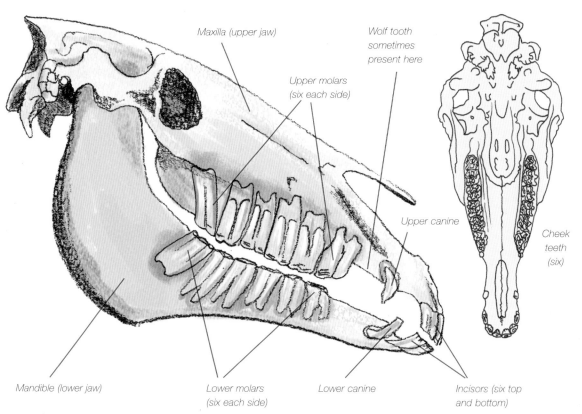

Maxilla (upper jaw)

Wolf tooth sometimes present here

Upper molars (six each side)

Upper canine

Cheek teeth (six)

Mandible (lower jaw)

Lower molars (six each side)

Lower canine

Incisors (six top and bottom)

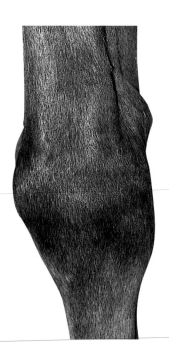

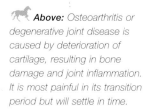

Above: *Osteoarthritis or degenerative joint disease is caused by deterioration of cartilage, resulting in bone damage and joint inflammation. It is most painful in its transition period but will settle in time.*

hacking, they are usually very easy to handle and great confidence givers. They are a lot more tolerant and have learned our language and foibles, even if we do not understand theirs.

If you have owned your horse from its younger years, then you will appreciate how much the horse has given you in his youth. You should be prepared to repay this dedication with the extra attention required in his twilight years – all these animals deserve our respect.

Health Problems

The onset of physical problems such as arthritis, which is very common in animals of this age, especially those who have led an active life, may well cost you financially more in vet's bills. It is worth noting that some forms of osteoarthritis which cause inflammation and pain as the synovial fluid and underlying bones are affected will, once the bones have fused after a year or more, cause little or no pain thereafter. The animal may become more sound although the joint will be less mobile.

In the wild, problems associated with age usually lead to the gradual demise of the animal, through not being able to keep up with the herd or through starvation caused by an inability to eat properly due to lack of teeth. We are able to alleviate these problems through dental work, veterinary attention, or by the assistance that herbal and alternative therapies have to offer.

The more the horse is kept mobile, through gentle exercise and turnout, the longer it will be able to carry on and keep joints and the stomach functioning well.

Feeding Recommendations

In old age, the bacteria in the gut diminish. Their ability to break down and absorb food is lessened. It is important that we make their job easier in order to maintain the horse's good health and condition.

❏ Feed little and often.
❏ Feed foods higher in protein, calcium, oil, and probiotics to aid gut function.
❏ If chewing is difficult, feed short-chop feeds as an alternative to hay, e.g., alfalfa/chaff and soaked pellets.
❏ Allow grazing and turnout as much as possible.
❏ Garlic and herbs can be added to alleviate health problems without recourse to drugs.

Horses and ponies which have been active in their youth should not merely be "put out to grass" and left with no more reason for living. It is very hard for them to cope without the attention and excitement which went with their job. They should not be fully retired unless health problems dictate otherwise. Sometimes, even at such an advanced age, their skills can be redirected into other paths, such as driving. Here a greater proportion of the weight is borne by the horse's chest and shoulders and by the forward motion of the cart itself rather than the concentrated vertical load acting directly on the spine which is experienced in riding.

Even an animal which cannot be ridden will appreciate being taken to a show with the other horses just to soak up the atmosphere. This will, in return, help calm down any over-exuberant youngsters or bad loaders.

25 YEARS ONWARD

Very few people would actually buy a horse or pony of such an age. However, they can be of great benefit to us, such as by being a companion to another animal, for example. In return, we can give them an easy and stress-free life. It is important to make them feel a valued part of the barnyard and not just a worthless animal that is biding his time. Time spent grooming and caring for them will help keep their brains active. An elderly animal just left in the field can easily become depressed and introverted with no interaction with other horses or humans. On the other hand, it can equally become the target of bullies in the herd if socializing arrangements are not regularly monitored.

Total retirement, even at this age, usually brings on only physical and mental deterioration. It is far better to take such horses on the occasional hack, ridden or being led off another horse or on foot, or even taken for a walk with the dog! It is essential to judge your own animal – you know if it is struggling to keep up. Quite often, if they are kept with a close companion, they are happy to go out with them but become quite stressed if they have to leave the safety of their field to be taken out alone. In the wild, veteran horses do not venture away from the herd as they are easy prey or become stranded should the herd move on without them. This could be the reason why an old animal will pull out all the stops in order to keep up during a day's hunting or a group ride but shows reluctance and only plods along dolefully when asked to go out alone, calling persistently to its companions while it is out. In earlier years, it would have been quite happy to go out alone.

If trips away are out of the question, give your old companion more general freedom by allowing him to roam loose round the barn, perhaps when the other horses are shut in, or letting him act as lawn mower in the garden while you are doing the weeding. My old mare attended a barbecue at a stable and lined up with all the guests for the buffet, much to everyone's amusement. She even begged with her foreleg for second helpings!

Below: It is both beneficial and enjoyable to take elderly horses for a gentle walk to keep them supple and maintain a sense of purpose in their lives. Standing in cool water soothes inflamed limbs.

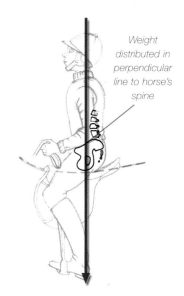

Weight distributed in perpendicular line to horse's spine

WEIGHT DISTRIBUTION
In a classical position, the rider's weight falls in a perpendicular line down onto the horse's spine. With unfit or weak animals, it helps if you tilt forward slightly to push more weight onto their forehand.

 **Above:** *Elderly animals are often harassed and intimidated by other horses or taken advantage of by children. They may appear very tolerant but could be suffering stress silently. Every effort should be taken to make sure they receive the love, care, and respect that they deserve.*

> 66 The coat is nature's way of trying to prevent heat loss. If these animals feel the cold and shiver, any condition they are holding will soon be lost and be very difficult to reestablish. 99

Horses seem to get either more crabby or more lovable as they get older. Even if yours falls into the adorable category, it does not mean he is able to tolerate more than a younger animal. It is not fair to let your good-natured animal be the entertainment at a five-year-old's birthday party because he does not have the heart or energy to give them a sharp nip on the backside for pulling his tail!

In the same way, the elderly horse or pony may suffer from bullying in the field as he is unable to hold his own against the others. Nature can be cruel when animals are competing for survival. This problem can root itself deeply, causing great stress to the animal. You may not be aware of it until physical signs are evident. My own elderly mare suffered epileptic-type fits caused by the stress of being bullied when kept in a large herd environment. It is essential to pick suitable companions or perhaps only one best friend who will value and enjoy the company of the old horse as an equal.

A horse over 25 is likely to suffer muscle loss and can be prone to brittle bones, as we humans are. As with the foal, it is important to feed high levels of protein and calcium to maintain muscle bulk and strengthen the bone structure. The volume of food needs to be increased as a significant proportion may not be getting properly digested. The ability of the enzymes and bacteria to digest the food eaten and of the lymphatic system to absorb the nutrients is compromised in old age. Avoid obesity, however, as extra weight will put further strain on organs and limbs.

Signs of Aging

The classic signs of aging are now likely to be very apparent – a dipped back and sagging stomach, stiffness in the legs, graying hairs on the muzzle or other areas, and generally a thicker coat than in younger days.

The coat is nature's way of trying to prevent heat loss. If these animals feel the cold and shiver, any condition they are holding will soon be lost and be very difficult to re-establish. Even in the summer months, they may still hold on to their coats. If living out, this helps to compensate for the temperature drop on a clear night. They are able to trap air within the coat or let it lie flat in warm weather to control its properties of insulation and heat retention.

A stabled horse is just as likely to need rugs as a field-kept animal as lack of movement will slow the blood flow and make the animal feel colder. Buy one or two good waterproof rugs and several thin underblankets so that you can add layers gradually depending on the ambient temperature. Trickle feeding will help to keep the animal warm as the body digests the food. So a constant supply of good-quality forage in the form of grazing or alfalfa or hay plus short feeds will maintain both the bulk and vitamin requirements of the diet.

Offer treats such as carrots and use soaked pellets/cubes and short-chop or soaked sugar beet if you feel your horse or pony is not able to chew the food properly. Generally, spoil the animal unashamedly, but this does not mean fussing over it unless it enjoys the attention. Some horses and ponies have sensitive skin and simply do not like being groomed for hours on end. If you have a good relationship with your animal, you will understand the body language for "leave me alone" or "more fuss please."

Minor health problems may now become more significant. Slight stiffness and loss of muscle may eventually result in the horse being unable to get up. It takes a lot of effort for an animal as large as a horse to stand after lying down. Their lungs become congested if they recline for too long. It is rare for horses simply to die of old age. Horses just do not live to such an age in a wild environment. As soon as they became less agile and weaker, they are killed by predators or die a slow death due to starvation or injury. Death is one area that is *improved* for captive horse as, thankfully for them, more often than not an illness or injury dictates that we decide to have the animal put to sleep to alleviate further suffering.

It is very important to know your own horse. Although they may be old and slow with a few aches and pains, you should recognize whether they are generally bright, happy, and healthy and whether they still have the will to live. It is only when this inner light fades, or it is no longer possible for us to look after them as they would want, that we should consider saying good-bye.

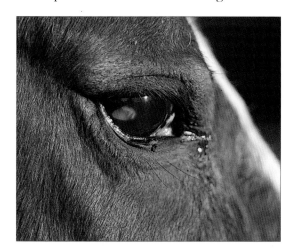

🐎 **Above:** Many elderly horses develop a dipped back, which may make them unsuitable for riding. If they are still active, they could be driven in a lightweight exercise cart to avoid full retirement.

🐎 **Above top:** Cataracts may develop which limit vision, but in a familiar environment this should not be too much of a handicap. Elderly horses may not move out of the way if threatened, so match companions wisely.

🐎 **Above:** Although many old horses tend to hold onto their winter coats and may never shed them fully, abnormally thick, curly coats should be investigated as they can be a symptom of Cushing's disease.

🐎 **Left:** As in humans, graying hairs and general stiffness come with age! Elderly horses sometimes have to get up in stages from a lying position – by stretching out their forelegs and "sitting up" on their backsides and hocks, then summoning up the energy to "flick" the hindlegs out behind them to reach a standing position.

VALUES

Horses are as individual as you or I. They deserve good care from birth until death. Unfortunately, some people use them like disposable toys. To these owners, once a horse's "usefulness" is over, so is its worth.

❝ **While we may have to watch the painful and undignified demise of a relative with a degenerative disease helplessly, our animals are more fortunate – they can be spared long-term pain and suffering.** ❞

EUTHANASIA OR HUMANE DESTRUCTION

Unfortunately for owners, it is rare that their animals will pass away naturally in the field or stable and even less likely that they will simply succumb to old age. Some horses are killed outright in dreadful accidents, but fortunately this is rare.

Feral horses face a bleak end, often starving to death on their own. They may have been injured by a predator or another horse and bleed to death or be too lame or weak through old age to keep up with the rest of the herd. For them, there is no owner or veterinarian around to ease the pain. The outlook is better for our domestic horses. We tend to treat them as members of the family. While we may have to watch the painful and undignified demise of a relative with a degenerative disease helplessly, our animals are more fortunate – they can be spared long-term pain and suffering.

Euthanasia is defined in the dictionary as "the intentional causing of a painless and easy death to a patient suffering from an incurable or painful disease." There are several situations in which euthanasia may be regarded as being the most humane option available.

❏ An emergency condition brought on suddenly. In some cases, the animal may undergo surgery in an attempt to treat the condition. Investigation may prove that the outlook is hopeless, and the decision is taken not to bring the animal around from the anesthetic.

❏ An accident causing serious internal injury or extensive loss of tissue, a bad fracture, or loss of a limb. There may be severe pain associated with such an injury. A veterinarian is the only person able to give a reliable prognosis on the likely chances of recovery.

❏ The horse's quality of life becomes seriously compromised, possibly due to a degenerative or chronic condition. The animal should be assessed as an individual. Some people live happy lives while coping with painful joints or stiffness, but others find that the constant discomfort causes depression. The same holds true for horses. If an acceptable level of comfort cannot be established for a particular animal with permanent unsoundness, or if there is mental anxiety or distress (from whatever cause) which cannot be alleviated, then putting the animal down may realistically be the kindest option.

❏ Financial or practical situations. I would never consider putting down a healthy animal as I would feel morally obliged to look after it or find it a suitable home. In some situations, this may be totally impractical. An animal may not be suitable for a new home. Putting a demanding animal into the wrong hands could lead to further mental or physical suffering for the horse, which could even become a danger to human life. We all have a duty to care for our animals, but it is a sad fact that many are disposed to put down old horses in favor of newer models. However, this may be preferable to their abandonment or passing them through the salesrooms to a new, unsuspecting owner. Sadly, there are always more horses and ponies available than there are good homes.

Although ultimately it usually falls on the owner to make the decision to put the animal to sleep, and it can be a heart-wrenching decision to make, generally we should be guided by the facts and impartial advice offered by a veterinarian.

Methods of Humane Destruction

There are really only two acceptable methods for inducing euthanasia in horses:

❏ Injections of drugs (barbiturates and anesthetics) that depress the central nervous system leading to cessation of respiratory function and cardiac arrest.

❑ A gunshot or captive bolt gun fired directly into the brain, causing destruction of the brain tissue vital for life and ensuring instantaneous death.

Euthanasia should be carried out by a veterinarian, particularly if the animal is insured. In all cases, there is likely to be a financial charge.

Both methods can, however, be very distressing to watch. It can be a profound shock for an owner to see such a large animal fall to the ground or exhibit uncontrolled reflex movements of the limbs. Although watching a horse have an injection sounds less horrific than hearing the bang of the gun, as many as five injections may have to be given. On occasions, horses have been seen to rear up as the drugs take effect. Be assured that both methods are entirely swift, painless, and have high regard for the horse's ultimate welfare. However, they can cause lasting emotional upset for an owner who witnesses them.

It is, therefore, worth considering saying your good-byes in a private moment and then allowing a trusted veterinarian or assistant to be with the animal out of your sight when the time comes.

Methods of Disposal

It is far less stressful for the animal if no traveling is involved and the act of euthanasia can take place at home where the horse will be relaxed in familiar surroundings. Although it may be legal to bury horses on land under your ownership, depending on the laws in your area, most people do not have the large machinery available to organize this at short notice. So removal of the carcass from the site is usually necessary.

This can be arranged by calling a rendering plants. For your peace of mind, it is worth asking whether the animal can be incinerated. Otherwise, a rendering plant will process the carcass.

In some areas, pet crematoriums offer a very sympathetic service to owners and may be able to collect the body and cremate your animal with others, or individually, allowing you to collect their ashes if desired. Although an expensive option, it is becoming the preferred choice for many owners and can assist them in coping with their natural grief.

> 66 Although ultimately it usually falls on the owner to make the decision to put the animal to sleep, and it can be a heart-wrenching decision to make, generally we should be guided by the facts and impartial advice offered by a veterinarian. 99

Above: Horses are majestic, intelligent, and sociable animals. We can form powerful attachments to them, equal to or even greater in intensity than a relationship with a pet dog or even a friend or relative. It is possible to own a horse or pony for 40 years and care for him or her daily. So it can make a very dramatic change to your lifestyle when it is gone.

CHAPTER 6

Tack, Bits, and Gadgets

Horses have an extraordinary ability to sense our feelings – whether they are of apprehension, concentration, or excitement. They frequently try to anticipate our thoughts relating to the matter in hand in order to please us. They can be taught voice commands. Generally, our instructions to them come in the form of touch signals and visual guidance from our body language both on the ground and when mounted. They have a very acute sense of tactile sensation. By reciprocating in a similarly sensitive manner, we can develop understanding and a good partnership.

Above: *Horses have enough to contend with. Never use tack on a whim or for appearance's sake. Understand the action of each piece of equipment used and its consequence for the horse.*
Right: *Whatever your chosen sphere of riding, you should be aiming to achieve a good partnership with your horse rather than simply control of him. There are many ways to achieve a chosen goal, though some may involve more effort on our part!*

> 66 Nowadays, it is quite possible for you and your horse to attend clinics and courses to relearn how to ride. These courses teach you communication skills and the art of riding from the horse's point of view. 99

TACTILE SENSATION

All equines have an acute sense of tactile sensation. Their sensory nerves send messages of pressure, pain, heat, and cold to the horse's central nervous system. The motor nerves respond by reacting to the message, e.g., stimulating the hair erector muscles, increasing blood flow through the blood vessels, or making the horse move away.

Some riders are born with good "hands" and possess a wonderful ability to communicate by subtle aids alone. It is fascinating that contact between a rider's seat, thighs, calves, heels, and hands can produce such a specific type of two-way "conversation." The concentration of a horse on his rider is apparent. Although the rider may not be audibly giving commands, the horse's ears will appear to be "listening" to instructions, with perhaps one ear pointed forward on the direction of travel and one ear back, directed on the rider.

After having broken in several youngsters, I find it incredible how horses manage to learn our universal leg aids and hand movements so quickly and easily. We can switch from one horse to another and they will (nearly) all instinctively understand that we wish them to move forward or sideways in a particular direction and gait.

It is a pity that instead of learning to communicate clearly with our horses and consequently riding in a sympathetic manner, we often get into a vicious circle of sending confusing signals to our mounts. They then react in an unpredictable way, causing us to use yet more severe aids or instruments to force the desired result.

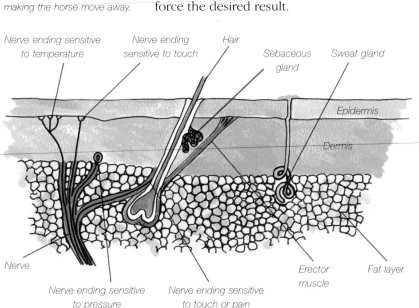

Nerve ending sensitive to temperature

Nerve ending sensitive to touch

Hair

Sebaceous gland

Sweat gland

Epidermis

Dermis

Nerve

Nerve ending sensitive to pressure

Nerve ending sensitive to touch or pain

Erector muscle

Fat layer

Too many novice riders have no "hand sense" and reduce the art of riding into crudely using "legs to go" and hands to stop. Fortunately, horses are very tolerant in these early days. Riders do usually try to improve their understanding and technique.

I have great admiration for riders who can communicate with and control their horses with the minimum of force (and tack).

Left: Whether you ride western or English style, your hands should be light. The western style of riding proves that you do not have to have a constant contact to have a light, responsive horse. More emphasis is put on weight aids than rein communication.

Above: An excellent example of a heavily built horse showing true lightness in his rider's hands. The horse's mouth is open. This should not be seen as a sign of resistance but as a natural consequence of exertion.

Below right: Although this Spanish horse appears to be overembellished in gadgets, they are simply for decorative purposes and are neither excessively severe nor hamper his movement. This type of bit would need sympathetic handling.

Nowadays, it is quite possible for you and your horse to attend clinics and courses to relearn how to ride. These courses teach you communication skills and the art of riding from the horse's point of view. This, in turn, deepens the understanding between horse and rider. It helps to improve performance and potential in such a horse/rider combination.

THE CHOICE OF TACK

I believe that the principal reason we use the abundance of tack that we do is because we are influenced by the attitudes and practices of people around us. When we buy or breed a horse, we should *go back to basics*. Any tack used should be applied in the interests of promoting safety and to assist communication – not to restrict or force it.

HALTERS AND BITS

From foalhood horses are led about in halters which control them by pressure on their nose and poll. "Bitting" is very alien and should be done progressively.

🐎 **Far right:** *English saddles are designed to assist a rider's position with knee rolls of varying cuts, from very straight (dressage and showing – left) to more forward cut and padded knee rolls for general purpose or jumping (center and right).*

Most tack used on horses is 80 percent for our benefit and only 20 percent for the benefit of the horse. While a saddle primarily provides a comfortable and safe seat for the rider, it can help increase the flexibility of weight relocation by the rider, which is important to the horse when he is moving at high speeds or over fences. There are few riders who have the ability to ride bareback from a gallop to a standstill or go flying over fences and around tight bends without slamming down on the horse's back or flying out of the side door! A saddle will, to a degree, compensate for poor balance on the part of the rider. What type of saddle you choose (English general purpose, dressage, jumping, western pleasure, roping, Australian, sidesaddle, etc.) will depend on the style and purpose of your riding.

Bridles, bits, and reins form an important link in the chain of communication between the rider's hands and the horse. Again, they can

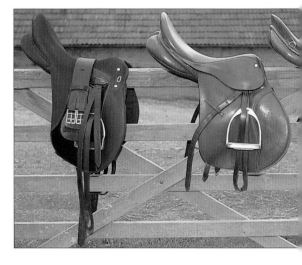

make or break a partnership. Unfortunately, if a horse is broken unsympathetically or without allowing time for the tender skin of the mouth cheeks to become accustomed to an iron bit, this sensitive line of contact can be physically damaged or deadened.

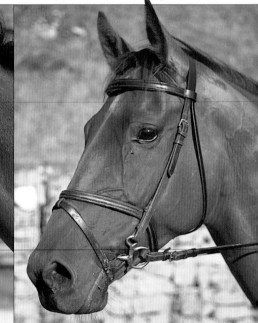

🐎 **Above:** *Take care with a loose-ring bit that the horse's lips do not get pinched between the ring and the hole. A cavesson noseband is smart and nonrestrictive.*

🐎 **Above:** *A hackamore uses pressure on the nose, poll, and jaw for control. As there is nothing inside the horse's mouth, it is useful for child riders or horses with sensitive/deadened mouths.*

🐎 **Above:** *A flash noseband – an unnecessary evil! It may keep the horse's mouth closed, but this just causes tension in the jaw when we really need the horse to be soft and flexible.*

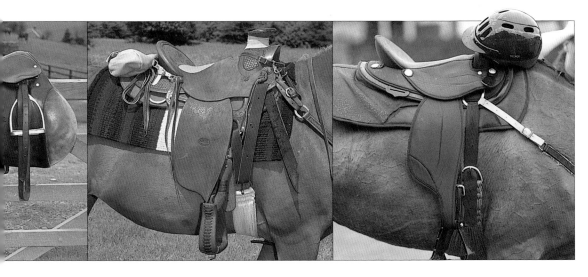

Unfortunately, all competitive riders are constrained when choosing tack by the rules prescribed by the governing bodies of the various riding disciplines or by fashion. It also follows that up-and-coming riders are influenced by their peers. For example, in the world of English showing or dressage, other than in classes for novice horses/ponies, most animals are required to be shown in a double bridle or a Pelham bit. Show jumpers tend to choose drop or grackle nosebands and martingales as a matter of course. In polo,

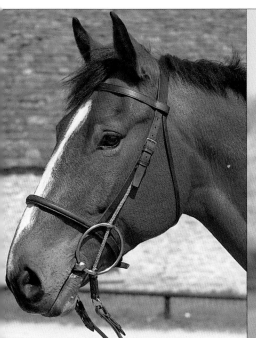

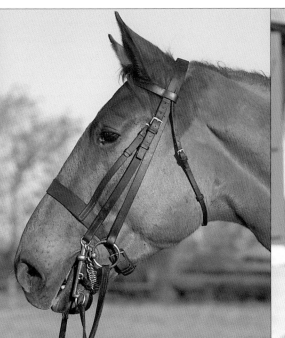

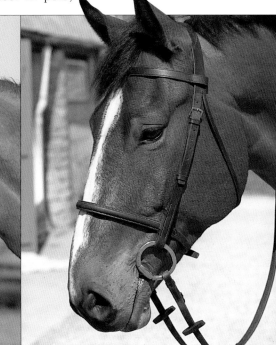

🐴 **Above:** *The action of a gag snaffle works in two directions – pulling down on the poll and up on the cheeks. It is useful on strong horses as they are pulling against themselves.*

🐴 **Above:** *The double bridle consists of two bits, a bradoon snaffle and a weymouth curb which are used with two sets of reins. It is not for novices as there is little room for error.*

🐴 **Above:** *An eggbutt snaffle has fixed rings with smooth sides. They are popular with either a single- or double-jointed mouthpiece and are probably one of the least severe bits available.*

Above: An eggbutt or French link full cheek (Fulmer) snaffle gives added assistance with steering.

Below: This martingale is too small for the horse and creates a constant downward pull. The reins should always follow a straight line from the bit to the rider's hands.

we see gags and Pelham bits with two sets of reins which surely cannot be used effectively with only one hand!

While there is nothing wrong with using any or all of the variety of bits on offer (and I am a fan of the Pelham but admit that this is probably because it helps to mask my shortfalls as a rider!), I believe there are no hard-and-fast rules. Tack and bits should be used that assist and improve the going of the *individual horse and rider combination.*

You know from personal experience that the inside of your mouth, gums, and tongue are far more sensitive than the skin on your nose and face – the same is true of a horse. When breaking in horses, I find it beneficial to attach one set of reins to the bit and another set to the cavesson noseband. A youngster will have spent most of his life being led about by a halter (which exerts pressure mainly on the nose). This sensation can be extended easily to ridden work by attaching reins to the noseband on the bridle and thereby directing the horse in a similar fashion. This eases the sudden transition to pressure in the mouth from the bit, making the whole process of education less painful and less demanding. The bit reins can gradually be used more and more until the reins from the noseband can be removed altogether.

We all want to achieve "lightness" with our horses. I would like to see the rules changed so that milder snaffle

> 66 To watch someone perform a dressage test riding western style with loose reins, or even in the equivalent of a halter, really is an awesome sight. Subtle changes in position or shifting of the rider's weight are all that is needed to perform the most advanced of movements. 99

bits, hackamores, and even halter-type bitless bridles could be used. To watch someone perform a dressage test riding western style with loose reins, or even in the equivalent of a halter, really is an awesome sight. Subtle changes in position or shifting of the rider's weight are all that is needed to perform the most advanced of movements. This is not a criticism of traditional dressage riders, I would just like to see alternative methods *allowed* in the dressage arena, not excluded, as they are now. It seems disgraceful that, at present, one item of equipment which can aid animal welfare and relieve respiratory allergic problems, the nose net, is forbidden in competition when such a profusion of other gadgets can be used.

Unfortunately, over the years, we have tended to get bogged down by image and the acquisition of accessories that actually hinder rather than enhance a true partnership with your horse. Image consciousness can be a good thing as it does mean that all horses taken out in public tend to be healthy but, in the case of tack, we should primarily be concerned with concentrating on safety, comfort, and good communication between horse and rider. It is good to have fun, and a colored saddle cloth will certainly do no harm to the horse, but using a training aid just for the sake of "image" is not right. All too often, we see horses strapped down by martingales, side reins, and drop nosebands, for example. If these are used, they should only be temporary measures and not form part of the daily tack.

People seem to be obsessed with keeping their horse's mouth shut. In fact, we need the horse to have a *relaxed* jaw which is able to play with the bit, salivate, and flex freely.

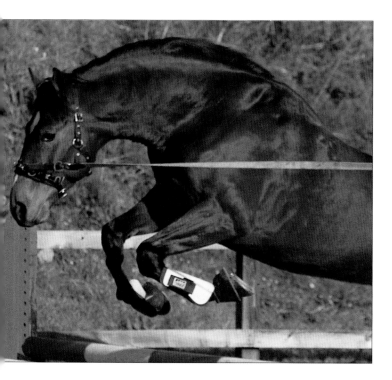

Martingales – Pros and Cons

A martingale is used to prevent the horse from raising his head and neck too high or throwing his head around, which he does often to evade the action of the bit. Many horses benefit from wearing one *in the short term*, but why are martingales so commonplace? The neck of a horse needs to be free and supple for balance and bend. However, it is often forward-going horses that are seen wearing martingales. As this problem may well have been caused by the rider hanging on his mouth in an unsuccessful bid to gain collection, it is more likely that the horse would actually benefit from being ridden forward long and low on a loose rein.

It seems ludicrous that so many hunters and jumping ponies are ridden in martingales while, at the same time, they are expected to stretch out over wide ditches or high fences and perhaps stop suddenly.

Gadgets are often classed as "performance or training aids," but really they should be called "teaching aids" as they can be useful in showing the horse what is required of him. The best gadgets are those that reward the horse immediately when the desired action is achieved. In this way, a horse that lifts his head, leans, or pulls can be more quickly and humanely taught by using a Market Harborough, Harbridge, martingale, or gag bit in the short term, for example, than by constant nagging and pulling on his mouth with no respite. Side reins can also be useful in the short term when schooling ponies whose riders may not have the strength or ability to communicate their instructions correctly. This exercise must always be supervised by an experienced person to avoid misuse.

A horse will use his head as a counter-balance, moving it upward, downward, or sideways to balance his gait or direction of travel. By using rein aids, we create direct or indirect pressure via the bit on several areas of the horse's head – the corners and bars of the mouth, tongue, poll, and curb groove (the chin area behind the lower lip). Generally speaking, pressure on the poll and lower bars

Both above: *A horse needs to really stretch his frame to clear a jump (big or small) with a smooth action. Confidence can be quashed by the fear of being jabbed in the mouth and many horses then choose to "cat leap" and snatch their hind legs over jumps rather than stretching and basculing freely. The breastplate worn by this horse will help keep the saddle in place, but the martingale is likely to be a hindrance.*

DOUBLE BRIDLE

A double bridle combines the actions of a snaffle to aid lateral flexion and a curb bit to encourage vertical flexion, straightness, and engagement/ elevation.

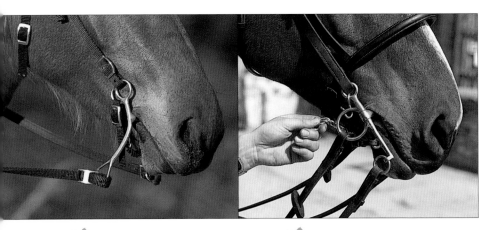

🐎 **Above:** *This western bit may look similar to a Weymouth, but its use could not be more different! Rather than using the two reins independently, a western rider neck reins.*

🐎 **Above:** *Pelham bits encourage flexion from the poll. A jointed Pelham is better if your horse has a tendency to lean on your hands. Curb chains should lie flat.*

I believe that it can be beneficial to change a horse's bit from time to time, or for one particular discipline. This can have the effect of encouraging the horse to perform every time he wears that particular bit.

However, without the immediate reward of the release of any pain or restrictions as a result of performing correctly, horses tend to fix themselves in contorted positions or try to compensate in other ways to alleviate the pain or restriction imposed on them. By restricting their movements, you will never achieve harmony. Long-term use may cause stiffness, unnatural muscle tone, tension, and spinal problems.

It is certainly the case that horses and ponies can only ever be as good as their riders. No amount of gadgets can compensate fully for lack of riding ability.

Tack, Bits, and Gadgets for Ponies

Again, parents and children alike are often influenced by friends and also by what is deemed the correct choice for tack to be used on their ponies. It certainly alarms me to see very young children in show pony classes riding ponies in double bridles. I know there are many excellent young riders. However, there are also many who simply have to look the part, to the detriment of their tolerant mounts.

When I learned to ride, we did a great deal of work riding bareback with just a halter with lead rope attached. This included schooling, hacking, and jumping. In this way, we really learned to feel the horse and improve our sense of balance. Unfortunately, riding schools have to be so conscious of safety that this style of riding is rarely offered nowadays, which is a shame. Kitted out in an approved safety hat/helmet and back protector (with a soft surface for any sudden "dismounts"), children should be more than adequately protected to try learning this way. In the long run, it would actually improve the riding skill, and therefore the safety, of

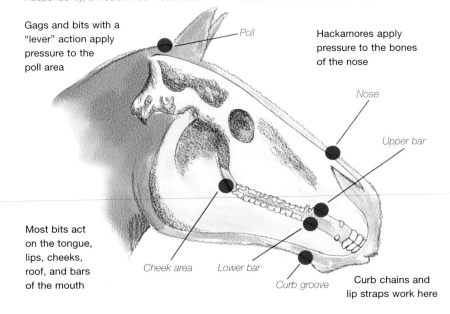

Gags and bits with a "lever" action apply pressure to the poll area

Poll

Hackamores apply pressure to the bones of the nose

Nose

Upper bar

Most bits act on the tongue, lips, cheeks, roof, and bars of the mouth

Cheek area

Lower bar

Curb groove

Curb chains and lip straps work here

How Bits and Bridles Work

This diagram shows how careful positioning of bits and bridles is crucial to avoid discomfort and achieve the desired assistance with control. As well as causing pain, bad handling or incessant nagging on the mouth can deaden sensation there.

of the mouth will cause a horse to lower his head. Pressure on the corners and upper bars of the mouth will encourage him to raise his head. Pressure on the curb groove will have the effect of making him tilt his nose toward his chest. Bits vary in their action by directing the force from our hands to one or a combination of these pressure points. The double bridle allows greater precision as it combines the action of both a snaffle and a curb to be used separately or in unison.

any child learning this way. I also feel that bareback equitation competitions should be actively encouraged to improve the skills of riders generally.

CHOOSING AND FITTING TACK

We all know the importance of correctly fitting tack. The saddle should merely be an extension of the horse to aid our comfort and that of our mount. An incorrectly fitting saddle can quickly result in soreness, misalignment of vertebrae, unbalanced development of muscles, and generally a very miserable animal who may even seem badly behaved and aggressive. Similar problems occur with other poorly fitting tack and buckles which may pinch or rub in certain places.

The most common mistake we make is to trust other people's judgment automatically without question, especially when buying a new horse or pony. We may be happy that the deal struck includes the tack with the horse. As the previous owners may have used it for years, we assume that it must be a perfect fit. In reality, we should have the saddle checked by a qualified saddle fitter at the earliest opportunity. The old saddle may have fit for many years. After that period of time, though, it may well be in dire need of restuffing.

The previous owner may have had a peculiar position, slightly weighted to the off-side, for example. This, in turn, will have flattened that area of the padding and caused a build-up of extra muscle on the horse in this area. It is worth acquiring the peace of mind of knowing that you can at least rule out saddle or back trouble as the cause of any problems with your new horse. You can probably blame your riding for the trouble instead!

 Above left and above:
These show hunter ponies look a picture, but are they all in capable hands? I feel that some children's ponies are overproduced for five minutes of fame in the showring. Bareback riding (above) should be more common as it improves the rider's balance and awareness of the horse or pony's movements.

The upper body should be straight but not stiff. The lower spine and seat should be fluid, following the movement of the horse.

Free hand can take up excess rope, rest against thigh or hang straight down.

The eyes focus on the direction of travel. To change direction point the eyes, followed by the head, shoulders, hips and toes in that same direction.

The back should be straight, not leaning back as here. The lower back and seat should be fluid, following the movement of the horse.

Steering is predominantly from leg pressure rather than rein aids. The stirrups are longer than in English riding.

The reining hand is held just in front of the horn of the saddle.

Pressure on the bit is released as soon as the horse responds.

The horse is asked to work with his hocks "underneath him" with more elevated paces.

Above: In western pleasure classes, riders will be asked to walk, jog, and lope in both directions and on the correct lead. In a trail class, horses have to work over and through obstacles including gates, bridges, and logs.

Above right: A very different style of riding is exhibited by this novice dressage rider. Dressage riders are asked to perform pre-defined patterns of movements and paces in an arena and judged on accuracy and the horse's responsiveness.

Another problem may be the *amount* of tack you receive. By this I mean all the added extras, like martingales and peculiar bits, etc. Often this is simply the result of fashion and people wanting their horses to look difficult to ride. They believe that it will give the impression that they have experimented with what tack is "needed" for their animal, but more often than not, this is not the case at all. Many people automatically use martingales when they are not needed and often this has a completely adverse affect on the horse's outline, especially when jumping when this restriction is certainly not desired in most animals. Always bear in mind how you would

feel subjected to a piece of equipment and whether it would help or hamper you. You don't see ballet dancers or athletes trussed up with gadgets, and yet we expect our horses to perform like them.

The same is true of bits. Start off with a standard snaffle and if *you* (not the previous owner or someone else) really cannot get on with it, then borrow bits from a bit library or friends. Use them during different disciplines, e.g., hacking, jumping, and flatwork *for several days* before making up your mind what to use. You may find that for everyday work, your horse is perfectly comfortable and well behaved in a snaffle, but for cross-country

The hands are held low, just in front of the pommel of the saddle. The elbows should be slightly bent and follow the movement of the horse. There should be a straight line from elbow to hand to the horse's mouth.

There is likely to be a contact on the horse's mouth at all times although this rider is leaning back and hauling on the bit excessively.

toward enabling you to transmit your wishes to your horse in a manner that he finds easier to comprehend and with minimal force.

Western Style

The western style of riding allows far more freedom for the horse to "hold" himself and practice "self-carriage." (Self-carriage is when the horse's energy is compacted, known as "collection" – a bit like a coiled spring. The impulsion goes in an upward as well as forward direction. The horse's paces are lifted and floating so that he feels "light" to ride, rather than flat and hanging on the reins.) Far less force is exerted by the rider's hands. There is more emphasis on "thinking and feeling" the direction or gait, rather than ordering or forcing it.

Try riding your horse (in an enclosed space or manège) with only a rug or bareback pad on and a halter with two lead ropes attached and tied together. The rug will stop you from slipping around on the horse's back but still enable you to feel its every movement. The halter *will prevent* you from hanging on its mouth.

You should find riding this way surprisingly easy. Without a saddle, you will benefit from being able to feel how quickly your horse responds to the correct aids. Most horses can be ridden purely from the leg with just a little tweak on the relevant "rope" for guidance. It is also within most people's capabilities to get their horse "down on the bit" without a bit!

This is great fun and should inspire you to improve your riding techniques now that you can feel the difference you can make without the use of fancy bits, martingales, and pink fluffy numnahs!

or dressage, a Pelham or a double bridle is preferred because of the added control it affords. Horses can sometimes benefit from a change for specific events, and they often seem to learn that this means they have to "perform" while wearing a certain bit.

The answer is often *less is more*.

Less force, *fewer* gadgets, and *more* sensitive and accurate riding lead to a better partnership between horse and rider. This is especially important with youngstock whose mouths (and mental attitude) can be ruined for good by an overzealous rider, however good his or her intentions may be. Learning your horse's language will go a long way

> " *Less* force, *fewer* gadgets, and *more* sensitive and accurate riding lead to a better partnership between horse and rider. "

🐴 *Above:* For everyday work, your horse may perform well in a snaffle. For cross-country, a change of bit may be required.

❝ **A horse with good conformation and a reasonable leg action should have no need for any type of protective bandaging for general riding.** ❞

CORRECT BANDAGING
Exercise bandages employing cotton or fleece bandages wrapped over gamgee padding provide excellent protection and support for the legs, but still have a certain amount of "give." Polo riders favor this type of bandaging.

To summarize, give your horse the benefit of the doubt, and believe that he does not need the gadgets until he proves otherwise. Even then, speak to your instructor in order to have a second opinion.

Physical Influences on Horse and Rider

The physical size and shape of the horse and rider combination plays a big part in the nature of the communication between them. Although a good rider is able to convey instructions to any size horse or pony, the volume and frequency of these aids may change with each animal.

I adore riding large, heavy-boned horses. I feel safe and relish being in control of the power of such a large animal beneath me when I weigh a mere 112 pounds (50 kg). I do feel, however, that I am far more of a passenger on these animals – if I shift my weight slightly or move my leg position, it is of less consequence than it would be on a slighter-built animal. For fast work like cross-country, this is probably a bonus as I am less likely to confuse my mount and therefore should stay in the saddle!

When I ride finer-built horses and ponies, there is a different pleasure in the preciseness with which my body can influence the movements of my mount. Simply twisting my shoulders or pushing down with my spine or tailbone can produce a change of direction or pace which would require a more detectable

leg or rein aid on a less sensitive animal. Certainly, there are very responsive large-set horses and cobs. Generally, though, finer-bred, thinner-skinned animals can be more easily influenced (for better or worse) by a rider's actions. This may be due to temperament as well, as highly strung animals will react more dramatically to stimuli coming from the world around them.

Bandages: Pros and Cons

Bandages, such as tendon boots, brushing boots, overreach boots, knee boots, and hock boots, all have their place in the tack room for use on more demanding outings or on animals who have a tendency to harm themselves accidentally, by overreaching for example. These are generally classed as "protection aids."

I feel they are used unnecessarily on many horses for daily riding in good, safe conditions simply because the rider desires their horse to wear them, either for the sake of appearances or because they worry about their horse too much. Wearing any type of support bandage unnecessarily will actually instigate a dependency on such items, weakening limb strength in the long term as the muscles and tendons will be supported by the bandage and therefore not harden to the same degree as they would without them. It will then actually become risky for the horse to be ridden without the bandages to which he has become so accustomed.

Another problem is that sweat, lack of air, and the warm conditions that prevail under these bandages can provide a fertile breeding ground for harmful bacteria. If possible, use breathable materials and remove the bandages as soon as possible.

A horse with good conformation and a reasonable leg action should have no need for any type of protective bandaging for general riding. Polo horses and those competing cross-country will require protection from the impacts or abrasions that are a hazard of these

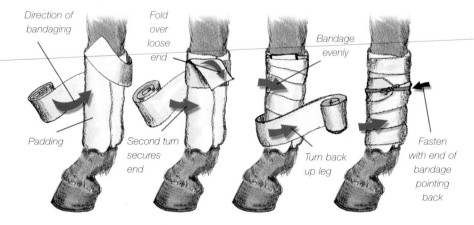

Direction of bandaging

Padding

Fold over loose end

Second turn secures end

Bandage evenly

Turn back up leg

Fasten with end of bandage pointing back

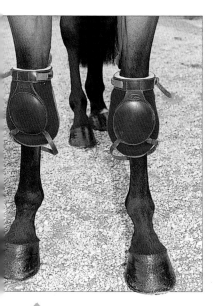

🐎 **Above:** *Knee boots are only really necessary on young, unbalanced horses or, perhaps, if you are doing a lot of road work (including driving horses).*

🐎 **Above:** *Tendon boots support the ligaments and tendons at the back of the leg. Overreach boots are useful for horses who forge or overstep with their hind legs.*

🐎 **Above:** *Fetlock and brushing boots are useful if a horse has a "plaiting" action or is close behind. Bear in mind that any horse with good conformation that is "fit" for the work he does should **rarely** need to wear boots or bandages.*

sports. Youngsters and green horses may not have perfected their coordination, and knee boots and bandages can be beneficial to avoid splints or broken knees.

For the most part, provided horses are exercised correctly and are fit for the job that they are expected to do, bandages should not be required.

CHOOSING THE RIGHT BLANKET

Horses and ponies have a very effective form of protection from the elements because their coats can lie flat or trap air between the hairs as insulation. I am quite happy seeing horses *of any breed* kept year-round without rugs, provided they have shelter and are able to grow adequately thick coats for protection. Many people could do away with their rugs for the sake of their horses. I know owners who put blankets onto fat horses and ponies and then try to limit their food intake in order to knock some weight off them. Leave the rugs off, and let them use their food and body fat for warmth, as nature intended!

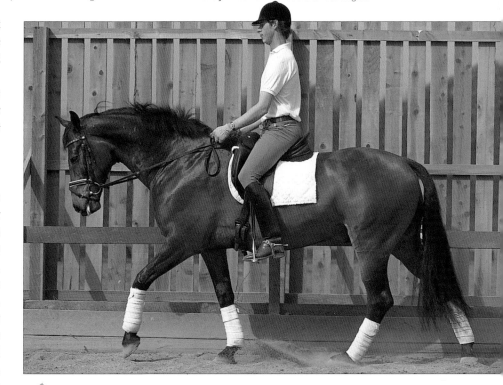

🐎 **Above:** *Leg bandages are commonplace on the dressage circuit as they visually accentuate the movement of the horse's limbs. Most horses do not **need** them.*

FATTIES!

Many stabled equines (ponies especially) are overrugged and underfed to keep a desired weight. They would be happier and healthier if fed larger quantities of hay and allowed to let the digestion of this keep them warm.

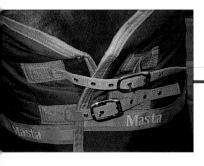

Below: Although modern rugs are designed superbly, many fit perfectly when the horse has his head raised but constrict the windpipe and gullet when the horse grazes. Always adjust the straps to accommodate this – it may mean having the top strap one or two holes looser than the bottom one.

FITTING BLANKETS

Blankets should not only be the correct length and depth for the horse, but the neck aperture should be the correct size to hold the rug in place. Too small a fit and the movement of the shoulders will be restricted, too large and the whole rug will slip back and rub on the horse's withers. Leg straps and cross surcingles (under the belly) should have about a hand's width of slack.

Having said that, although many animals winter out well, extremely cold or wet weather conditions over long periods can cause weight loss or rain scald. We should endeavor to prevent this in horses in our care.

Thin-skinned horses with sensitive skins may also need to be protected from biting insects during hot weather as their bites can easily cause sweet-itch or other allergic reactions. If you have felt the contrasting surface temperature of a gray horse compared with a bay or black animal, you will appreciate the benefit of using a light-colored cotton sheet on a dark-colored animal to help reflect the Sun's rays. So, most horses will need some kind of rug at some point during the year,

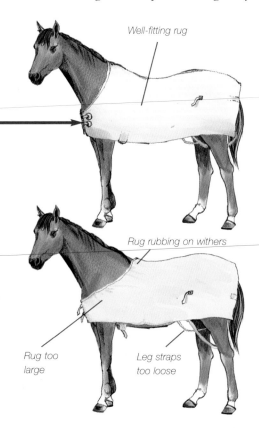

Well-fitting rug

Rug rubbing on withers

Rug too large

Leg straps too loose

> 66 **If you have felt the contrasting surface temperature of a gray horse compared with a bay or black animal, you will appreciate the benefit of using a light-colored cotton sheet on a dark-colored animal to help reflect the Sun's rays.** 99

for warmth, for protection against heat and flies, or to keep them clean before a competition.

When deciding what rug(s) to buy, remember to take into consideration the following factors rather than just buying the latest type or a bargain offer which may be false economy.

Breed/type This should dictate the weight of the lining required.

Usage Indoor/outdoor or both – this should dictate the material. There are now excellent waterproof breathable rugs that can double for outdoor and indoor use.

Careful or destructive horse Many a beautiful rug has been ruined in just a few days – if your horse is destructive, it may be prudent to purchase two cheaper rugs so you will not be so heartbroken when yours begins to look as if Edward Scissorhands has been at it!

Weather If your horse lives out, you may need two outdoor rugs so a rain-saturated rug can be allowed to dry out while the other rug is used in its place. In hot climates or after exercise, a cooler blanket can be beneficial. These are designed to assist the evaporation of sweat at a steady rate during the drying-off process, preventing the horse getting a chill.

High humidity Constant high humidity and heat can be distressing to horses which seem better able to withstand cold than intense heat and humidity. No rugs can regulate humidity. It is kinder in such circumstances to keep horses indoors during the day and turn them out at night to graze.

Note: It is better to have several thin rugs that can be used in conjunction with one another or a rug with a detachable lining so that sudden changes in the weather can be accommodated by removing or adding some extra layers.

Fitting Blankets

Horse rugs are generally sized by measuring from the middle of the chest of the horse to the point of the hip. It is important that the rug sits correctly and does not slip backward, forward, or sideways easily, even when the horse lies down or rolls.

Horses generally eat off the ground. However, most owners fasten the front chest straps while the horse has his head up. Many rugs are made to come quite high up the neck

1. Adequate length covering from top of withers to dock.
2. Darts and shaping along the back to improve fit.
3. Breathable material to wick away moisture.
4. Preferably no seam along the back where dampness could seep through.
5. Deep enough to prevent drafts and cover the animal when lying down.
6. Correct size of neck aperture to fit the horse.
7. Shoulder pleats here on an outdoor rug would allow for freer movement.
8. Adjustable, secure fastenings.
9. Tail guards reduce drafts and rubbing (especially pulled tails).
10. Leg straps fitted through each other reduce slippage but can rub fine horses.

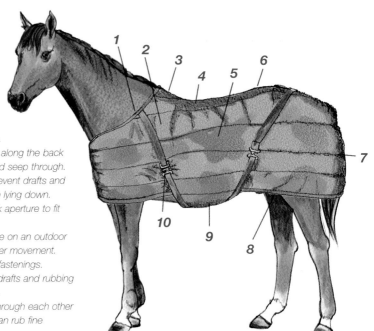

POINTS OF A BLANKET
Blankets should be chosen of a material and weight best suited to the horse, climate, and location (indoor or outdoor). A horse's wardrobe can be quite large if you include a summer sheet, sweat/cooler rug, and exercise sheet (useful to keep the chill off when riding on cool, damp days) as well as a waterproof outdoor rug and insulated indoor rug.

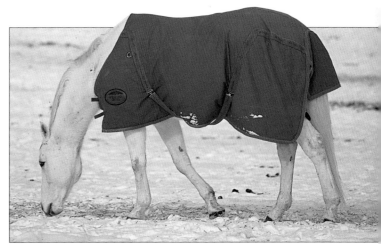

for warmth. In almost every case, the top chest strap will need to be much looser than the bottom strap to allow the horse to stretch down to the ground to eat without this action causing the strap to grow tight, squashing and restricting his trachea and esophagus.

 Above left and right: *Most horses can withstand freezing temperatures, particularly those with long winter coats (left), but they suffer when there is prolonged wet weather. After exercise (when a horse has sweated) or after a downpour are the times when a horse is most likely to shiver. For elderly animals or poor doers, rugs are beneficial to prevent them from losing weight.*

🐎 **Neck and chest clip:** *Ideal for horses that live out but sweat up when ridden. I prefer **not** to extend this along the belly as a rug offers no protection here.*

🐎 **Trace clip:** *A very useful clip for working horses that maintains protection but removes hair from areas which sweat.*

🐎 **Chaser clip:** *Similar to the trace, but all or part of the hair on the face is clipped. It looks smart, but removing facial hair is unkind.*

CLIPPING PATTERNS

Clipping looks smart, aids grooming, and is beneficial to hard-working horses that sweat a lot. If you only ride once or twice a week, however, it is more valuable to the horse to leave the hair in place.

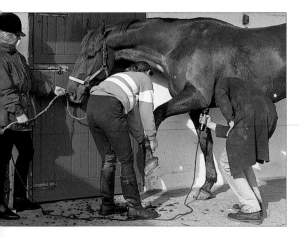

🐎 **Above:** *You will almost certainly need an assistant to help maneuver limbs to stretch the skin on wrinkly areas, such as the elbows. If you have a fidgety horse, your assistant can hold up one foreleg to encourage him to stand, but change legs frequently so he doesn't tire.*

IS CLIPPING A GOOD IDEA?

Most horses tend to grow longer, denser coats in the winter, which provides good body insulation but causes them to sweat in hard work. This can make them uncomfortable and may lead to loss of condition. Clipping the coat is generally done for the comfort of the horse and, provided the type of clip is matched to the level of work undertaken by the horse, there should be no problems.

Summer Clipping

Some horses do not lose their coats readily or they naturally have thick coats year-round. It is kinder for them to be clipped during the summer to keep them more comfortable. Owners should consider what will ensure the horse's comfort rather than simply doing what their friends do.

Unclipped For all horses and ponies ridden for short periods of time or just a couple of times a week. It is preferable for a horse to sweat for a couple of hours a week after exertion rather than shiver for the remaining 166 hours!

Neck and chest clip This is suitable for most horses and ponies who may live out but which sweat up when ridden.

Trace clip, chaser clip, low chaser (Irish) clip These clips remove hair from the neck, belly, and flanks (the areas that sweat most) and aid grooming. The hair remains on the back and legs, but horses will require blankets in cool weather.

Blanket clip, hunter clip The hair is clipped off, leaving just a covering over the back in the shape of a blanket or a saddle. The hair on the head and legs can be left on or clipped off. These horses will need blankets cool weather.

Full clip All the hair is removed from head to hoof. This is only suitable for horses in hard work or in hot climates. When I clip horses in the summer, I usually clip under the jaw (leaving the hair on the face), the entire body, and just trim up the long hairs and feathers from the legs.

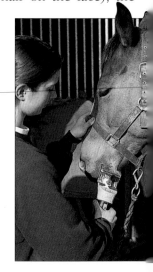

🐎 **Right:** *Removing the whiskers and jaw hair gives a finished appearance, although some of the horse's facial sensation and protection is lost by doing so. If you do have to clip your horse and he is not keen on the idea, using a humane twitch is preferable to having a battle with an angry and fidgety horse.*

Irish clip or low trace: *Another very useful clip as only the areas prone to sweat are removed. It can follow a line above or below the shoulder.*

Blanket clip: *Smart and useful for hard-working horses or for cobs with hogged (shorn off) manes (to avoid lots of tramlines).*

Hunter clip: *This removes all body hair apart from an area the shape of the saddle. Some people take off facial and leg hair too.*

> **66** Owners should consider what will ensure the horse's comfort rather than simply doing what their friends do. **99**

I do not agree with clipping the hair from a horse's head. The skin on the face is very thin, and this is not an area where horses sweat. So clipping is completely unnecessary. For appearance's sake, it is quite acceptable to trim up the jaw line and any long hairs to smarten and sharpen the outline without clipping the whole head. I also do not recommend clipping the hair from the legs of fine-bred horses as you will remove a valuable and natural layer of protection that guards against bruising, grazing, and irritants.

I find that it is beneficial to leave the hair on horses with a small amount of feather during the winter but to remove the bulk of hair of horses that are exposed to muddy, wet conditions if their feathers are extremely heavy and long. These seem to trap moisture and mud, which never fully dries out and so encourages harmful bacteria such as the organisms that cause mud fever. Once clipped, these areas are exposed to the air and dry out quickly.

Ears and Whiskers

During the months when I am competing, I do trim off the larger whiskers. I will trim the edges of the ears but never trim inside the ears as there is too great a risk of hair falling inside. My horses lead a very natural life, but I suppose I want them to look as smart as the next horse in the showring. So I hope they forgive me for this little blip in my natural methods.

Below: *Having your horse shod by a qualified farrier ensures that his feet are kept in good condition and are regularly checked. Many pleasure horses can be worked without shoes.*

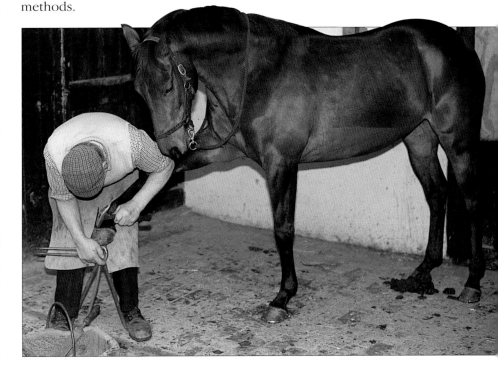

TO SHOE OR NOT TO SHOE?

Rather like the choice of tack, shoeing seems to be greatly influenced by peer pressure and geographic location.

> **Specialized shoeing can compensate for deformities, disease, and aging traits such as crooked limbs, laminitis, and contracted tendons which may otherwise cause discomfort and render the horse useless as a working animal.**

Whether a horse needs shoes or not depends on

❏ his conformation and hoof structure,
❏ whether he has been shod in the past,
❏ the type of work he undertakes, and
❏ whether he is (or can be) comfortable without shoes.

A hoof can be compared loosely with a fingertip or toe. If we were to tap or drag our fingertip or toe along on an abrasive surface, the nail will normally protect the sensitive tip, and we would feel very little. However, if it is cracked, chipped, or worn away, our sensitive fingertip or toe will bear the brunt of the rough surface. This could lead to soreness or bruising. However, over time, a more even pattern of skin growth and wear would be established. Our skin would toughen up and thicken (as bare feet do over time), allowing painless exposure to most types of surfaces.

Wild horses cope very well without shoes on all kinds of terrain. Their active lifestyle assists in creating a regular pattern of hoof wear and regrowth. The friction and compression directly on the frog and sole promote blood flow to the hoof to stimulate

growth. An even climate, whether it be hot and dry or cool and wet, means that the water content of the hoof remains more stable than that of a domestic horse (moving regularly from sodden fields onto drying, absorbent bedding). All these factors (along with diet) help to encourage stronger, healthy hooves.

We shoe and trim the hooves of domestic animals primarily for their welfare. We expect them to move over a variety of surfaces, including grass, sand, and concrete, and to experience great pressures on their limbs, for example, by carrying a rider or jumping. It would certainly be unusual (but not impossible) for driving horses, who cover great distances mainly on the roads, to manage without shoes.

A small minority abuse the use of shoes, using weights and abnormal blocks which work *against nature* to corrupt and contrive the natural movement of the horse for their own entertainment. This can only cause discomfort. In my opinion, it is a practice that should be condemned.

In most cases, shoeing our animals means they will receive regular care from a qualified

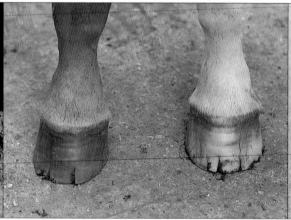

Above: This hoof has grown too long and the clenches have risen. The angle of the hoof and long toe puts extra strain on the limbs and makes tripping very likely.

Above: The condition of these hooves is poor, with splits and cracks from toe to the coronary band. Not only will these need careful trimming, but the cracks may have to be "filled" until they grow out. Good general nutrition will also be essential to promote healthy regrowth.

Above: This pony has a well-shod, compact hoof, although its boxy shape and upright conformation may possibly predispose it to other forms of lameness.

Above: The shape of this hoof resembles that of a feral, unshod hoof with weight carried over a wider area. The long toe and low heels would need to be addressed in a working animal.

farrier to keep them pain free and sound during their lifetime. Specialized shoeing can compensate for deformities, disease, and aging traits such as crooked limbs, laminitis, and contracted tendons which may otherwise cause discomfort and render the horse useless as a working animal.

Equally, it is possible to leave many animals unshod for they will remain comfortable to perform well on any terrain. In many countries, including Argentina, South Africa, and many parts of the United States, unshod horses of a variety of breeds are ridden on uneven, rocky terrain which would make the English grimace in horror! Although in the U.K. ponies are often kept unshod, it is rare to see horses kept in this way. The owner of an unshod horse runs the risk of being labeled uncaring (rather than being applauded for using more natural methods).

It may be the case that only front shoes are required to make the animal comfortable. Your farrier will be able to advise you on

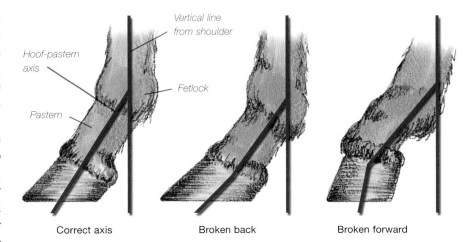

Correct axis   Broken back   Broken forward

alternatives such as glue-on shoes or more temporary solutions such as a removable "equi-boot," or similar. In the matter of shoeing, there is neither a right way nor a wrong way. It is a question of weighing what is most beneficial for the individual horse or pony.

The best candidates for going unshod are youngstock and those that have never been shod or have had a period without shoes (perhaps having been wintered out or rested after injury or illness). The hoof walls of any horse that has been shod regularly in the past will have been weakened by the presence of nails and their residual holes. So be aware of this if you decide to remove the shoes. There is likely to be a period of discomfort until the hoof wall, sole, heels, and frog all harden. So it is unlikely that you will be able to continue an unchanged active work program with your horse immediately.

Horses living out that experience gradual climatic and dietary changes are likely to have fewer problems than stable-kept animals. However, although stabled animals should not be precluded from going shoeless.

The only worry of establishing a trend for "natural" hoof care is that it could be used by some people as an excuse for neglect. It is necessary to balance the natural benefits with possible detrimental effects and look at each animal individually before making a decision.

CORRECT/INCORRECT HOOF-PASTERN AXIS

Remedial foot care by a farrier is really the only way to balance or attempt to correct weaknesses caused by poor conformation or injury (such as contracted tendons). The length and the angle of the pastern in relation to the line of the hoof make a huge difference to the displacement of force when each hoof hits the ground. If the axis is broken back, collapsed heels, bruised soles, and tendon strains are likely. If it is broken forward, the horse is likely to suffer from concussive injury and have a choppy gait.

Left: *English riders tend to baulk at an unshod horse (other than youngstock or a child's pony), associating the lack of a shoe with lack of care by the owner. Anyone lucky enough to ride in countries such as Argentina, South Africa, and the United States will find that horses cope brilliantly on rocky terrain over which an English rider would never venture even on a shod horse!*

CHAPTER 7

Nutrition The Natural Way

I n recent years, the number of products available for consumption by domestic equines has increased tenfold. It almost seems that you need to have a degree in horse nutrition to understand fully what these "new advances" in feed substances have to offer! In fact, becoming a horse nutritionist to develop new formulations and subsequently advise on their benefits to the horse owner is now a lucrative career path in its own right.

Certainly, there really are some superb feeds on the market. Do we really need to make life so complicated, especially considering that even after thousands of years of domestication, horses are still designed to thrive on a diet that consists of predominantly grass?

Above: Even after thousands of years of domestication, all horses are designed to thrive on a diet of predominantly grass.
Right: Keeping horses in peak health is as easy or as complicated as you make it. The key is providing a good basis of forage plus a ration matched to the needs of the individual animal.

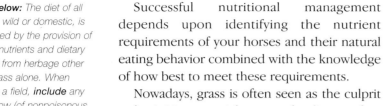

Below: *The diet of all horses, wild or domestic, is enhanced by the provision of added nutrients and dietary interest from herbage other than grass alone. When fencing a field, **include** any hedgerow (of nonpoisonous plants) on the inside of the fence rather than outside the boundary.*

Above: *Horses are trickle feeders, designed to snatch at food while on the move. Many domestic horses have an unnatural feeding pattern – gorging on food and then standing immobile for hours.*

Successful nutritional management depends upon identifying the nutrient requirements of your horses and their natural eating behavior combined with the knowledge of how best to meet these requirements.

Nowadays, grass is often seen as the culprit as laminitis, grass sickness, and colic are often directly linked to the consumption of grass. What we tend to forget is that few such problems occur in horses that have access to grass year-round and grass of a moderate quality and quantity rather than the lawnlike lush pastures we see today. Many breeds of horses and ponies most susceptible to laminitis originally come from feeding grounds of sparse grass and fibrous herbage. They would have lost a great deal of condition over the winter period. When their diet was enhanced with an improving supply of grass and plant sources in the spring, the change would have been a gradual process to which they would become acclimatized.

Different Energy Requirements

That said, it must be appreciated that many horses cannot thrive or perform to the best of their ability living on a diet of grass alone. A horse participating in a three-day event requires some 160 megajoules (MJ) of available energy (see also page 154). If supplied solely by grass or hay, this would amount to more than 44 pounds (20 kg) a day, an amount which the horse would struggle to consume. By introducing cereals and oils, these energy levels can be derived from a more manageable diet. The nature of some of the breeds we have introduced, the demands of domesticity, and the performance we expect from our working equines

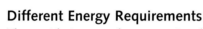

> 66 Do we really need to make life so complicated, especially considering that even after thousands of years of domestication, horses are still designed to thrive on a diet of predominantly grass? 99

necessitates an improved and enhanced diet. We also expect a certain standard of weight, health, and condition. We endeavor to retain this throughout the full 20–30+-year span of a domestic horse's life, far longer than a wild horse could hope to remain in full health.

In this chapter, I shall try to provide what I believe to be a balanced picture of what is available and how we can best provide a ration for our horses and ponies. It must fulfill both the requirements to provide a nutritious diet to enhance performance and maintain a reasonable weight with the horse's own psychological need to be eating little and often.

Horses are trickle feeders. Although their feeding is interspersed with moving around, lying down, socializing, and simply standing still, they will eat for about 14–16 hours out of a 24-hour period. They do not intentionally go for more than a couple of hours at most without feeding. Wild horses are often seen snatching at grass and plants while actively on the move. Domestic horses do not prosper if they are forced to have empty stomachs for prolonged periods.

All equines need a balanced diet containing water, fiber, protein, fats, starches, sugar, vitamins, and minerals. This diet will maintain good functioning of all the life-sustaining body systems, replenish and repair body tissues, maintain body temperature, and provide sufficient energy to fuel body processes, such as blood circulation and digestion as well as actual limb movements.

DIGESTIVE ANATOMY

To appreciate the nutrient needs of a horse, it is useful to have an understanding of the anatomy of the digestive tract and the digestive processes. The entire digestive tract of a mature horse is approximately 100 feet (30 m) long, coiled within the body. The stomach of the adult horse is roughly the size of a rugby ball. This is relatively small, representing only 10 percent of the overall area of the gut, compared with the small intestine (30 percent) and large intestine (60 percent). The stomach of a human being comprises 30 percent of the digestive system and of a dog 60 percent.

Rate of food passage through the digestive system is very rapid. It moves through the intestines at the rate of 12 inches (30 cm) per minute. Any feed not digested in the small intestine is passed on to the cecum and colon within two to four hours. Whatever the horse is fed, whether it be solely grass or a combination of concentrates, dried forage, and grass, etc., it is dealt with in the same way. The digestive system breaks down and separates the chemical components into substances which combine with oxygen to produce energy. Enzymes and bacteria break down the food into nutrients, which are absorbed. Any indigestible or waste matter travels to the rectum and is passed out of the body.

The horse's gastrointestinal system has not changed over thousands of years of evolution and is still designed to digest primarily forage. So fewer problems will occur when a natural diet of grass, herbage, or other forage forms the bulk of the ration.

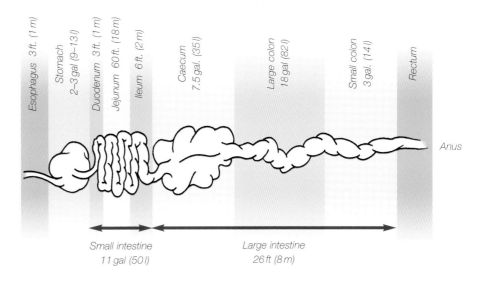

Esophagus 3 ft. (1 m)

Stomach 2–3 gal. (9–13 l)

Duodenum 3 ft. (1 m)

Jejunum 60 ft. (18 m)

Ileum 6 ft. (2 m)

Caecum 7.5 gal. (35 l)

Large colon 18 gal. (82 l)

Small colon 3 gal. (14 l)

Rectum

Anus

Small intestine 11 gal (50 l)

Large intestine 26 ft (8 m)

The most serious nutritionally related problems in mature horses are colic and laminitis (founder). Laminitis is a disease of the hoof that causes severe lameness. Although there are many causes of laminitis, eating high-energy grass or concentrates is probably the most common cause.

Colic, or abdominal pain, is often associated with impactions and twisted intestines in the horse. Sudden changes in diet, bolting food, and eating feeds with a low-fiber content are frequent causes. Because of the rapid rate of passage of food through the upper gut, it is

THE DIGESTIVE TRACT

For such a large animal, the stomach of a horse is really very small – roughly the size of a rugby ball and making up only 10 percent of the overall area of the gut. Food passes through the digestive system very quickly, and trickle feeding allows for optimum absorption of nutrients.

Left: Grass is often seen as the enemy when it is actually the cheapest and best form of feed available. Unfortunately, unlike a bag of feed bought from a feed merchant, the energy and nutrient levels are not listed on the side nor do they remain constant throughout the year. The art lies in cultivating the crop of grass to make it suitable for the type of animals you have (see also Chapter 4).

easy to overwhelm the digestive capacity of the stomach and small intestine. This forces excess cereals to pass through to the cecum and colon, where rapid fermentation can produce too much gas and lactic acid, resulting in the onset of colic. For this reason, it is important to feed relatively small amounts at a time, dividing the feed into several smaller portions to slow down consumption if required.

Below: *Good teeth are a fundamental part of survival in the wild. Domestic horses are lucky that good dentistry and the broad spectrum of feeds available to them can eliminate suffering and keep them healthy even in their later years.*

Above: *An equine dentist can rasp any sharp tooth edges which may be cutting into the gums and causing problems when the horse is eating or being ridden. Many youngsters have some pain when their teeth are erupting, and all horses should have their teeth checked annually. Never attempt tooth care on your horse yourself.*

TEETH

Horses chew forage at a rate of about one chew per second. This amounts to a total of approximately 54,000 chews a day (estimating on a total of 15 hours of grazing/feeding). Although the number of bites will be dictated by whether grazing is plentiful or sparse, the grinding action of the large, flat molars serves to shred and masticate each mouthful into segments that are only a few millimeters long before they are swallowed.

Having good teeth is an essential part of survival for any wild or feral animal. Coping with dental problems, such as jaw abscesses or missing teeth, will severely compromise their health. If forage is not chewed adequately, the fibrous cell walls are not broken down sufficiently to enable the enzymes and bacteria in the small and large intestines to digest the available nutrients. Impaction of long-stem fiber may occur, resulting in colic. Longer-term effects include poor nutrient absorption leading to poor health or starvation in some cases.

Fortunately, because of the nutritious short-chops and easily digestible feeds on the market today, elderly domestic animals with worn, loose, or missing teeth are still able to digest adequate levels of nutrients and fiber to maintain their health.

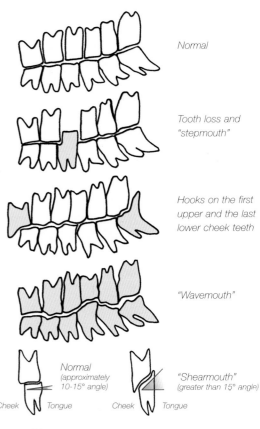

Normal

Tooth loss and "stepmouth"

Hooks on the first upper and the last lower cheek teeth

"Wavemouth"

Normal (approximately 10-15° angle)

Cheek   *Tongue*

"Shearmouth" (greater than 15° angle)

Cheek   *Tongue*

DENTAL MISALIGNMENTS

This diagram illustrates some common patterns of tooth wear resulting in the formation of sharp hooks and irregular alignment of the eating surface of the molar teeth.

ENERGY REQUIREMENTS

The feed our horses receive provides energy to fuel the muscles and various nutrients, vitamins, and minerals to keep the entire body functioning correctly. Too little energy causes a horse to become lethargic and lose weight. Whereas too much, or the wrong type, can cause unsettled behavior or too much weight gain, leading to health problems due to an unbalanced diet. Energy itself is not a nutrient or a vitamin.

Energy is measured in calories. One calorie (kilocalorie) is equivalent to 4.2 kilojoules. Because of the large body weight of the horse, energy is normally measured in megajoules (1 MJ = 1,000 kJ). An "average" 1,100-pound (500 kg) horse may require 27.5 pounds

(12.5 kg) (in weight) of food a day, which must provide 70 MJ of energy. In human calorie terms, this equates to approximately 16,666 calories!

It is easier to understand just how much effect the energy levels of a horse can have on his performance, temperament, and weight when you consider that the digestion process is remarkably fast in equines. While in humans food may take up to 48 hours to be digested, moving through the intestines at a rate of about 0.4 inches (1 cm) per minute, in horses the speed is a staggering 12 inches (30 cm) per minute. Therefore, feeds are absorbed quickly and can have quite dramatic consequences.

Energy is obtained from the various components that make up a well-structured horse feed:

Structural/insoluble carbohydrates Mainly fiber, which contains relatively low levels of energy. These are principally digested in the hind gut. Because of the coarse cell structure of fibrous feeds and the lower levels of bacteria and enzymes present in the hind gut, the whole process of digestion of these feeds is slower. Although fiber does not have dramatic short-term results on energy levels, the longer digestion period has the effect of generating warmth and a feeling of well-being in the horse. High-fiber feeds should make up the greatest part of the horse's ration.

Soluble carbohydrates and sugars These are mainly made up of glucose, which is rapidly broken down by enzymes in the small intestine. Grass can contain up to 30 percent sugar. A field-kept horse on good pasture may well consume between 22–33 pounds (10–15 kg) of grass (dry weight), which translates into the equivalent of four to five bags of sugar! The rapid absorption of simple sugars accounts for the hyperactivity of horses and ponies put out on spring grass.

Starches Present in all plants and vegetables but found in high levels in cereals. The starchy part is found in the center of a grain of cereal, inside the fibrous shell (the flour part of a grain of corn, for example). In modern compound feed mixes, the cereals are generally bruised, crushed, and/or extruded (pressure cooked) to help break down the starch molecules to aid digestion. Excess starches can result in problems like laminitis and lymphangitis.

Oils Only low levels of oil are present in a horse's natural diet. These have, in recent years, become the wonder feed of modern equine diets. Obtained from refined plants and cereals, soy, corn, sunflower, and linseed, they contain fatty acids and glycerol which are easily digested and can be an excellent slow-release source of energy. Oils contain two and a half times more energy than the same weight of carbohydrates, so they are ideal to top up rations to promote stamina and weight gain. Oil also has the added benefit of lubricating joints and enhancing the appearance of the horse's skin, coat, and hooves. Take care when feeding oil, however. It can actually increase the need for antioxidants, which are required to control damaging free radicals in the body. So a balanced vitamin intake is required. It is common to add from one tablespoon up to two cupfuls of oil to a horse's diet. As most proprietary brands of coarse mixes contain oil in their composition, take care. Too much oil can not only upset the balance of the diet but also make it unpalatable with an undesirable laxative effect. The energy value of 2.2 pounds (1 kg) of oil is equivalent to feeding 8.8 pounds (4 kg) of hay, but oil should make up only a *tiny* percentage of your horse's overall diet.

Energy Levels of Different Feeds (MJ/kg)			
	GE	DE	NE
Hay	16	8	5.5
Oats	17	11.5	8.7
Corn oil	39	32	28
Coarse mix low energy	16	10	7.3
50:50 Hay:oats	16.2	9.8	7.2
45:45:10 Hay:oats:oil	18.5	12	9.3

DIFFERENT FEEDS
*Energy levels are important when formulating a diet, but a high-energy level is **not** a prerequisite of a good diet. It should be matched to the requirements of the horse or pony. (GE: gross energy; DE: digestible energy; NE: net or usable energy.)*

Above: Pony nuts are a cheap compound feed which are often overlooked as they are not so pleasing to the human eye as a mix is. They comprise good-quality fiber, cereals, and a vitamin/minerals premix in an easily digestible form.

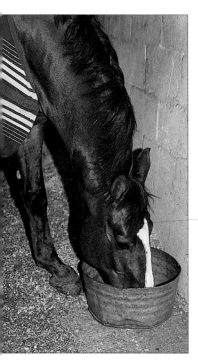

🐎 **Left:** *Diets should be dictated by the temperament, body condition, and work load that the horse undertakes. Food passes through a horse's digestive system quickly so feed your horse for work already done rather than for work to be done in several days' time.*

Although commonly fed to horses, it should be noted that oil derived from sources other than plants (such as cod liver oil from fish) is an unnatural diet for a herbivore.

How much energy does my horse need?

There are several factors to be considered when analyzing exactly how much feed your horse or pony should consume and the desired calorie content.

Type and temperament I prefer the term "type" to "breed" here as all animals are very individual in the way their bodies utilize feed. Some can almost live on fresh air, and these are termed as *good doers* or *easy keepers*. Then there are those that can be pumped full of nutritious feeds but still look like a bag of bones; they are known as *poor doers*. Usually, though not by any means always, good doers tend to have more laid-back characters whereas poor doers can be worriers or have

sharper personalities. The physical reason for this is that stress causes changes in the acidity levels of the gut and causes the beneficial bacteria which aid digestion to become detached from the gut wall, hence compromising the absorption of nutrients by the body. Visually, this can be seen by the frequent and loose droppings passed by anxious or highly strung animals. An already naturally lively horse will not require high levels of fast-acting energy-boosting food, although it may well still require high levels of calories to maintain weight.

Performance and workload Misconceptions often arise when people try to assess workload. Many people assume that hacking or schooling for an hour three or four times a week is moderate work. When you consider that a wild horse would be constantly moving from one feeding ground to another – and possibly exerting himself by fleeing from

Maintenance	Light Work	Moderate Work	Hard Work
80 percent forage 20 percent hard feed or up to 100 percent forage	70 percent forage 30 percent hard feed	60 percent forage 40 percent hard feed	50 percent forage 50 percent hard feed
Resting horses, e.g., those being roughed off at pasture	Retired horses needing more calories	Riding school horses working for four hours a day	Advanced event horses
			Racehorses
Retired horses who are good doers	Active child's pony or adult's riding club horse	Grade A show jumper competing regularly	75-mile+ (120 km) endurance horses
Convalescent horses	Growing youngsters	Advanced dressage horse	
Young child's riding pony	Horses/ponies requiring more condition	Intermediate event horse	
Ponies/horses: good doers used for hacking and schooling for one hour, three to four times a week	Novice show jumpers or novice event horses	50-mile (80 km) endurance horses in work	*It can be seen that most pleasure horses fall into the maintenance and light work categories.*
	Prelim dressage horses		
Polo ponies or hunters at rest out of season	20-mile (32 km) endurance horses	Lactating brood mare or stallion at stud	
	Driving horses and ponies	Hunters or polo ponies in work	

danger – while living only on a maintenance diet, the workload of our domestic animal does not look so arduous. Domestic animals, especially those stabled for long periods, are at rest for the vast majority of their day, munching at hay, warm, and well fed. They are actually exerting very little energy.

The examples given in the table opposite are only intended as a guideline. Age (e.g., a growing youngster), an impaired ability to digest food efficiently (e.g., a veteran, recuperating, or stressed animal), as well as individual type should all be taken into account in conjunction with actual workload. Therefore, a growing colt or a 30-year-old veteran may both have a workload score of nil. Yet they may well require a caloric intake equal to that of an intermediate event horse – it is just the forage-to-hard feed ratio that may be different.

A horse is, by design, an athletic animal which can easily cope with walking 20 miles (32 km) in a day on a maintenance diet, provided his level of fitness is also built up efficiently. It is no good simply feeding a high-energy diet and then expecting your horse to spring into action if he has not built up stamina and muscle tone to match! You may only succeed in causing overexuberance, resulting in strains or other injury to your horse and yourself.

Weight This applies not only to the fat and muscular weight carried by the horse or pony but also to the weight of his skeletal framework. A heavy-boned animal may require more weight and bulk of food than a lighter-framed animal. However, the other factors of temperament and workload should also be taken into account. His overall condition should correspond with his build and height.

For a 100 percent accurate measurement of weight, it is necessary to transport your horse to a weighbridge. However, there are calculations which help you to estimate your horse's or pony's overall weight and the corresponding weight of feed (hay and short feed) he should be receiving. Unfortunately,

after speaking to various nutritionists, I have found that there are discrepancies between the figures used in the calculations that lead to enormous variations in the result.

One calculation to gauge the body weight of an animal is

$$\frac{\text{Girth (cm)}^2 \text{ x Length (cm)}}{11,900}$$

(however, another formula gives a much lower dividing figure (denominator) – 8,717).

I used the formula to calculate the weight of my 15.1hh heavyweight Shire X cob gelding. The results ranged from 1,367 pounds (620 kg) with the first calculation up to a whopping 1,867 pounds (847 kg) with the second calculation.

Calibrated weigh tapes are available, but these again work on specific calculations. When using a weigh tape, my cob was estimated to weigh 1,630 pounds (740 kg), which appears to be a reasonable and logical weight for his build.

Once weight is established, you can use the formula **(Body weight in kg ÷ 100) x 2.5** to work out the approximate weight of feed required (total of hay plus hard feed). By using the body weight of 1,630 pounds (740 kg), this computation resulted in an estimated feed intake of just over 41 pounds (18.5 kg). This horse generally gets a daily ration of approximately 31 pounds (14 kg) of hay and 13 pounds (6 kg) of hard feed, totaling 44 pounds (20 kg) (when not at grass).

In my opinion, the only way to assess your horse fully is by sight and touch.

Left: *Taking your horse to a weighbridge is the only truly accurate way of finding out your horse's weight.*

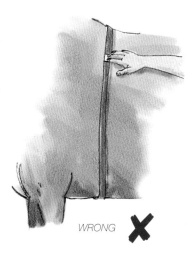

CORRECT

WRONG

CORRECT MEASURING
When using calculations to assess the weight of a horse, the positioning of the tape measure is crucial in order to be as accurate as possible. When using a calibrated weigh tape, only the girth measurement needs to be taken, aligning the tape as shown above.

Type Versus Condition Versus Weight

Poor condition   Good condition   Fat horse

Pads of fat over the horse's rump will give you an idea of his condition score, although muscle tone and breeding are other contributing factors which should be taken into account. This horse is overweight.

Young horses often appear underweight and bony, but they will generally fill out by the time that they are three years old.

When judging condition, assess each horse individually and as a whole. Not all horses have perfect conformation and muscle tone, so consider these points rather than focusing on the type alone.

A novice may mistakenly assume this horse with a large belly is overweight, but it carries no excess fat on its shoulders or flanks. In fact, it is more likely that it is either in foal or malnourished with a massive worm burden.

Many horses native to hot countries look leaner than our ideal picture; however, excessive body fat would only make them uncomfortably hot.

Poor condition is indicated by protruding hips and "sucked in" flanks.

REAR VIEW

The back view of a horse can reveal weight distribution more accurately than the front view. A protruding belly seen from the front may only be visible because the horse is narrow chested.

Condition Scoring

Assessing the physical health and weight held by a horse is known as "condition" scoring, and I find it the most accurate guide. Condition scoring is a way of assessing a horse's body fat by observing it visually and feeling manually for fat deposits, normally at six body sites (back, ribs, neck, behind the shoulders, at the fore rib, withers, and tail head). Some experts advise that estimates of fat cover should then be compared with a numerical description of a condition score system to determine a condition score, but I believe that this can be misleading. Tables of figures cannot be standardized too specifically, as all horses are individual. Instead, I will explain what to look out for and caution about some of the areas where people mistakenly think horses are too thin or too fat.

First, observe your horses visually. Be warned: long hair will interfere with scoring. So palpation of fat cover (i.e., over the ribs) will be necessary. Do not confuse fat for the muscle tone of a physically fit horse.

Whereas most people look at the neck and the flanks when assessing weight, this can be misleading. Conformational traits and the size of the animal should also be taken into account. A crested neck in a cob type of horse may just be a sign of his heavy horse ancestry. In a pony, though, this feature would be a lot less desirable and could well be a symptom of obesity. Similarly, a lighter-bred pony with perhaps some Thoroughbred blood may seem underweight with, perhaps, an upside-down weak neck and poor topline, but this could simply be lack of muscle tone.

Veteran horses and ponies may well be underweight because their bodies are less able to digest nutrients. Often, their appearance is simply a sign of their being old rather than being underweight. They may have visible ribs and sunken flanks but still have a large belly and be perfectly healthy. This is simply a sign that everything sags with age, just as in humans where it is rare to see a 70 year old without a bony rib cage and flabby belly!

Signs of Obesity

A sign of an overweight horse is one with pads of fat on either side of the withers and over the shoulder (just in front of where the knee rolls are on the saddle). If you cannot feel any ribs when you run your fingers along the horse's sides and if the belly protrudes further than the hips and flanks (when viewed from behind), then the animal is probably carrying more than its fair share of fat.

An underweight horse cannot simply be diagnosed because it looks thin, with easily visible ribs and bony flanks and backbone. This may simply be a sign of lack of muscle tone or of a lanky two- or three-year-old who has not fully matured. An underweight animal will look poor, have a dull coat, and lack energy.

Feeding cannot simply be learned from the pages of a book or by calculations alone. Good horse ownership still depends on careful observation and accurate judgment of each individual animal. The owner also needs to determine what body fat condition score is most suitable for the workload undertaken by the horse and also the effect of the climate in which the animal is living.

Conformation and Lifestyle Play a Big Part

Performance horses, such as eventers and race horses, may visually appear leaner than is ideal, but overfeeding will actually have detrimental effects on them. The horse is less able to cover the ground with a heavier body weight. There may be potential strain on the heart. The full feeling could also hamper lung function and make the horse feel as we would if we tried to run a marathon after consuming a huge meal!

On the other hand, a heavy horse such as a Shire or an Irish Draft or cob type may appear fat when he is in fact in good condition, as he simply carries a thick covering of fleshy tissue and fat over his heavy-boned skeleton. Horses of this type are actually underweight if they do not display a large crested neck and bulbous flanks. These animals are bred for their bulk and strength rather than speed, and their conformation matches this.

In hot countries, horses can appear to be underweight by our standards. Generally, this is because it is not beneficial for horses to carry too much weight in a hot climate. Feed is not required to the same extent to maintain body temperature, and the extra weight would cause further sweating and lethargy. The body regulates its own feed-to-water ratio to take into account temperature and levels of activity. The diet we offer should mirror these requirements.

The digestible energy (DE) is the available energy in the feed minus any energy that passes through the body and is expelled in the feces. Therefore, DE is the actual energy that is fully digested and absorbed in the body.

> **Whereas most people look at the neck and the flanks when assessing weight, this can be misleading. Conformational traits and the size of the animal should also be taken into account.**

DIGESTIBLE ENERGY
Energy can be derived from many sources. This comparison of common feeds assists in formulating a suitable diet for an individual using the components most readily available to you.

Energy Levels of Different Feed (in MJ per kilo weight)

Alfalfa	9MJ
Coarse mix (cool-medium)	10-14MJ
Dried grass	13MJ
Good hay	8MJ
Haylage	7-9MJ
Oats	11.5MJ
Oil	32MJ
Spring grass	10-13MJ
Summer/winter grass	7-9MJ

Signs of Dehydration

- Lethargy or fatigue
- Loss of appetite
- Tying up or cramps
- Sunken eyes
- Depression and poor recovery after exercise
- Loose skin which, when pinched, does not quickly return flat

Below: A hard-working horse can lose 4.5 gallons (20l) of fluids a day through sweat alone. This must be replaced by water. Traces of ammonia, nitrates, and nitrite in a good water source should ideally be less than 1 mg/l with a lead content of less than 0.05 mg/l.

WATER – THE VITAL ELEMENT

The horse's body is made up of about 70 percent water; therefore a 1,320-pound (600 kg) horse comprises 925 pounds (420 kg) of water and only 395 pounds (180 kg) of bones, soft tissues, muscles, and fat. Without water, the nutrients in food cannot be utilized. Water is essential for digestion as it transports nutrients in soluble form to be absorbed. Lack of water can be a factor in colic. A horse dehydrated by a factor of only 20 percent could die. So it is essential that water is *always* freely available.

The breed of a horse affects its water intake to some degree. For example, Thoroughbreds sweat heavily whereas Arabs, bred to exist in the desert, sweat very little. Body mass also dictates the volume of water required – a 15hh heavyweight horse with a large covering of fat and flesh generally requires more than a 17hh finer-bred animal.

A mature, idle horse will drink approximately 8–10 gallons (38–45l) of water daily, more if lactating or sweating. The average working horse requires 9–13 gallons (40–60l) of water a day depending on temperature and work load. You can appreciate just

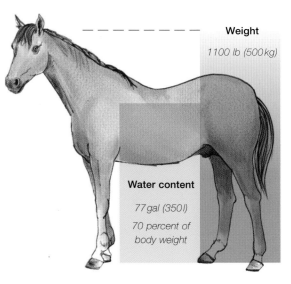

Weight
1100 lb (500 kg)

Water content
77 gal (350l)
70 percent of body weight

WATER CONTENT
Seventy percent of a horse's body weight comprises water, so it is vital that horses always have drinking water available.

how vital water is when you consider that a hard-working horse can lose 4.5 gallons (20l) of sweat in a day and up to 13 gallons (60l) of total excreted fluid.

A lactating mare loses water through the milk she produces, which can be as much as 35 pints (20l) a day. Therefore, a constantly available water supply is essential for her and for her youngstock, who requires a higher water intake in relation to this weight to prevent dehydration than an adult horse does.

> 66 A horse dehydrated by a factor of only 20 percent could die. So it is essential that water is *always* freely available. 99

Dehydration can occur even in winter. A horse may be reluctant to break the ice on his water trough or to drink ice-cold water. As a consequence of this, his feed intake will be reduced. There is also an increased susceptibility to colic caused by impaction. The optimum temperature for water consumption

by a horse is between 41–50°F (5–10°C). So take care to add warm water to raise the temperature of water buckets and troughs in cold weather to encourage drinking.

The required water intake of horses put out to graze on lush pasture will be partially met by the high moisture content in the grass. So you may notice that the amount of water consumed from buckets or water troughs is dramatically reduced, especially if the temperature is cool. All feeds contain moisture, ranging from about 10 percent in cereals, to 15 percent in hay, to 70–90 percent in succulents and grass. Warm water, succulents, and soaked sugar beets can be added to feeds to increase water intake. Take care, though, not to make the meal sloppy as this actually decreases stimulation of the salivary glands.

Above left: Break ice on troughs daily in winter if water is frozen. Regularly empty and clean troughs in summer to remove the buildup of algae and rotting leaves.

Above right: A horse can break ice on a puddle with his hoof but may be reluctant to drink from a water trough if he has to break the ice using his muzzle.

Top: A lactating mare will have a greater need for water to replenish fluids lost in the milk she is producing, which may be as much as 35 pints (20l) per day.

Composition of Hay and Other High-Fiber Feeds

FEED	Crude Protein (%)	Crude Fiber (%)	Digestible Energy (MJ DE/kg)	Dry Matter (%)
Hay	4.5-10	30-40	7-10	80
Haylage	8-14	30-38	9-11.5	55-65
Straw	3	40	6	88
Sugar beet pulp	7	34	10.5	Feed soaked
Alfalfa chaff	15-16	32	9-10	80
Alfalfa/straw chaff	10.5	38	7	80
High-fiber cubes	9	20	8.5	85
Grass meal	16	36	9-10	85

SOLID FEEDS
Fiber

This should constitute the greatest percentage of your horse's or pony's diet. Horses evolved to eat digestible fiber from which they could extract beneficial nutrients. Although fibrous roughage may be somewhat indigestible in itself, it aids the breakdown and digestion of other foods. You may consider that the most natural diet in the world would be grass alone. In fact, spring grass actually has such a high water level and relatively low fiber content it can result in poor gut function and sloppy, loose droppings. A low-fiber diet will reduce the levels of beneficial microorganisms in the gut and inhibit digestive function leading to a buildup of gas, resulting in a potential attack of colic or poor nutrient absorption. Wild horses naturally seek out and eat fibrous branches and a greater variety of herbage to balance this effect. Hay or chaff should actually be offered to domestic horses on lush spring grass to add fiber to their diet to aid gut function.

Above: Horses enjoy the variation and palatability of different herbage and shrubs which are often selected to assist gut function or to dose as a medication for a deficiency or ailment.

Whereas most cereals are digested within three or four hours, fiber can take up to two days to pass through the body. This thereby generates heat and is a source of slow-release energy as it is digested.

Horses also have a psychological need to chew. Fiber provides the best way to satisfy this grazing instinct. Unfortunately, in performance horses whose diets may consist of only 50 percent forage with the remainder coming in the form of cereals and concentrates, the horse will take fewer chews to consume the ration. A field-kept horse or one on a high-fiber diet may spend 16 hours a day eating. In contrast, a performance animal may receive a higher calorie intake, but his chewing time can be reduced by half, leaving this chewing instinct unsatisfied. Vices such as cribbing often manifest themselves in horses on a low-fiber diet.

Grass

This is the mainstay of the diet of wild horses. A diet of grass supplemented by other herbage providing additional nutrients offers an excellent and simple diet. Unfortunately, overgrazed paddocks, limited species of grasses and herbs, and low soil nutrients either do not provide enough sustenance for most working animals or have the adverse effect of being too high in available carbohydrates and sugars, etc., for others.

Grass consists of two main constituents. The cell wall is partly indigestible. It consists of high fiber and complex carbohydrates. The cell contents provide the highly nutritious proteins, starches, sugars and fructans, vitamins, minerals, and fats. High in energy, it provides about 10–13 MJ/kg of energy.

For large yards with horses on limited turnout, a hydroponic grass machine is a great asset. This provides a constant crop of grass, grown from seed without soil, which provides live enzymes, proteins and amino acids, vitamins, mobilized starch, and sugars. All are

obtained from the seed and root, which is eaten as well as the leaf and stem. It offers a fresh and appetizing addition to the diet of stabled animals that are otherwise fed on a predominantly dry diet.

Hay

Hay is dried grass that may have been harvested from established pasture or from one-to three-year leas (untilled land). Its feed value depends on a number of factors.

If the crop has been planted in order to extract grass seed, the resulting hay is known as "thrashed grass" or "seed hay." This is coarse grass with tough stems of lignin and little leaf. Its fiber content is high (similar to straw), and the nutrient level is low. This is, however, ideal for overweight animals who still require high-volume forage to satisfy their grazing needs.

Ideally, hay is obtained from a blend of different grass varieties (see Chapter 4 for suggested species). These contribute different nutrients and vitamins – hay obtained from pasture such as this is known as "meadow hay." Provided that it has been harvested correctly, this should have a good energy value of around 8MJ per kilo gram and contain acceptable levels of vitamins and minerals,

depending on the soil quality where it was grown.

The best hay in the world can be ruined by bad timing (and bad luck!) when it comes to harvesting the crop. The cut grass has to be partially dried over a period of a couple of days to reduce its moisture content to around 15 percent. If rain or high humidity prevent this, any baled crop will have too high a moisture content, causing spores of mold to germinate and rendering it totally unsuitable for feeding. On the other hand, too much Sun will actually bleach the hay, reducing vitamin levels. The low moisture content will render the leaves brittle, causing a high level of disintegration into dust.

Typically, hay alone will provide enough energy to satisfy a horse at rest or in light work. It is very likely to be deficient in the levels of nutrients offered. It is probable that, if no coarse mix is being fed, then a broad-spectrum vitamin supplement will be required to prevent poor health. Horses fed a diet of 100 percent hay, although possibly carrying enough weight, may show external signs of nutrient deficiencies, including a dull coat and poor hoof quality.

Before purchasing hay, get a guarantee that it is free from weeds like ragwort and from toxins.

Above left: *Winter grass will have lost much of its nutrient content. While it may be adequate for some animals, for others it may not provide enough sustenance to cover their energy requirements. Hay will need to be provided to cater to even a maintenance diet.*

Above right: *Hay should provide the mainstay of the diet if grass is not available. Its nutrient composition will vary greatly depending on whether you use meadow hay, thrashed grass, or legume hay. Any supplementary food should take this into account.*

66 Horses also have a psychological need to chew. Fiber provides the best way to satisfy this grazing instinct. 99

Haylage

This is grass that has been cut but only semiwilted, meaning that it maintains a moisture content of around 35–50 percent water. It is compressed and sealed in airtight bags to eliminate air. Because of the reduced drying time, it is easier to produce and crops are more consistent.

It is ideal for horses with chronic obstructive pulmonary disease (COPD) or other respiratory problems. Its dust levels are negligible, and any spores tend to stick to the haylage rather than being inhaled.

The main disadvantage is that once a bag is opened, its shelf life is only four days. Mold can readily populate the stalks once it is exposed to the air. Any haylage purchased should state its moisture content. Too high a water content, e.g., 50 percent, will dramatically reduce both the fiber level as well as the available protein, energy, and other nutrients, and feeding by weight will be inaccurate.

> 66 **If both legumes and grasses are available to you, a mixed hay is an ideal forage for horses.** 99

Alfalfa

This is actually not a grass at all, but a legume related to the clover family. In my opinion, this is something that any owner of a poor doer or veteran animal should not be without.

In many countries, this is the primary source of hay. It is actually far more nutritious than even most meadow hay, having high protein and calcium levels and available energy of approximately 9MJ per kilogram. It can be fed as the primary source of fiber in long-stem form. It should require only a small ration of coarse feed to supplement the diet of most horses in light work. You may find you actually have to dilute the ration with hay or straw to prevent weight gain!

Legume hays (alfalfa, lespedeza, bird's-foot trefoil, and clover) provide higher levels of protein, calcium, and vitamin A (carotene) than do grasses. Grass hays (timothy, orchard grass, fescue, ryegrass, etc.) are lower in

Alfalfa or lucerne (below) is a highly valued forage for horses as it is rich in protein, vitamins and minerals but still high in digestible fibre. Can be fed longstem (hay) or short chop.

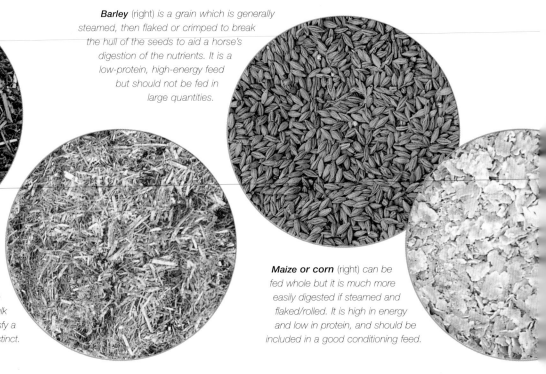

Barley (right) is a grain which is generally steamed, then flaked or crimped to break the hull of the seeds to aid a horse's digestion of the nutrients. It is a low-protein, high-energy feed but should not be fed in large quantities.

Chaff (right) consists of chopped straw (usually lightly molassed to make it more palatable and less dusty). Chaff serves to bulk out a ration and therefore satisfy a horse's chewing instinct.

Maize or corn (right) can be fed whole but it is much more easily digested if steamed and flaked/rolled. It is high in energy and low in protein, and should be included in a good conditioning feed.

calcium and protein and higher in fiber than legumes. If both legumes and grasses are available to you, a mixed hay is an ideal forage for horses. Alfalfa is also available as a short-chop. It is an extremely useful product to bulk up feeds and enhance protein and calcium levels in the diet.

One word of caution: a small proportion of animals, particularly Arab types, have been found to have an allergic reaction to alfalfa. This results in symptoms including scabs (similar in appearance to those of mud fever) and inflamed skin on the lower limbs.

Straw

Oat straw and barley straw can be used as a partial hay replacer when caloric intake has to be reduced without reducing fiber intake. I am quite happy for my horses to eat straw from their beds. I often leave a section un-fluffed for them to chew on – it usually looks and smells equally as nice as any hay. I view it as both a cheap feed and a good additional source of fiber.

You must be aware that a greater proportion of straw is indigestible than is hay. Eating it may result in a hay belly or impaction if water is unavailable to the horse for any reason.

Chaff

These are usually straw/hay/alfalfa mixes in varying proportions, chopped to a length of approximately 1.5-inch (4-cm) stems. These are ideal for bulking up a feed or slowing down the speed at which it is eaten as they require a lot of chewing. Depending on their composition, they can replace part of the hay and all or part of the short-feed for a resting animal or a good doer. However, a broad-spectrum vitamin supplement will also be required. Take care not to feed large quantities of molasses-containing chaff as the high sugar content is undesirable in large volume.

High-Fiber Cubes

Another invaluable addition to your feed room if you have fat, laminitic, or over-exuberant horses and ponies who do not want

Below: Mangers are especially useful for field-kept horses, as buckets are easily knocked over. Widely spaced mangers help to prevent confrontations over food although some "thieving" horses may still need to be tied up at feed time.

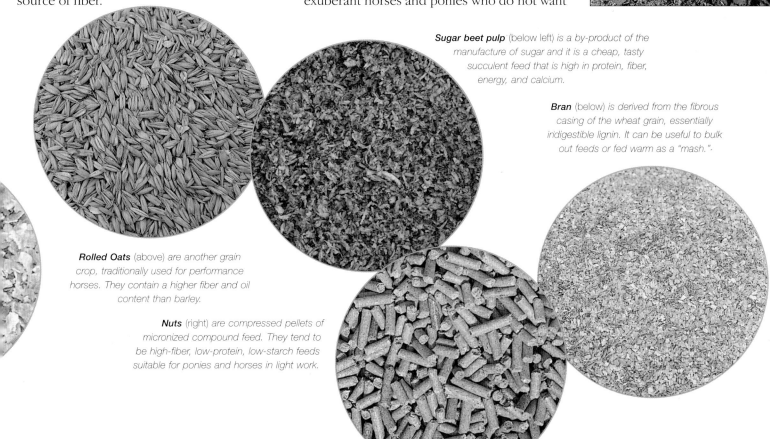

Sugar beet pulp (below left) *is a by-product of the manufacture of sugar and it is a cheap, tasty succulent feed that is high in protein, fiber, energy, and calcium.*

Bran (below) *is derived from the fibrous casing of the wheat grain, essentially indigestible lignin. It can be useful to bulk out feeds or fed warm as a "mash."*

Rolled Oats (above) *are another grain crop, traditionally used for performance horses. They contain a higher fiber and oil content than barley.*

Nuts (right) *are compressed pellets of micronized compound feed. They tend to be high-fiber, low-protein, low-starch feeds suitable for ponies and horses in light work.*

🐎 **Below:** *Nothing can compare with a natural diet, both for mental and physical satisfaction. Fresh herbage will supply most, if not all, of the essential nutrients.*

🐎 **Above:** *Carrots and parsnips will tempt the fussiest of feeders. With a high-fiber, water, and vitamin content they should be utilized as a valuable addition to **every** feed (or as a snack for fatties!).*

to be left out at feeding time! These should contain at least 20 percent fiber and added vitamins and minerals. Although they may look unexciting, my horses seem to prefer these to any of the expensive mixes they are given.

High-fiber cubes are also an excellent way of increasing the fiber intake of veteran animals who may not be able to chew and fully digest long fiber. They can be soaked in water or mixed with sloppy sugar beet if they need to be broken down further.

OTHER ESSENTIAL COMPONENTS

All compound feeds include a high-spectrum vitamin and mineral premix which should be adequate for most animals, other than those with a very low intake. These are essential for many biological processes. While in its natural state, a horse could probably obtain sufficient levels of these from the variety of plant sources growing on different soils, but modern farming methods, restricted grazing, and demanding workloads imposed onto domestic horses may cause deficiencies.

You will see that horses kept outside with access to a variety of fresh herbage are naturally exposed to most, if not all, of the essential components necessary for their well-being (vitamins, minerals, fiber, proteins, energy, etc.). Absorption of these substances is often enhanced by sunlight and the higher levels present in a natural diet. Horses stabled for long periods of time will almost certainly be predisposed to deficiencies and require supplemented diets.

Protein and Amino Acids

Although protein itself is actually low in energy, these are essential to restore and maintain body tissues, especially for horses or ponies in hard work. Without adequate levels of protein, a working horse will lose condition as muscle tissues will not be sufficiently replenished. Amino acids are the building blocks of

proteins. All the major organs, such as the heart and lungs, use high levels of proteins. Although they can be manufactured by the body, deficiencies can occur especially in foals, breeding stock, and elderly animals. Lysine and methionine are two commonly found in supplements, although there are at least 22 different types of amino acids.

Ash

Often seen on the analysis of the contents of a sack of feed, ash is the residue left once the organic portion of feed has been processed. A higher level tends to indicate a higher level of minerals included.

Calcium

All horses and ponies require a calcium-rich diet. For lactating mares, youngstock and veteran animals, adequate levels of this mineral are essential. Calcium, in conjunction with phosphorous and vitamin D, helps production of healthy bone and tissue. Even grass-kept horses may not obtain sufficient calcium in their diet during the winter because the level available decreases as the growth rate of the grass decelerates. Most commercial feed mixes, pellets, and short-chops have good levels of calcium. Limestone flour can be added to the diet if necessary.

When buying a sack of feed, make a point of examining what ingredients, vitamins, and minerals are included. The following will help you to interpret the contents.

Vitamins

These organic substances are vital for overall optimum body functioning. They are classed as either fat soluble for long-term use, such as A, D, E and K, or water-soluble, the B vitamins and vitamin C. Water-soluble vitamins cannot be stored for long periods and must be replenished. Whereas overdoses of fat-soluble vitamins can be toxic as the excesses cannot be readily excreted out of the body. Most horses and ponies out at grass will take in good levels of these essential vitamins. Stabled horses receiving minimal exposure to fresh leafy herbage and sunlight will almost certainly be deficient. Traces of most vitamins are present in good-quality leafy hay but to a far lesser degree than available from fresh grass.

The main properties of the vitamins are as follows:

Vitamin A (retinol) This is important for vision, growth and repair of skin, hooves, and soft tissues. Derived from carotenoid pigments (e.g., beta carotene) present in fresh herbage, it can be found in high levels in leafy pasture and, of course, in carrots, which are a well-known source. Unfortunately, dried forage provides meager amounts. The level in hay will drop to almost zero when it is more than six months old. Amazingly, horses have the ability to store vitamin A in their bodies for up to six months. Wild horses were able to cope when levels available to them fell, for example, during winter or times of drought, as their bodies had stored reserves to see them through the difficult times. Similarly, a domestic horse grazing for one month can (in theory) store enough vitamin A to last him for the next six months.

Symptoms of vitamin A deficiency include weak horn growth of the hooves, slow development in youngstock, poor performance and recurrent strains, poor night vision, and infertility in mares.

B-complex vitamins Although synthesized naturally by bacteria in the large intestine, these water-soluble vitamins are *not* stored in the body. The B vitamins aid nutrient absorption when fiber intake is low or in stressed animals. They support the nervous system and blood composition to promote health and vitality and to combat stress. They are also important for the correct functioning of the adrenal and thyroid glands.

Vitamin C (ascorbic acid) This works as an antioxidant and promotes resistance to

bacterial and viral infection. By being water soluble, it cannot be retained in the body for long periods. Again, this is a naturally occurring vitamin in fresh herbage.

Vitamin D The sunlight vitamin. This assists with the metabolism of calcium and phosphorous and with the absorption of zinc, iron, cobalt, and magnesium, which, among other things, assist in the formation of strong bones. Vitamin D is converted by precursors present in the skin which require exposure to sunlight. Rugged or stabled horses will only receive limited amounts of natural sunlight, resulting in their ability to produce sufficient vitamin D being compromised.

Vitamin E Essential for breeding stock but also useful for horses in hard work. When administered in conjunction with selenium, it can help prevent cell damage and tying up (azoturia). It aids fat metabolism.

Vitamin K This is associated with the blood-clotting mechanism and the proper functioning of the nervous system.

Biotin This is a vitamin which is synthesized in the gut and utilized in conjunction with the amino acid methionine.

Nutrient	Available From	
Vitamin A	Carrots Colostrum milk (for foals only) Fresh grass and herbage including dandelions	
Vitamin B1 (Thiamine) Vitamin B2 (Riboflavin) Vitamin B3 (Niacin) Vitamin B12 (Cyanocobalamin)	Alfalfa Cereals Cod liver oil/soybean oil Fresh grass/herbage Peas and beans Yeast	
Vitamin C	Carrots/apples Fresh grass/herbage	✔
Vitamin D	Colostrum milk (for foals only) Fresh herbage Sunlight	✔
Vitamin E	Alfalfa Cereal germ Fresh grass/herbage	✔
Vitamin K	Alfalfa Fresh grass/herbage	✔

✔ Fat soluble

✔ Water soluble

✔ Small amounts synthesized by bacteria in hind gut

- **Biotin** Fresh grass and herbage Maize Rose hips Yeast
- **Calcium** Alfalfa Limestone flour Seaweed Sugar beet
- **Phosphorus** Bran Dandelions Oats/barley/maize
- **Protein** Alfalfa Cereals Fresh grass and herbage Linseed
- **Manganese and zinc** Alfalfa Bran Cereals Fresh grass and herbage including dandelions Yeast

66 **The whole of the dandelion plant can be fed – flowers, stem, leaves, and root. What a cheap, tasty, natural, and nutritious feed supplement for your horse!** 99

It plays a part in improving skin and hoof quality. It is often given to horses with historically weak hooves, although the benefit may not be apparent until after several months of supplementing the diet with biotin. Natural sources are grass, yeast, maize, and rose hips.

Dandelions Usually regarded as worthless weeds, these common yellow flowering plants should have their status reviewed, as they are one of the most nutrient-rich plants in the world! They contain more available vitamin A than even carrots as well as lesser amounts of vitamins B, C, and D. They also provide a source of potassium, sodium, phosphorus, zinc, magnesium, and iron.

As well as being a source of valuable nutrients, other beneficial effects of feeding dandelion plants are as a liver and kidney tonic, blood purifier, and diuretic. Dandelions are the only natural diuretic not to deplete potassium levels in the body due to their high potassium content.

Feed one or two plants daily. The whole plant can be fed – flowers, stem, leaves, and root. What a cheap, tasty, natural, and nutritious feed supplement for your horse!

Minerals and Trace Elements

These include:

Salts Essential for many biological processes including maintaining the acid balance in the body and regulating fluid and body temperature, salts are lost through sweating and urination. Therefore, it may be beneficial to supplement these for horses in hard work, especially in hot weather or to stimulate drinking. All horses require about 1 ounce (28 g) of salt (to provide 0.1 ppm of selenium) daily. Free access to a salt/mineral block will enable them to replenish any shortfall in their diet, although water *must always* be available to them.

Zinc and selenium Together with vitamins A, C, and E, these elements help in the formation of white blood cells to strengthen the immune system and general respiratory and circulatory health. Selenium levels in the soil vary dramatically by geographic location. As it is only required in small quantities (0.15 mg/kg), toxicity can occur from overexposure.

MSM (methylsulfonyl methane) Essential for healthy muscles and connective tissues, this is a naturally occurring form of sulfur to replenish the body's own sources. It increases cell oxygenation and tissue repair after strenuous exercise or stress. Needed also for the efficient metabolism of carbohydrates.

Manganese and zinc They activate the enzymes in the horse's gut to break down food and release energy for cell metabolism. Raw plants contain enzymes, but these can be destroyed by processing or cooking. So a stabled horse may be deficient. High levels can be found in sprouting plants, such as broccoli and alfalfa.

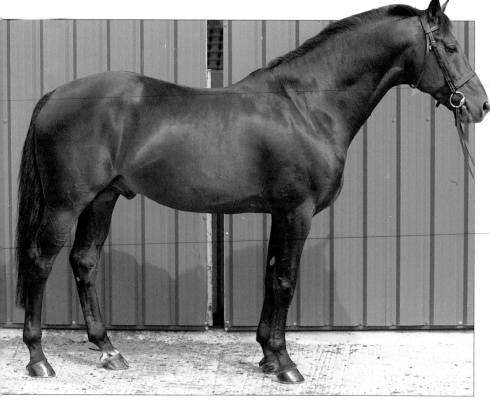

Left: A horse requires over 40 nutrients in the correct balance to remain healthy and fit. A shiny coat, bright eyes, and contented demeanor show that you are on track.

Magnesium An essential component for strong bone and teeth development, magnesium is also required for effective metabolism of vitamin C, phosphorus, potassium, and sodium. Magnesium affects blood pressure and supports the nervous system to reduce the harmful effects of stress.

Iron and copper These elements are necessary for the formation of hemoglobin in the blood and cartilage formation. Significant quantities are lost through sweating, which could result in lack of stamina and poor performance. So it is essential for these substances to be supplemented in hard-working animals.

Feed Supplements – Do Horses Need Them?

Often owners are influenced by advertising and commercial scare tactics into assuming that their horse needs some form or other of supplement. Proprietary formulations come in a variety of packages containing wide-spectrum vitamins and minerals, or individual dietary components such as biotin, or as combination, such as oil, zinc, and methionine. Herbs can also be purchased in individual or composite forms.

Probiotics containing yeast cultures to aid the friendly bacteria in the hind gut are also becoming popular for enhancing the body's ability to digest and utilize food effectively.

Supplements are there, as their name suggests, to supplement any deficiencies in the horse's diet and should not be added just "to be on the safe side."

Here are some guidelines to help you assess whether your horse needs a supplement added to his diet.
❏ If your horse has bright eyes, a shiny coat, good hoof strength, and appears generally happy and healthy, then it is unlikely he needs any form of supplementation to his existing diet. Good management and access to a natural lifestyle and diet will play a more significant part in maintaining good health.

❏ You may want to feed herbs to enhance the natural diet of a stabled animal. It is best to feed these by hand rather than mixing them with the food, and rotate the herbs used (see Chapter 8 for further advice).
❏ Horses fed on grass or forage alone may benefit from a broad-spectrum vitamin/mineral supplement.
❏ Horses fed more than one scoop of a proprietary-made mix or pelleted feed should not need diet supplementation. Check the levels present in the feed by reading the information on the bag or asking the manufacturer. Double dosing by adding a general supplement to this type of feed could lead to *toxic* levels of certain elements being absorbed and is very unwise.
❏ Horses fed on straight cereals, such as oats, barley, or bran, may need greater proportions of specific supplements, such as calcium or phosphorus, to rebalance the intake.
❏ Feed supplements often relate directly to a *problem that your horse possesses*, such as weak hooves, mineral deficiency, hormonal imbalance, respiratory trouble, etc., but look also at the lifestyle of the animal and other contributory factors.
❏ Licking the soil or chewing wood or bark from trees can be a sign of a mineral deficiency and should be investigated further.

DIET REQUIREMENTS FOR TYPICAL EQUINES

A horse must have a food intake of between 1.5–3 percent of his body weight depending on workload and condition. For the average horse, this translates to receiving 2.5 percent of his body weight in dry weight of feed per

Above: *Horses fed on grass alone will benefit from a broad-spectrum vitamin/mineral supplement, and not only in winter as seen here.*

Both above: *Eating wood and soil are symptoms of a mineral deficiency that the horse is trying to rectify. The provision of a mineral lick (center picture) helps to prevent this.*

Above: *The restricted lifestyle we impose on horses means they are unable to select their own herbage to satisfy their cravings. Regular turnout is much better than stabling them and providing an unchanging daily diet.*

❝ A domestic horse is totally reliant on us for the food to which he has access and also for those elements of a natural diet that we may deprive him of. ❞

day. The majority of ponies, however, are able to use smaller quantities of feed efficiently and do well receiving only 1.5–2 percent of their body weight in dry weight of feed.

The major factors to consider when formulating a diet are the type of animal being fed (workload, weight, age, etc.) and the kind of forage available. A good ration will start with a high-quality forage. Large amounts of cereals will not fully compensate for poor-quality hay. It is more economical and better for the health of the horse to have a good-quality hay or pasture as the foundation of the feeding program. Then supplement the hay ration with concentrates, vitamins, minerals, and probiotics as necessary.

Ideally, horses should spend as much time out at pasture as possible. They will naturally receive an unmeasured quantity of feed during this time. It is extremely difficult to quantify the weight and feed value of grass eaten as this fluctuates with the seasons. A horse or pony on good pasture could consume approximately 1.75 pounds (0.8 kg) of grass (dry weight) per hour but only 0.2 pounds (0.1 kg) per hour on poached or barren fields.

For the purposes of these calculations, I have assumed 1.75 pounds (0.8 kg) per hour (dry weight) of grass received in the summer and 0.88 pounds (0.4 kg) per hour in the winter.

I believe in keeping things simple. All feeds on the market are good quality. By mixing rations together, you simply undo all the hard work done by the feed company in providing a balanced ration.

It is important to treat each horse or pony as an individual. Although we often categorize animals and standardize their average requirements, it is essential to assess regularly physical performance, visual external signs of health, and mental well-being and to adjust the diet accordingly. A domestic horse is totally reliant on us for the food to which he has access and also for those elements of a natural diet that we may deprive him of.

General Feeding Tips

❑ **Stable horses for as little time as possible.** If grazing is limited or weather conditions are unsuitable, turn horses out in barns or yards if possible rather than confining them to individual stables. Hay can be put out in piles (more piles than there are animals). They need only be separated to allow those receiving additional feed to be able to eat in peace. Avoid overgrazed, weedy pastures and hays. If the pasture is expected to contribute the majority of the nutrients all year round, allow at least 1.5–2 acres (0.75 ha) per horse.

❑ **Feed hay (or equivalent) at ground level if possible.** This reduces exposure to dust and is a more natural feeding position, allowing better mucus drainage. If a horse or pony spends most of its time grazing outside, it will naturally assume this position for eating. A stabled animal may spend hours on end contorted in an unnatural position if fed from a high hayrack or hay net. I discovered that feeding hay from a hay net hung from the top hinges of the top stable door resulted in an obvious, unnaturally developed line of muscle on the left side of my heavy cob's neck. This was caused by the action of bending to the right to pull hay from this hay net. If you do use a hay net, be aware of this problem and adjust its position from time to time. Obviously, it is undesirable to feed hay off the floor if your horse has a bed of wood shavings or paper, which should not be ingested. It is also unwise to fix hayracks or hay nets low down for fear of legs getting trapped in them. In these circumstances, feed from some kind of crate or manger that can be fixed nearer to ground level.

❑ **Soak hay for only two to five minutes.** Fully immersing hay for only a few minutes will cause the dust particles to swell and stick to the stems, preventing them from being inhaled, but to not dilute or wash away the nutrients. Horses predisposed to respiratory problems such as COPD should have their hay soaked as a preventative measure against the inhalation of dust or spores. However, for animals out at grass or in open barn areas with good ventilation, soaking forage is usually not required provided the animals have good access to fresh water. In fact, some animals will not eat wet hay at all, especially if they are out in cold, wet conditions where soaked hay may further chill an already cold animal.

❑ **Feed concentrates in small quantities.** Horses and ponies often gorge their feed of concentrates, which can swell up to three times its initial volume when mixed with saliva and stomach juices. After swallowing, the food passes to the stomach, which is the size of only a rugby ball. In view of this, split feeds into at least two meals. Ideally, do not feed more than 6.6 pounds (3 kg) of concentrates at a time. Overloading the stomach simply pushes the food through the system faster, resulting in the likelihood of nutrients going to waste.

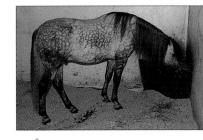

 Both above: A high hay rack is undesirable as it will cause dust to fall into the eyes or be inhaled more easily. Feed hay at a low level or off the ground but choose an interesting vantage point rather than a blank wall.

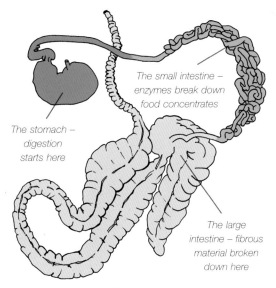

The small intestine – enzymes break down food concentrates

The stomach – digestion starts here

The large intestine – fibrous material broken down here

THE STOMACH'S CAPACITY
A horse's stomach is designed for trickle feeding. Overloading it with large meals simply pushes the food through the system faster, resulting in nutrients not being absorbed.

 Above: If you need to soak hay, only immerse it for about five minutes. Take climatic conditions into consideration – cold, wet hay will chill an already cold horse but refresh a hot animal.

❏ **There are many ways to achieve similar results.** Different combinations of different concentrates and forage can result in the same end result of energy obtained or benefits derived. All feeds are simply broken down into chemicals by the stomach, but some nutrients may be more readily available in one feed than another.

❏ **Feed forage before concentrates.** This is important for two reasons. First, forage should form the main part of the diet, and concentrates should be added only if forage alone does not provide enough fuel. Second, as fiber sinks to the bottom of the stomach, it takes a far greater time overall to be digested. By filling up a greedy horse on hay or short-chop fiber *before* he receives his concentrate ration, he is less likely to overload his system by bolting the food.

❏ **Fresh water should be available at all times.**

❏ **A mineral/salt lick** should ideally be available to all horses and ponies, whether stabled or free grazing.

❏ **Analyze hay carefully.** Then develop the rest of the ration based on the forage quality. Look for hay that smells clean, has fine stems and lots of leaves, and is not dusty, damp, or contaminated by poisonous weeds. Dusts and molds can contribute to indigestion and respiratory problems.

❏ **Make changes to the diet gradually over a seven- to ten-day period.** This practice allows the digestive system to adapt to different levels and forms of nutrients and is especially important when feeding energy-dense rations. When changing from one coarse mix to another, if both have similar energy levels, the change is minimal and can be completed over a few days. However, if there is a significant increase in the energy level, it is best to mix the new and old rations for each feed and gradually increase the amount of the new ration while decreasing the old.

Similar precautions should be taken when weaning a horse from an all-hay diet to lush pasture. Horses should be turned out for only a few hours for the first couple of days, then gradually have the time at grass increased over the next week until they can be left out permanently. If this gradual introduction is not possible, it is advisable to offer hay to horses to satisfy their hunger before turning them onto lush pasture. It should be emphasized that the effects of a change in diet should be closely observed for a period of at least two weeks to determine any changes in the animal's condition or eating behavior.

❏ **Avoid overzealous use of supplements, conditioners, tonics, etc.** Feed only if the basic ration requires supplementation, for example if feeding "straights," i.e., basic individual cereals rather than a compound feed. Commercial feeds are usually balanced to provide adequate levels of all the main vitamins and trace minerals required. It may, however, be useful to add a broad-spectrum vitamin supplement to animals receiving only a handful of concentrates or living on forage alone.

❏ **Feed all feeds by weight not by volume.**

❏ **Feed horses individually if it is at all possible.** This is to prevent aggressive horses from overeating and intimidating more submissive horses. Usually, foals and youngsters can be fed in groups with minimal problems. As they age, however, horses develop pecking orders. Unfortunately, some horses can naturally be very competitive when it comes to feeding, to the detriment of others. Do not simply put down the buckets or fill the trough and leave.

❏ **Never feed cereal mixes or supplements containing rumensin.** Found in some cattle feeds, this additive enhances growth. It is lethal to horses.

❏ **Allow horses one hour to digest a meal before forced exercise.**

Above: A (small) bale of hay weighs between 55–77 lb. (25–35 kg), a scoop of feed between 10 oz. (300 g) (chaff) and 4.4 lb. (2 kg) (oats/cubes). There is scope for getting things wrong, so weigh the ration. Guesswork will not do!

Above: Analyze the quality of hay being used and develop the rest of the ration based on this knowledge.

❏ **Have your horses' teeth checked.** A checkup should be carried out by an equine dentist at least once a year. Study the way they eat for early signs of dental problems. A horse that drops food from his mouth (known as quidding) could have sharp or loose teeth.

❏ **Examine the appearance of droppings.** The presence of long fibers or whole grains in the horse's droppings can be significant as they may be a sign of insufficient chewing or poor digestion.

❏ **Maintain an efficient worming program.** This helps to prevent parasitic damage (see Chapter 8).

❏ **Be vigilant.** Sudden changes in appetite should alert you to a potential problem.

Feeding Youngstock

A suckling foal will receive adequate nutrition from its mother's milk. In my opinion, it is not wise or natural to wean a foal before four months of age. You may wish to offer small amounts of concentrates after about one month. This is the one time in a horse's life where he may be receiving a higher ration of concentrates to forage. This is because the hind gut takes several months to develop fully to cope with forage. It is unlikely that your foal will do little more than nibble at grass before about three months old.

It is still beneficial for him to be turned out for the greater portion of the day. In dry, good weather, a spring foal can live out permanently. Energy expended playing and

Above: Water accounts for a vast proportion of body weight and is essential for all biochemical functions.

Above: Horses rely on their teeth to grind food before swallowing it. Have them checked regularly.

> 66 Succulents and fresh herbs are very useful as these are high in fiber and nutrients and are especially beneficial for horses stabled for long periods who appreciate fresh food. 99

Below: *This horse is certainly displaying his satisfaction with life! Freedom, friends, forage, and food are the makings of a good horse who will thrive on the attention we give him and the job that he has to do.*

Succulents – Adding Variety and Vitamins to a Horse's Diet
All must be fed fresh and free from mold. Feed whole or cut in half rather than chopped up.

Sugar beet – Sugar beet is the residue of beet after the sugar has been extracted. It is high in fiber, energy, and calcium. It is usually fed in the form of shreds or pellets, which are soaked. It can be fed in quantities of up to 3 pounds (1.4 kg) dry weight per day

Carrots, parsnips, rutabagas – Can be given daily in quantities of up to 4 pounds (1.8 kg) per day. Low calorie and every horse's favorite!

Apples (cooking, eating, and crab) – Horses do not have to eat Granny Smiths, *any* type will do. Feed a couple a day but not just before exercise.

Cauliflower, broccoli, sprouts, peas – Most sprouting vegetables, peas, and beans are palatable in small amounts.

Corn on the cob – Horses enjoy the taste and the challenge of a whole cob. This is where maize comes from.

Cabbage, turnips – Very palatable, but feed in only small quantities as they can inhibit iodine intake and affect the thyroid gland.

Cherries, melon, vegetable marrow, papaya, blackberries, mango, pumpkin – Full of vitamins, feed as a treat.

Dates, prunes, apricots, grapes – These can be fed as a treat, fresh or dried, but with no added sugar.

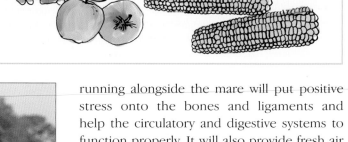

running alongside the mare will put positive stress onto the bones and ligaments and help the circulatory and digestive systems to function properly. It will also provide fresh air for his developing lungs.

A horse or pony does not reach full skeletal maturity until around six years old. Up until the age of two or three, great changes are occurring throughout the body, including the transition from cartilage to bone in some areas.

Getting the balance right so as to sustain a natural growth pattern can be difficult to gauge. If a colt is becoming fat, then you may assume that he is receiving too much feed and simply reduce his feed ration. It is likely that only the energy (calorie) intake needs to be reduced without compromising the protein, calcium, vitamin, and mineral levels which are required in greater amounts for growth.

Suckling foal 1–6 months

- 1.1–1.2 pounds (0.5–1 kg) specialist foal mix offered over four feeds
- Plus mother's milk
- Calcium to phosphorus ratio 1.25:1

- High protein
- High calcium
- High vitamins and minerals
- Keep outside or turn out as much as possible

Weanling 6 months to 18 months

- Specialist youngsters coarse mix
- Plus alfalfa and hay
- Calcium to phosphorus ratio 1.75:1

16.2hh Hunter Type/Dressage Horse/Warmblood

Many of these types are unfortunately kept stabled for long periods due to the nature of their work. This enforced lack of activity predisposes them to laying down too much fat. They also tend to be rugged up and pampered like no other horses, perhaps because of their value and for appearance's sake. For optimum health and performance, we still want to maintain an active, energetic animal. So a high-fiber diet enhanced with small quantities of a high-energy mix is preferable to a greater quantity of a medium-energy mix that may just be laid down as fat. Succulents and fresh herbs are very useful as these are high in fiber and nutrients and are especially beneficial for horses stabled for long periods who appreciate fresh food. These horses may require only 1.5–2 percent of their body weight in food.

Daily ration: 1.5–2 percent of body weight

80% Forage
- Grass/hay

20% Concentrates
- Competition–type mix
- High-fiber cubes/chaff

Dietary Extras
- Succulents
- Fresh (or dried) herbs
- Turn out in yard to restrict grazing
- Feed **small** quantities of a higher-energy mix
- Garlic, hawthorn, and cleavers are useful herbs

Feeding a Poor Doer or Spirited Type

Often of Thoroughbred ancestry, these types may cause a problem as forage alone does not provide the caloric intake they require to maintain a good weight.

Too much energy will make their already exuberant character unmanageable. Turning them out for as long as possible will help them to relax and allow them to expend some energy. The slightest distraction or a stressful situation will hamper their nutrient absorption still further. Yeast or probiotics added to the diet will assist in optimum gut function.

Daily ration: 2.5–3 percent of body weight

70% Forage
- Grass/hay

30% Concentrates
- Conditioning mix
- Alfalfa
- Probiotics
- Oil

Dietary Extras
- Succulents
- Fresh (or dried) herbs
- Turn out as much as possible
- Valerian, hawthorn, chamomile, and meadowsweet are useful herbs

Intermediate Event Horse (Hard Work)

These horses work consistently hard across a wide spectrum of activities requiring precision as well as power. They may find it hard to switch off and recharge their batteries. So it is essential to assist their mental and physical well-being to achieve optimum results.

Daily ration: 2.5 percent of body weight

65% Forage
• Grass/hay

35% Concentrates
• Working/competition mix
• Alfalfa
• Vitamin/mineral supplement
• Probiotics
• Oil

Dietary Extras
• Succulents
• Fresh (or dried) herbs
• Turn out as much as possible
• Electrolytes may be needed occasionally
• Ginkgo biloba, watercress, dandelions, beech, and hazel branches enhance the diet
• Whole corncobs (maize) provide energy as well as stimulation while being eaten

Endurance/Arab (Medium-Hard Work)

These horses normally thrive on their work and have naturally active dispositions and stamina because of their breeding. The key is to provide the right level of slow-release energy feed and to avoid weight loss coming about through nervous activity.

Daily ration: 2.5 percent of body weight

70% Forage
• Grass/hay

30% Concentrates
• Working mix/weight gain mix
• High-fiber cubes
• Probiotics/yeast
• Oil

Dietary Extras
• Succulents
• Fresh (or dried) herbs
• Turn out as much as possible
• Electrolytes may be needed occasionally
• Take care with alfalfa as some Arabs can be allergic to it
• Valerian, hawthorn, chamomile, and meadowsweet are useful herbs

Pleasure Horse (Light Work)

This is a horse or pony ridden about three times a week and rarely pushed to exert himself for long periods. Most of his fuel should come from grazing or forage with any vitamin/mineral shortfalls being supplemented.

Daily ration: 2–2.5 percent of body weight

80% Forage
• Grass/hay

20% Concentrates
• Maintenance mix
• High-fibre cubes

Dietary Extras
• Succulents
• Fresh (or dried) herbs
• Turn out as much as possible
• Hawthorn, rosebay, willow herb, rose hips

Veteran Over 20 Years (Retired or Semiretired)

Older animals often have a decreased ability to absorb nutrients effectively. They often lose condition and may have problems chewing due to worn or loose teeth. Despite their light workload, they need higher sources of energy/calories and also good available protein and calcium. If they have trouble eating hay or grass, high-fiber cubes can be fed with sugar beet pulp to provide fiber.

Daily ration: 2.5–3 percent of body weight

70% Forage
- Grass/hay

30% Concentrates
- Veteran/conditioning mix
- High-fiber cubes
- Alfalfa
- Oil
- Sugar beet pulp
- Probiotics/yeast

Dietary Extras
- Succulents
- Fresh (or dried) herbs
- High calcium, high protein
- Turn out as much as possible
- Cider vinegar is a useful addition to the diet
- Willow, meadowsweet, and comfrey are useful herbs for animals with arthritis

Games Pony/4-H Pony/Show Jumping Pony/Show Pony

An active pony but one which may only be required to work hard at weekends, having several days off work each week which may predispose him to weight gain. A higher-energy mix could be used on the days where he is working hard, reverting back to high-fibre cubes on rest days.

Daily ration: 2–2.5 percent of body weight

70% Forage
- Grass/hay

30% Concentrates
- Maintenance mix
- High-fiber cubes

Dietary Extras
- Succulents
- Fresh (or dried) herbs
- Turn out as much as possible, in barn if necessary
- Hawthorn, garlic, cleavers, and meadowsweet are useful herbs

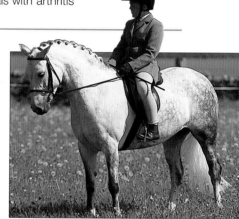

Ponies Susceptible to Laminitis

Laminitis is a common complaint. Unfortunately, once a pony has succumbed to this disease, it is often recurrent.

To prevent laminitis in the first place, I firmly believe that ponies who live out year-round on unfertilized grazing (supplemented with hay in winter) acclimatize better to changes in grass composition throughout the seasons and are less likely to develop laminitis than stabled ponies who are only turned out for short periods. Their weight may fluctuate dramatically throughout the year. However, the same cycle can be observed in wild horses who do not develop this disease.

A pony with laminitis will require veterinary treatment to control it. The pony will probably have to be kept on stall rest and a restricted diet.

Daily Ration: 1–2 percent of body weight

95% Forage
- Grass/hay

5% Concentrates
- High-fiber cubes
- Soybean oil
- Probiotics/yeast

Dietary Extras
- Fresh (or dried) herbs
- Succulents
- Year-round turnout on unfertilized grazing will avoid changes in dietary content
- Barn turnout if grazing has to be restricted
- Cleavers, hawthorn, buckwheat, and yarrow are useful herbs to assist with blood flow to the hooves, and rose hips contain biotin

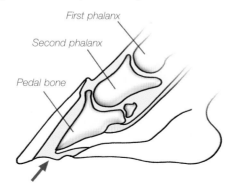

First phalanx

Second phalanx

Pedal bone

LAMINITIS
The rotated pedal bone of a laminitic animal. A high-fiber, low-starch diet would help to avoid this in the first place.

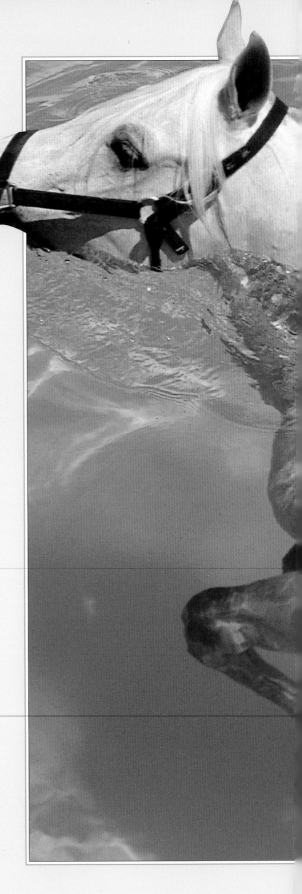

CHAPTER 8

Healing and Natural Remedies

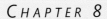

Owning a horse comes with its pleasures and its pit-falls. Injury and illness add to the worry and expense so knowledge of preventative measures and good aftercare is essential for both the horse's and the owner's welfare.

The most important part of the daily routine of looking after a horse is *watching it*. Studying your horse is the best route to understanding it and becoming aware of any warning signs of abnormal behavior or symptoms of trouble, whether mental or physical.

Above: *Many plants, such as this evening primrose, contain natural substances that are beneficial in terms of tonics and treatments.*
Right: *A hydrotherapy pool assists with gentle, non-concussive exercise as the water helps to support the horse's frame. Although horses are good swimmers, this practice can alarm some animals.*

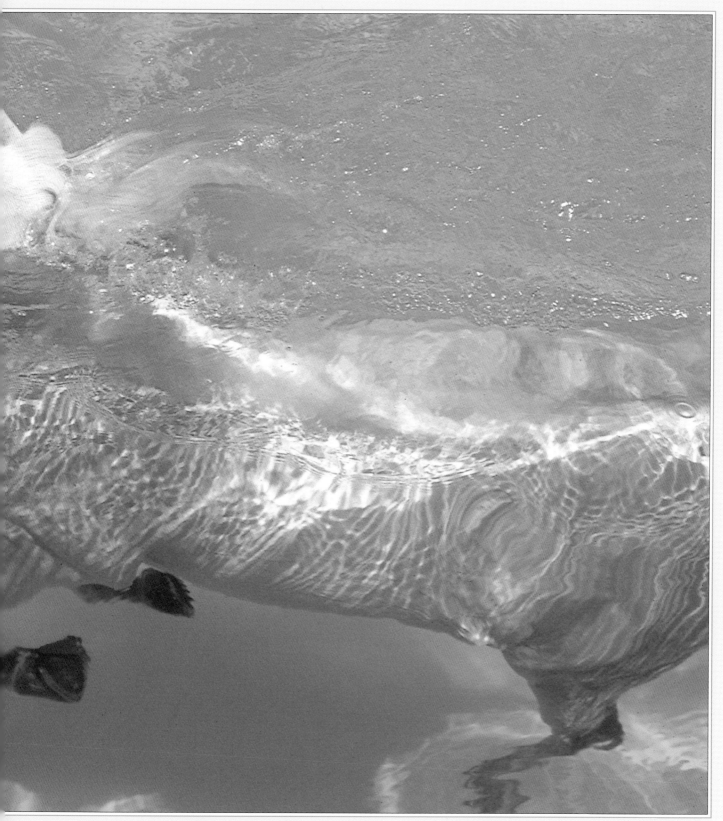

HYDRATION

To test if a horse is dehydrated, gently pinch the skin of the horse's neck or shoulder and then release it. It should spring back flat immediately. If it remains crimped for longer, it is quite likely that the horse is very dehydrated.

CHECKING THE PULSE

There are four ways in which you can check a horse's pulse/heart rate quite simply. The normal pulse rate should be 30-40 beats per minute.

Ideally, you should be aware of the following:

❏ *The previous medical history* of your horse, including any recurrent problems or conformational defects that may potentially cause a problem in the future

❏ *His overall demeanor when healthy* including his stance (whether he commonly rests a back leg, etc.) and the colour of mucous membranes (around the eyes and the gums in the mouth)

❏ His normal *frequency of urination or passing droppings* (and their consistency, taking into account his diet)

❏ His normal *appetite*

❏ His normal *temperature, pulse,* and *respiration* rates

By knowing what is the norm, it is easier to detect any abnormalities, which may be early symptoms that all is not well.

Temperature The normal temperature for a horse is 100.4°F (38°C). This is usually taken by inserting the end of a thermometer about 1.75 inches (4cm) inside the rectum and

> 66 The mortality rate of horses and ponies with tetanus is up to 90 percent, which demonstrates why vaccination is essential. 99

holding it against the wall of the intestine for about a minute.

Pulse/heart rate A horse's pulse at rest should be between 30 and 40 beats per minute. It can be taken by pressing a finger onto any artery but is commonly taken under the horse's jaw.

Respiration This is the number of breaths a horse takes per minute. It should be between eight and 12 breaths in a resting horse but will increase after exercise.

Hydration and blood circulation When the skin of the neck, shoulder, or flank is pinched, it should spring back quickly. If it is slow to return flat, this may be a sign of dehydration. The color of the mucous membranes around the nostrils, eyes, and gums should be salmon pink. A paler color may be a sign of anemia or low blood pressure.

The next port of call is your vet Although *you* should be the best person to advise if your animal is off-color, your vet is trained to diagnose and pinpoint the specific problem and treat it accordingly.

The heartbeat can be heard through a stethoscope placed just behind the elbow.

The heartbeat can be felt and counted behind the elbow where the girth lies.

Feel and count the heartbeat with your fingers (not thumb) placed on the artery under the jaw.

Feel and count the heartbeat with your fingers on the artery under the fetlock.

VACCINATIONS

Prevention is better than cure, and a responsible horse owner should inoculate animals against common debilitating diseases. Many competitions demand proof of vaccinations as a condition of entry. Your veterinarian can recommend an appropriate vaccination program and booster schedule for your horse, based on the needs and risks of the area where you live.

All horses need to be vaccinated against tetanus, also known as lockjaw. The condition, which causes muscle paralysis and rigidity, has an extremely high mortality rate. The bacteria, present in the soil, usually enter the body through a wound, such as a puncture in the skin or hoof.

Horses should also be vaccinated against rabies in areas where this disease occurs. Although the incidence of rabies in horses is quite low, they can contract the fatal virus through the bite of an infected wild or domestic animal and then transmit it to their human caretakers.

A typical vaccination program may also include routine protection against encephalomyelitis (sleeping sickness), equine influenza, rhinopneumonitis (equine herpes virus), and Potomac horse fever. Equine encephalomyelitis, a mosquito-borne viral infection, has numerous strains. The most familiar in the United States are eastern (EEE), western (WEE), and Venezuelan (VEE).

Equine influenza, a highly contagious viral infection characterized by high fever, nasal discharge, and a dry cough, also has several strains that constantly change, like human flu viruses. Due to frequent contact with other horses, show horses are especially vulnerable and may require vaccinations more often than once a year.

Because new diseases and vaccines evolve over time, staying informed about your horse's health is imperative. A vaccine for the West Nile virus is one of the more recent products to become available after cases began to appear on the East Coast a few years ago.

Parasite control is another important consideration for horse owners. Most animals naturally carry some form of parasites from time to time. However, by confining animals to small areas of permanent grazing, we increase the chances of worm infestation. Weight loss or a potbelly, poor coat quality, tail rubbing, diarrhea, and anemia can be signs that parasitic infection has taken a stronghold. A heavy load of internal parasites can have serious health consequences, even leading to bouts of colic.

A good control program starts with having a sample of your horse's manure analyzed to determine what parasites are present. Your veterinarian can handle this procedure and then recommend an appropriate dewormer, such as ivermectin or oxibendazole. To be effective, medications must be administered based on the type of parasite and its life cycle.

Periodic deworming should also be combined with sanitation in the stable and good pasture management. This includes rotating grazing areas and removing droppings to reduce the number of infective larvae in the environment. Rotating grazing with sheep or cattle may also be of value, as these animals do not share parasites with the horse. Therefore, one grazing species can help remove larvae from a pasture that infect another species.

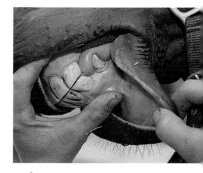

Above: Gums should be salmon pink in color. A paler color may possibly be an indication of anemia or low blood pressure.

Above: Domestic horses usually graze on the same small areas of pasture, increasing the chances of worm infestation. De-worming treatments may be needed.

Above: The color of the membrane around the eye should also be salmon pink. A yellow tinge indicates jaundice and liver damage, perhaps due to poisoning.

CHECKING FOR SHOCK

A symptom of shock is poor circulation indicated by slower capillary refill times. This can be viewed by pressing your thumb/finger on the horse's upper gum for two seconds. When the pressure is released the resulting "white" area should revert to pink within a second. A slow response should alert you to a problem.

COMMON SENSE

Think logically about the symptoms of any injury and whether you can adequately deal with it. Many veterinarians are happy to give you advice over the telephone.

Right: *A veterinarian is qualified to assess injury or illness in an impartial manner (unlike many well-meaning friends!). Although it is best to err on the side of caution, I have found that it is sensible not to demand a visit every time your horse is slighly lame. If the demeanour of the horse is poor, a visit is far more imperative.*

When To Call The Veterinarian

The main aim of this book is to encourage a more natural way of life for domestic horses. However, their well-being should always come first and must *never* be jeopardized by thinking you can let nature take its course and not seek medical advice. Nature can be cruel. Injury and disease act as a natural method of culling the weak or elderly to limit the equine population in the wild.

The very way we domesticate horses – using tack and rugs, transporting them in vehicles, fencing them in paddocks, feeding them contrived diets, and pushing them to their limits in the way we ride them – actually exposes them to more risk of injury than is the case with their wild relatives. We certainly owe it to them to be responsible owners and help with recovery from injury and illness as best we can.

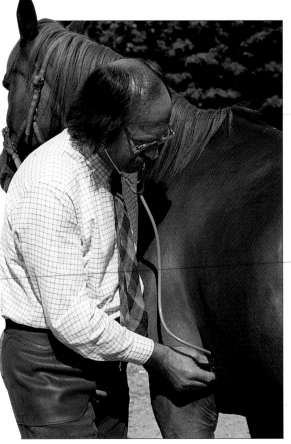

Call your vet immediately if there is

- Heavy bleeding.

- Severe pain. Obvious signs of distress include groaning, violent rolling, eyes rolling, straining.

- Sudden lameness or inability to move willingly.

- A foreign body puncturing or embedded in the skin, such as a piece of wire.

- Breathing difficulty.

- Joint oil (a yellowish fluid) leaking from the wound.

- An exposed bone.

Keep a close eye on your horse or pony and arrange for the vet to call as soon as possible if there is

- A cut or puncture wound that has not caused lameness but may require flushing out or stitching.

- Lameness, although the horse is able to walk.

- Diarrhea or loss of appetite.

- Mild colic (although this may pass before the vet arrives).

- Abnormal behavior, staggering or moving awkwardly, unusual aggression, or hypersensitive behavior.

- Lumps, swellings, or foul-smelling areas.

- Recurrent coughing or discharge from the nose.

Emergency Treatments
Before The Veterinarian Arrives

Owning a horse or pony brings with it the inevitable risk of injury and health problems. While it is essential that we consult a vet to ensure the correct diagnosis and treatment, there are certain things we can do in an emergency to try to lessen the problem.

❏ *Try not to panic.* You may be worried, and the animal will certainly be stressed or even in shock. So it is essential to stay calm and try to think clearly.

❏ *If in doubt, do nothing.* Do not aggravate the problem. Get advice from your vet before even cleaning a wound. You may feel you want to clean a laceration by hosing the area. Sometimes damage can actually be caused by overhosing as the water pressure is greater than the structure of the cell walls, and it can break the tissue down and impede healing.

❏ *Use your common sense.* If you carry a cellular phone and your horse has a fall or accident, telephone for help and just try to make the horse as comfortable as possible until the vet arrives. The vet may be able to give you advice over the phone before you attempt to transport or walk the animal back to the barn.

❏ *Stop any bleeding with pressure.* If your horse sustains an injury while you are out, you may need to improvise with what you have on hand. Firm pressure on a pad applied directly to the wound is essential to help the blood clot and avoid major blood loss.

You may find yourself in an unlucky situation where there is no phone or help at hand and it is necessary to improvise treatment to stabilize the situation before help arrives. Here are some simple remedies that can alleviate common problems.

❏ For minor cuts which do not require stitching, a clean, newly spun cobweb is an excellent aid to bridge the wound and help

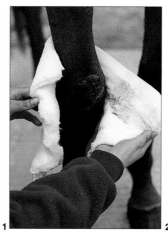
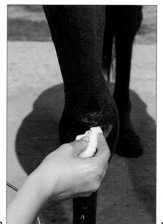
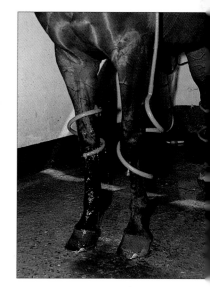

blood to clot. It is especially useful for applying to awkward or sensitive places.

❏ Sugar-free mints have successfully been used to alleviate mild colic. The mint oil present in the sweets is antispasmodic and helps soothe and relax the digestive tract while the sorbitol acts as a mild laxative to get the system moving again.

Note: Consult your veterinarian if systems persist as colic can be life threatening.

❏ To protect and support an injured leg, an improvised dressing can be made. First, put something nonadhesive over the wound (e.g., a large leaf or even part of a clean plastic bag). A scarf or necktie can be used to bandage the area firmly to give support. If the wound is bleeding profusely, use padding in the layers of the bandage to give added pressure. A handful of grass or leaves can act as padding in an emergency. Finally, use bailer twine or a belt to secure the bandage in place.

❏ For minor sprains and strains or just to relieve tired limbs, icepack leg wraps, refresher braces, and even standing in water are beneficial in reducing swelling and heat. Astringent witch hazel can be added to a wash to reduce inflammation and refresh and revitalize sore, tired muscles or can be used as a compress to stop bleeding.

1: Apply pressure to a bleeding wound using a thick pad – this may take a few minutes. Once the bleeding stops, remove the pad.
2: Clean the wound using a mild solution of salt water or iodine and water. Assess the extent of the injury.
3: You have used the time valuably while waiting for the veterinarian. The wound is now ready for him to stitch or bandage.

Above: Cold hosing the lower limbs reduces swelling and heat. However, open wounds should not be hosed.

Above: *Company and an interesting view will keep these horses happy and "sane." Lack of company is the single most significant cause of distress and disturbed behavior in horses.*

Below: *Although many people feel sorry for brood-mares, they are probably among the happiest horses around, usually being kept outside with an unchanging herd of other mares.*

MENTAL HEALTH

Physical distress is usually apparent at an early stage, whereas mental distress may be almost undetectable. It is, however, just as important to look after the mental health of your horse or pony as it is to care for his physical well-being if he is to reach his peak condition.

We may think that the pampered lives we offer horses are better for their well-being than life in the wild. Certainly, we do protect them from many physical dangers and shortages of food that they would naturally face. We can see just how healthy most domestic equines are by their superb condition and the amazing ages they attain in our care. Nevertheless, their mental health can suffer as a result of this protected form of life that we offer them. Often, they are not able to make choices or decisions for themselves, and they enjoy very little mental stimulation.

In their natural environment, horses experience many kinds of mental stimulation as a result of interacting with other members of the herd and having to search for food and water. They are exposed to all forms of weather and changing scenery. They have to cope with the difficulties of an unpredictable and sometimes inhospitable environment.

A horse stabled for more than a few hours a day is, in effect, a prisoner. In an ideal world, he would have the choice of grazing, resting, sleeping, playing, rolling, or simply standing in the open or under cover. The removal of this freedom of choice can have lasting consequences. In the same way, a solitary animal in a paddock can also be a prisoner. (See Chapter 4 for a more detailed analysis of this situation from the horse's point of view).

Mental well-being is of crucial importance for optimum performance in a horse and can enhance good physical health, personality, energy, and responsiveness. Psychological imbalances can show in the forms of introverted or nervous behavior, inability to bond or communicate with human or animal companions, aggressive behavior, lack of enthusiasm for work, and general depression or listlessness. Physical symptoms include cribbing and wind sucking, box walking, weaving, self mutilation, swollen legs, and dull coat.

We can help alleviate the stresses imposed on our horses and ponies by taking into account their mental needs. We can:
- provide company, both equine and human,
- provide stimulation in their surroundings,
- provide exercise requiring physical effort,
- provide work requiring mental effort, and
- provide relaxation time.

We must be aware that, like people, horses have different aptitudes and abilities. They cannot be all things to all people. We would not expect every teenager in a class to be an excellent sprinter or high jumper however much they trained. In the same way, we must accept the limitations of our horses and concentrate on their fortes and the disciplines they enjoy. If we don't do this, stress and resentment may set in.

Aromatherapy and various types of massage are among the simplest and most effective forms of alternative therapies found to release tension in horses and promote a feeling of mental well-being.

ALTERNATIVE THERAPIES

It would be pleasing if all equine diseases and injuries could be treated with natural therapies. However, they should not be seen as the end all and be all of equine medicine or as a replacement for conventional veterinary care. They do, however, come into their own as a way of promoting day-to-day health and well-being and as *complementary* therapies that can work in conjunction with orthodox drugs or which may help when drugs prove ineffective. What you have to remember is that most drugs administered by a vet are derived from natural sources and have been proven and tested in clinical trials. It is also the vet's extensive knowledge and training that is invaluable in diagnosing medical conditions as well as the pharmaceutical treatment he offers.

Alternative therapies should be viewed as complementary, rather than replacement, therapies. Advice should always be sought from a vet before employing them.

Many owners may like the idea of using complementary treatments, but they are often unsure how they can be effectively used in an everyday situation. From the advice available to us today, many of these treatments can be selected and easily administered by the average sensible owner. An example of a scenario in which complementary therapies can be beneficially introduced (based upon personal experience) is set out in the case study on the right.

Complementary Therapies – Do's and Don'ts

If you do use complementary therapies, here are some important dos and do:

Do make sure any plants you pick are correctly identified and free from chemical sprays or other pollutants.

Do inform your vet before using any type of complementary medicine or treatment.

Do check the qualifications of any practitioners you decide to use.

Do be aware that horses can be allergic to some plants, so stop using them if there are any signs of adverse reactions.

Don't expect miracles overnight. Some plant-based medicines take several days or weeks to get into the system.

Don't assume because it is natural that it must be safe. Natural substances can be toxic.

Don't use guesswork when administering treatments or remedies yourself. Always seek professional advice.

Remember that not all therapies discussed in this chapter can be practiced at home by the owner. Some require the services of a qualified, expert practitioner – if in doubt, seek advice.

Horse 1

Gets injured	Bach Rescue Remedy given to horse (and rider) to calm nerves while awaiting vet.
Goes to veterinary hospital	Conventional emergency treatment.
Returns home to convalesce	Maintenance diet including grass/alfalfa and carrots, supplemented with echinacea, blackberry leaves, white willow, rose hips.
Treatment for wounds and scarring	Homeopathic tablets – hypericum and arnica. Aromatherapy oils offered – neroli, comfrey. Topical application of – aloe vera and tea tree oil.
Returning to work	Massage and gentle limb stretches prior to exercise.

Horse 2 (mare)
Pair-bond

Distressed and lonely without Horse 1	Aromatherapy oils offered – neroli and rose. Plenty of attention and exercise. Diet supplemented with calming herbs such as valerian, meadowsweet, and chamomile.

> **❝ It is just as important to look after the mental health of your horse or pony as it is to care for his physical well-being if he is to reach his peak condition. ❞**

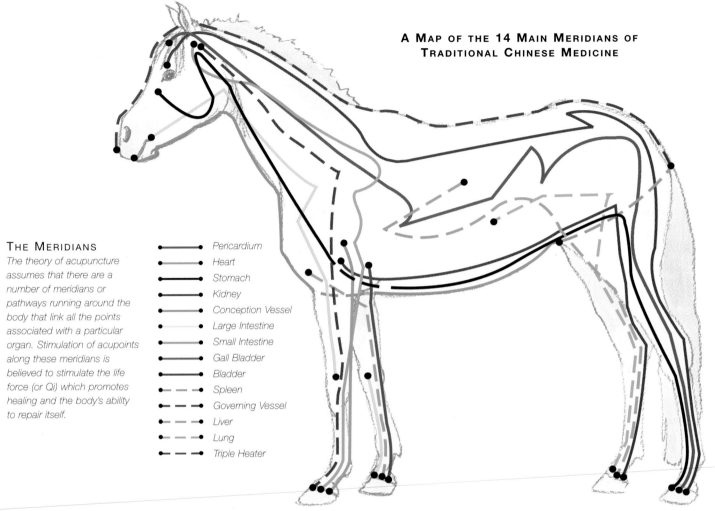

A Map of the 14 Main Meridians of Traditional Chinese Medicine

The Meridians

The theory of acupuncture assumes that there are a number of meridians or pathways running around the body that link all the points associated with a particular organ. Stimulation of acupoints along these meridians is believed to stimulate the life force (or Qi) which promotes healing and the body's ability to repair itself.

- Pericardium
- Heart
- Stomach
- Kidney
- Conception Vessel
- Large Intestine
- Small Intestine
- Gall Bladder
- Bladder
- Spleen
- Governing Vessel
- Liver
- Lung
- Triple Heater

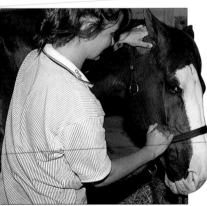

Above: Acupressure is a less invasive practice than acupuncture, but it still uses the same "map" of meridian lines to stimulate the flow of energy to promote healing.

Acupuncture

Eastern medicine believes that the correct balance of the two fundamental forces of nature, Yin and Yang, creates harmony and a healthy body. Meridian lines throughout the body are believed to channel energy (Qi). Acupuncture is used as a means of correcting disharmony and blockages in the flow of Qi (pronounched Chi), thereby stimulating the body's own healing powers and reducing pain.

Very fine hollow needles (usually made of steel) are inserted along specific points (acupoints) on the meridians just below the surface of the skin. It is interesting to note that the position of the needle may be located a long way from the corresponding site of pain.

The needles are gently agitated to stimulate the area under the skin and are sometimes heated or used in conjunction with Chinese herbs to enhance the treatment.

Acupressure uses the same meridian lines but aims to stimulate the flow of energy by fingertip pressure instead of the insertion of needles.

Aloe Vera

Aloe vera is a vegetable of the lily family, like onions and garlic. It is generally the sap that is used, although the whole plant contains an abundance of vitamins, minerals, amino acids and enzymes. It can be used for both internal and external treatments and has been found to be extremely effective on wounds. It kills bacteria, has a cooling and anti-inflammatory effect, and speeds healing by supplying the cells with nutrients. It also seems to reduce scar tissue and the white hair growth often associated with the site of an injury. Taken orally, it is effective as a detoxifying agent to help with urinary infections and troubling digestive disorders.

Aloe vera is widely available in liquid or pill form for internal absorption or cream or gel form for external use. It is a very versatile, safe product which is an invaluable addition to any equine (or human) first aid kit.

Aromatherapy

Aromatherapy uses the therapeutic properties of essential oils which are extracted from plants and fruits. Unlike homeopathic remedies which usually have a water/alcohol carrier, aromatherapy oils are bottled by infusing the highly concentrated oils in a carrier oil, such as almond or walnut oil.

Horses have a far more sensitive sense of smell than we do. The oils work to improve both the physical and emotional well-being of the animal. Just as horses in the wild would seek out plants to aid or relieve their ailments, horses should be allowed to *choose* the oils used in their treatment. They will usually show great interest in a desired oil and turn away from those that are not appropriate.

When I offered one of my mares essential rose oil, she was so keen on it that she tried to eat the bottle. However, when my gelding was offered the same oil under his nostrils, he shot to the back of the stable, spun around, and tried to force his way out to get away. His aversion to the potion was possibly quite understandable as rose is generally used to balance hormonal changes in mares! My advice would be to be prepared for possible dramatic reactions and ideally employ the services of an aromatherapist or kinesiologist to match the needs of the animal to the correct oil.

The horse's needs may change over time, so different oils may be useful in different situations. Horses will tend to lose interest or show dislike of an oil when their needs have been met. You should stop administering it rather than offering the same treatment time and time again. According to the composition of the oils, they can be used for their antiseptic, anti-inflammatory, decongestant, sedative, or stimulating attributes. They are used to treat a variety of both physical and emotional conditions ranging from respiratory complaints to distress or depression in horses.

A wide range of aromatherapy treatments are available to buy over-the-counter and they are usually administered by inhalation. The bottle containing the remedy is offered up to the horse's nostrils or sprayed into the air. Aromatherapy oils should be used only if favored by the horse. The oils he chooses will change periodically. Depending on the condition to be treated, they can also be massaged into the skin in dilute form. If the horse shows an interest, a couple of drops can be massaged onto the muzzle or forehead. This can be repeated for several days or until the horse loses interest or refuses treatment.

Unlike Bach Flower Remedies and homeopathic treatments, they should not be added to drinking water or fed internally unless directed by an expert.

Trained aromatherapists often combine the art of kinesiology as a way of diagnosing which oils should be selected for particular conditions. Seek the advice of a kineseologist or aromatherapist to assess the animal and advise on the most effective choice of oils.

Above: *Growing plants for aromatherapy purposes is big business – not surprisingly when you consider its popularity as a way of treating equines and humans.*

Above: *The aloe vera plant is unsurpassed in terms of its therapeutic benefits when used either internally (pill or juice) or externally. I have witnessed its quite exceptional healing qualities when used in concentrated gel form on wounds.*

🐴 **Below:** *Aromatherapy oils can be surprisingly effective. Lavender has a calming influence and is particularly good for nervous horses, or those stressed before an event or by the traveling involved.*

❝ **The most well-known composition formulation is the Rescue Remedy (made up of five ingredients) which has been found to be invaluable in the treatment of stress, shock or pre-show nerves and can be used by both horse and owner!** ❞

Harnessing The Power of Aromatherapy

Rose A useful hormone balancer for mares in and out of season and for horses that may have experienced past trauma.

Comfrey An uplifting oil to boost the immune system; useful in the treatment of wounds, warts, and sarcoids.

Neroli Useful for general depression and to comfort a horse following illness or the loss of a companion.

Vetiver and nutmeg Found to help strong-willed and "bargy" horses.

The oils recommended below can be added to water as a brace after exercise, or a couple of drops can be massaged into the limbs. Creams, gels and, sprays are also available for external use.

Oils from these plants are ideal for external application/massage	
After hard work/ to prevent bruising/ astringent:	Arnica, witch hazel
Buising:	Arnica, comfrey, yarrow
Calming, soothing:	Marigold/calendula, rosemary, tea tree, yarrow
Fly repellent:	Fennel, orange and lemon oil, tea tree
Stiffness/after hard work/arthritis:	Lavender, rosemary
Wounds:	Aloe vera, tea tree, vervain

Bach Flower Remedies

Dr. Edward Bach was born in 1886 in Britain and trained as a medical student at Birmingham University. His medical know-

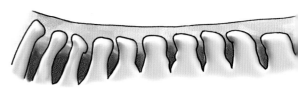

In a healthy spine there is a gap between each dorsal spinous process, the part of the vertebra that projects upwards.

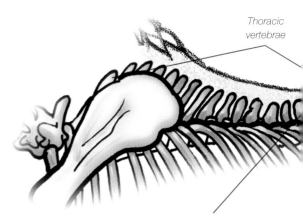

Thoracic vertebrae

Dorsal spinous process

ledge combined with his interest in nature led him to discover the healing power in flowers and plants. He believed that the energy that they contain could be bottled by infusing flowers in spring water exposed to sunlight. The resulting liquid could be used to energize, balance, and kick start the body into healing physical and emotional upsets.

Dr. Bach described the remedies as "a simple and natural method of establishing equilibrium and harmony through the personality by means of non-poisonous wild flowers". Although he developed these for use on humans, Bach flower remedies can safely be used on horses too. Usually about eight drops of the remedy are added to water or dropped onto a treat such as an apple. The frequency of dosing will depend on the gravity of the situation. They can also be made into ointment for external application on the skin.

Surprisingly, each of the 38 flower remedies in the range is usually only made up of one ingredient, specific to the corresponding

When the dorsal spinous processes rub together or impinge, the result is a painful condition known as "kissing spines."

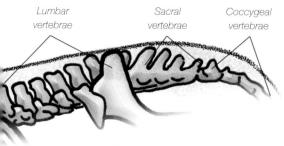

Lumbar vertebrae   Sacral vertebrae   Coccygeal vertebrae

BACK PROBLEMS

A painful spine is one of the most uncomfortable ailments you can suffer from, and in horses it is made all the more acute by the extra weight that bears on the back when the horse is ridden. "Kissing spines" is when two or more of the vertebrae rub together. Such problems can be remedied by a chiropractor.

Above: *Tenderness in the back or neck region should be investigated by a chiropractor, referred by your veterinarian.*

problems it treats. An example is Gorse, which is effective for depression, perhaps to be used during a period of stall rest when the animal is recuperating from illness or injury or after the loss of a companion. The most well-known composition formulation is the Rescue Remedy (made up of five ingredients) which has been found to be invaluable in the treatment of stress, shock, or preshow nerves and it can be used by both horse and owner!

Chiropractic

Chiropractic is a method of treating pain by external adjustment of the spinal column to release pressure on nerves. The treatment predominantly involves manipulation to promote a healthy nervous system and to treat joint disorders, especially those in the spine of the horse. It is primarily used to realign the vertebrae by low-velocity manipulative adjustments to correct incorrect pressure on the nerves and joints. It takes seven years to qualify as an animal chiropractor.

Chromotherapy

Chromotherapy uses color to restore and maintain good health. In 1665, Sir Isaac Newton discovered that sunlight is made up of seven individual colors or wavelengths. Chromotherapists believe that colors produce different vibrations in the environment which can affect our behavior. Strange as it may sound, just as sound waves can be altered to produce harmony or discord, colors can be used to stimulate or calm cells in the body.

The red side of the color spectrum is used in varying degrees to stimulate circulation and cell regeneration. The colors at the blue end of the spectrum have analgesic and anti-inflammatory influences. Chromotherapists use a handheld device called a Bioptron which emits varying intensities of specialist lights with color filters to treat problems as diverse as behavioral problems, arthritis, and skin irritations.

EMRT – Equine Muscle Release Therapy

The theory based on the Bowen technique that is used on humans has been developed as a treatment for horses. It uses noninvasive gentle pressure and massage of the muscles and soft

Above: *Some animals may have had misaligned vertebrae or conformational defects all their lives but a particular event or trauma may aggravate the condition and cause pain. Inform your chiropractor of any relevant history relating to the animal.*

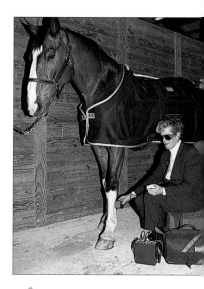

Above: *Chromotherapists use a hand-held device to emit varying intensities of colored light to stimulate or calm cells in the body. Lasers can also be used on acupoints.*

> **❝ Feng Shui works by identifying the energies and working to absorb any unhealthy Sha Qi, and transform it from a "black stream."❞**

tissue, usually in a specific order over key areas of the horse's body. It is used to relax muscles and correct overcompensation which could lead to an unbalanced animal. It has successfully been used to help animals that tend to favor one side or direction of movement or who seem restricted in their way of going.

Feng Shui

Feng Shui is not really a treatment for the horse itself but more of a specialist approach to harnessing Earth's energies to enhance the well-being and potential of the animals and people exposed to them.

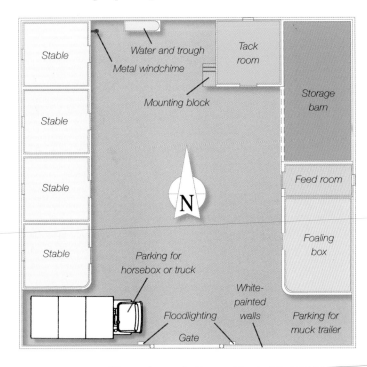

The aim of Feng Shui is to identify Earth's good energy currents (Sheng Qi) or vapors and neutralize unhealthy or blocked energies (Sha Qi). Bad energy currents or blockages are known as black streams and can be created by natural geologic faults, tunnels, quarries or power stations, and building foundations. Although many lea lines are invisible to the untrained eye, some can be easily identified on the surface of the ground

by bare patches of lawn, stunted growth of plants, or fungi growth. Insects and bacteria tend to thrive in these areas as well.

Feng Shui works by identifying the energies, and working to absorb any unhealthy Sha Qi, and transform it from a "black stream" into a "white stream." This can be done by strategically placing items such as wood, crystals, water, or fire to absorb, redirect, or enhance the energies. The idea is to balance the elements of Wood, Fire, Earth, Metal, and Water equally.

It is thought that birds are very sensitive to good and bad energy and that horses are quite resilient to its effects. However, a horse stabled over a "black stream" will never reach his full potential and may be more susceptible to injury or illness. We can therefore help achieve optimum health and performance by directing good energy into the barn and neutralizing any black streams.

Here are some basic principles of Feng Shui to try in the barnyard:

❑ Try and square off the shape of the barn. L- or U-shaped barns have corners missing and will therefore be leaking energy and lacking in certain life aspects. This can be achieved by fencing across the open side to create a whole square.

❑ Keep brooms out of sight. Although they are associated with sweeping away negative energy, they can also sweep away the good energy we want to keep.

❑ Use a compass to establish the Feng Shui directions:

❑ North is associated the element Water. It enhances wealth and career achievements. So having a water bucket, tap, or stream here should improve your horse's competition prospects! Make sure the water flows inwards and is not running behind the stables, as this would mean your wealth and opportunities are flowing *away* from you.

❑ South is associated with the element Fire. As fire and stables do not safely mix, adding a light in this area or a red object can help to

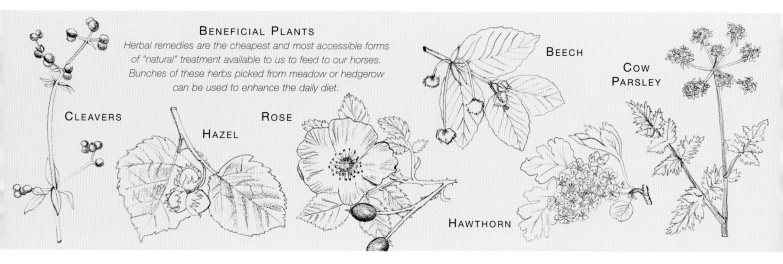

BENEFICIAL PLANTS

Herbal remedies are the cheapest and most accessible forms of "natural" treatment available to us to feed to our horses. Bunches of these herbs picked from meadow or hedgerow can be used to enhance the daily diet.

CLEAVERS

HAZEL

ROSE

BEECH

COW PARSLEY

HAWTHORN

boost this element and promote peace and harmony. Animals and livestock are represented by fire.

❏ East is associated with nourishment, growth, and the element Wood. There should be plenty of this around!

❏ West is associated with Metal. So wind chimes or a metal hanging basket in this sector will help bring good luck.

❏ Central, Southwest, and Northeast positions would benefit from earth, rocks, or crystals being positioned here.

Wood and *Water* should already be in the stable, and a crystal hanging from a red ribbon would provide the elements *Fire* and *Earth*. Any dangling crystals should be kept out of reach of inquisitive animals who may think they are the latest in horse treats!

A Feng Shui consultant will be able to dowse for lea lines and suggest specific ways to enhance the Feng Shui in your barnyard.

Herbal Remedies

This discipline covers a vast array of plant extracts or whole-leaf supplements which I consider the most accessible and useful way of maintaining a happy and healthy horse. Plant medicines have been used for thousand of years and are still the primary source of health remedies in many countries. Many modern

drugs originate from, or are direct copies of, chemicals present in plants.

By offering your horse herbs picked from the meadow, you are, in a small way, helping to redress the balance of modern field management which eliminates the vast majority of useful plants. Herbs offer stable-kept horses a more natural and varied diet.

I pick the following plants and young shoots (which are all easily recognizable). I feed them fresh when in season and also dry them in the Sun and store to use during the winter:

• Cow parsley (flowers, leaves, and stem)
• Willow (soft branches and leaves – feed whole branches when in season or dry out and chop up for easier storage – they can be added to feed in winter)
• Cleavers ("clingy" weed found in gardens and hedgerows)
• Rose hips
• Dandelion (leaves and flowers)
• Hazel (soft branches and leaves – save the nuts to eat yourself!)
• Beech (soft branches and leaves)
• Hawthorn (berries)

It is essential to be aware of exactly what you are feeding by identifying plants correctly.

Above: *Wild horses select plants for their therapeutic properties as well as their palatability.*

Above: *Rose hips are little gems! They contain a valuable natural source of vitamin C and biotin.*

Above: One of the benefits of long-standing permanent pasture is the variety of plants on offer.

Above: Thistles may seem unappetizing but the new shoots are palatable. The plant promotes a shiny coat.

Some plants may look very similar to others but actually be deadly poisonous. If in doubt, err on the side of caution.

By learning to recognize growing herbs and other plants and by harvesting them yourself, you will appreciate how horses relied on the changing seasons to take advantage of the ever-present tonics and nutrients provided by these invaluable plants. Horses are often really enthusiastic when offered a specific herb for the first few days. Then they seem to go off it as the shortfall in their body is replenished. After a break, they will be keen to feed on it again.

In an ideal world, horses would be able to select beneficial plants from the herbage they eat to compensate for any nutrients they were lacking. Modern herbal mixes of dried herbs or liquid preparations help to overcome the mystery of which herbs can benefit which complaint or disorder. These are now widely available.

Diarrhea Rose hips will help with scouring and diarrhea. The high level of vitamin C will help rehabilitate the animal and fight off infection. Mint and yeast are good general gut conditioners.

Inflammation Devil's claw with its anti-inflammatory and analgesic properties is a good alternative to phenylbutazone (bute). Other useful plant treatments for this disorder are comfrey, willow, and arnica.

Laminitis and navicular Nettles and hawthorn leaves and berries are an excellent circulatory stimulant and blood conditioner with a rich source of iron and vitamin C, making them excellent for anemia, arthritis, and laminitis. Cleavers, comfrey, and garlic will also help to support the lymphatic system.

Mental disorders Valerian has a sedative action that helps to calm horses without causing them to lose their faculties. It can be given prior to a stressful situation, e.g., traveling, clipping, etc. It has also been used successfully in the treatment of epilepsy. Chamomile and ginger also have beneficial calming properties.

Rehabilitation Echinacea is the most well-known immunostimulant, and kelp contains the best all-around source of vitamins. Cider vinegar and cleavers will act as a tonic for the whole body.

Respiratory problems Garlic, aniseed, and eucalyptus are expectorants and will clear mucus from the airways. Buckwheat has an antihistamine content to soothe irritation caused by allergies. A few drops of peppermint oil can also be added to the feed or hay to make breathing easier.

Skin problems Feeding kelp and cod liver oil will give the coat a good bloom. External treatments include tea tree oil with its antiseptic and antifungal properties and aloe vera to promote good tissue and hair regrowth.

There are many different herbal systems of treatment throughout the world. The Indian tradition of Ayurveda is becoming popular today for the treatment of equine ailments. It not only promotes the use of specific herbs but takes into consideration the physical makeup and personality traits of each horse before treatment. According to Ayurveda, a horse is made up from the five natural elements of Fire, Water, Ether, Air, and Earth. The three forces, known as doshas, dictate their physical and personality traits. The three doshas are Vata, Pitta, and Kapha and are present in all horses. However, it is the balance of these doshas and the dominant force in each animal that promotes individual characteristics. By identifying this, we can treat the animals more effectively. Ayurveda teaches that feeding herbs can increase or lower one specific dosha to help treat a specific condition and that herbs have a different effect on each horse depending on that horse's individual makeup.

Guidelines On Giving Herbal Remedies

Wild horses naturally select plants other than grasses to make up part of their diet. A domestic horse allowed access to a hedgerow of plants will benefit from the diversity of nutrients on offer. Failing this, horses can be offered a wide range of fresh or dried herbs, selected as best we can for their needs. When giving herbal remedies to your horse, remember the following points:

• Fresh herbs must be correctly identified. If in doubt, do not feed.

• Try to feed only herbs that the horse/pony *wants* to eat.

• Do not overdose. Generally offer only a couple of sprigs of fresh herbs each day (e.g., roughly a bunch of five rose hips, a double handful of cleavers, two thin branches of hazel or willow, one or two whole dandelion plants). You can use dried herbs as directed (usually one to two manufacturer's scoops per day).

• Alternate chosen herbs as dictated by the horse. Do not combine more than five per day,

Herbal Remedies To Be Taken Orally, Fresh, or Dried

Arthritis, joint stiffness Devil's claw, cider vinegar, hawthorn, white willow, meadowsweet, cleavers, celery leaves, saffron, yucca root, feverfew, milk thistle

Blood tonics/lamintis, organ cleansing Cleavers, hawthorn, echinacea, garlic, alfalfa, thistle, chicory, ginseng, gentian, bay leaves, prickly ash bark, yarrow, marigold/calendula, hazel leaves, buckwheat

Calming herbs Valerian, vervain, feverfew, rosemary, nutmeg, violet leaf, chamomile, meadowsweet, bergamot, lavender

Depression Rosemary, St. John's wort

Digestive aids Peppermint, rose hips, meadowsweet, vervain, fennel, ginseng, ginger

Diuretic Dandelion, hawthorn, meadowsweet, juniper berries, nettle

Fertility Echinacea, fennel

Fly repellent Garlic

High nutrient content Rose hips, dandelion, hawthorn leaves and berries, blackberries, seaweed, alfalfa, raspberry leaves, amaranth, rosebay, willow herb, carrots

Hoof conditioners Rose hips, cleavers

Hormonal balancers Raspberry leaves, chamomile, lemon balm, rosemary

Immune system, recovery from injury, wounds Echinacea, aloe vera, chamomile, garlic, nutmeg, seaweed, blackberry leaves, rose hips

Mental and physical stamina Ginkgo biloba, parsley, raspberry leaves, watercress

Respiratory problems Mint, cinnamon, fennel, feverfew, liquorice, coltsfoot, plantain, thyme, speedwell, ginseng, eucalyptus, ginger, beech leaves, evening primrose, fenugreek

Skin soothers and conditioners Thyme, rosemary, aloe vera, chamomile, rose hips, marigold/calendula, lemon grass, beech leaves, fenugreek

Worms Birch, pumpkin, wormwood, clove oil

and check the suitability of the combinations.

• Seek expert advice on the dosage of specific herbs to treat individual ailments.

• To remain effective, herbs taken over long periods should be used in the cycle of four weeks on and one week off.

• Herbs should be fed *in addition to*, not instead of, a balanced diet.

Helpful Homeopathic Treatments

Warning: Seek expert advice on the potency and frequency of treatment required before using homeopathic remedies

Acetic acid, abrotanum, and iodum For diarrhea

Aconite For shock and fear or panic

Apis For all types of swellings on limbs and also allergies and insect bites

Arnica (leopard's bane) Commonly used to reduce bruising and aid healing of bumps and strains
> Note: only use forms specifically made for internal use if you are intending to give this orally (as opposed to creams available for external application)

Arsenicum album (arsenic trioxide) Mud fever, rain scald, sweet itch

Belladonna (deadly nightshade) Treats acute laminitis, infections

Chamomilla To calm a restless horse

Colocynthis To relieve the intestinal spasms of colic

Echinacea Boosts the immune system to challenge infection and encourage healing

Hepar sulphuris calcareum For nasal discharge and coughs

Hypericum perfoliatum For lacerations and puncture wounds, to reduce pain and the risk of infection

Lachesis, platina, pulsatilla, sepia Sometimes used to improve the temperament of mares sensitive to their estrus hormone fluctuations

Lycopodium, bryonia (wild hops) For colic with gas buildup or impaction

Nux vomica For colic and general flushing of the digestive system and detoxifying of organs such as the liver which may have been damaged by ragwort or other poisoning substances

Rhus toxicodendron (poison ivy) For all types of arthritis

Sepia (cuttlefish ink) For improving fertility or hormonal imbalances

Silica Particularly useful to treat scabs and hair loss caused by allergy

Thuja occidentalis and hepar sulphuris calcareum To clear up mud fever

Urtica urens For bee stings and nettle rash

Homeopathy

Although the principle of treating like with like has been recognized in medical philosophy since the time of Hippocrates, it was the German physician Samuel Hahnemann who developed the system in the early nineteenth century by testing different ingredients on himself. He discovered that very diluted quantities of even *toxic* substances, when added to a water/alcohol base, rather than having a destructive effect could actually be beneficial and counterbalance a specific problem or stimulate a healing response. By extensive experimentation, he identified which plants and mineral derivatives could be used to treat specific conditions. A good example is Rhus tox, which comes from poison ivy. It causes stiffness in the joints of a healthy horse but actually gives relief to a horse with arthritis.

Nowadays, this therapeutic system is becoming increasingly popular. However, knowledge of the specific dilution or potency required is essential for effective treatment. The art is matching individual symptoms to the corresponding remedy and knowing how potent a preparation to choose and how frequently the tincture should be administered. An acute problem may need recurrent dosing every 10 minutes initially, whereas longer established chronic conditions may need application of the remedy only once a day. The idea is that the treatment kick starts healing. Watch for improvement in your horse. Then cease the treatment, and allow the body to heal itself. The remedy can be offered again if symptoms return, but continual exposure to the remedy will make it less effective.

Horses with sweet itch and pollen allergies have shown remarkable improvement when dosed with homeopathic remedies made from the substances which trigger their allergies, such as the colicoides midge or rapeseed oil.

Surprisingly, the greater the dilution of the mother tincture, the more potent the remedy becomes. For example, a remedy of 6 has been diluted 6 times in its carrier of water/alchohol. The suffix *c* (Roman numeral for 100) means the dilutions are carried out in steps of one part tincture to 99 parts carrier, and *x* (ten) means the dilutions are in steps of one part in

Left: Water is a useful natural element. A hydrotherapy pool lets a horse exercise gently against the resistance of the water.

Above: Specially designed cool boots soothe lower limbs and "whirlpool" boots include jets of water to gently massage the legs. These obviate the need for a tap to be running for 15 minutes (wasting water) when trying to reduce swelling.

nine. *There are many "over-the-counter" formulations available, but it is advisable to consult a trained homeopath for advice.* Most remedies are available in tablet, liquid, or powder form to be offered orally on food, in water, or directly on the gums or tongue. External homeopathic remedies such as tea tree and calendula are also available as a cream for the topical treatment of wounds.

Hydrotherapy

This comes in many forms, but it is based on the usefulness of a natural element, water. The properties of water are beneficial in several ways: for its cooling therapeutic effects, for the salt and other minerals contained in it, and for the supportive resistance it offers during immersed exercise.

Cold hosing has long been used to reduce soft tissue swelling. Immediately following an injury, the body's immune system triggers the release of chemicals and cells which are transported to the injury site. Although these are beneficial, the excess fluid that builds up can actually suffocate the healthy cells, depriving them of oxygen and exacerbating the situation. This inadequate supply of oxygen is known as hypoxia. Cold hosing, standing in water, or applying cold-water wraps causes the blood vessels to constrict, increases the external pressure, and helps to disperse the inflammation. It is important not to extend the treatment for more than about 20 minutes at a time and to *avoid* direct contact with any area of broken skin area as exposure to extremely cold temperatures will actually kill off healthy tissue. It is beneficial in the treatment of strains and sprains. It also helps to repeat the treatment over several short sessions. Contrast therapy using cold and warm water alternately is also effective. There are now various specially designed ice boots on the market which are more labor saving. There are also reusable cold wraps which are applied to the limb after injury or exercise and boots that have an attachment to keep the hose in place.

If you have access to a river, stream, or even the sea, standing your horse in the flow of the

Above: Hosing is useful to refresh a horse after exercise, but do not hose directly onto broken skin.

ARTHRITIS

Using travel bandages on arthritic horses in winter will help to improve blood flow and keep the joints warm. They can be used on field-kept animals and washed when muddy.

66 Pulses penetrate deep into the tissues to increase blood flow, remove toxins, and stimulate regeneration of cells. **99**

Below: *Magnetic therapy stimulates cell regeneration and increases blood flow. It has also proved an effective form of pain relief.*

water will gently invigorate and massage his body. Walking the horse through varying depths of water or even allowing him to swim is an excellent way of improving cardiovascular strength and muscle tone. The sea also has the added benefit of its natural salt content to help clear up any infection that may be present.

Hydrotherapy pools with adjustable jets are sometimes used in veterinary centers or racing barns for rehabilitating animals.

Kinesiology

Kinesiology is holistic method of muscle testing and energy balancing using the same meridians as used in Chinese medicines such as acupuncture. In the treatment of horses, a surrogate (human) is needed to assess any weaknesses of muscle function which will, in turn, pinpoint weaknesses in the organs or glands which share the same vessel of acupuncture meridian.

Practitioners are trained to feel physical weaknesses and also deep-seated emotional disorders, perhaps caused by past anguish or maltreatment. This can even be detected from hair samples taken from the horse's mane or tail.

Applied kinesiology is often used in association with aromatherapy, and it suggests which oils should be selected for treatment. These oils can then be taken orally (with a practitioner's advice), inhaled, or applied to the skin. Their beneficial effects are usually obvious three to seven days after application and sometimes within hours of the treatment.

Magnetic Therapy

Once again, the Chinese were the first to recognize the properties of magnets to promote healing. Magnetic therapy is found, by some, to be an effective form of pain relief. It can be particularly useful in alleviating the symptoms of arthritis, rheumatism, navicular, tendon problems, and muscle cramps. Pulses penetrate deep into the tissues to increase blood flow, remove toxins, and stimulate regeneration of cells. The magnetic waves should be set at the specific frequency for the condition being treated.

Nowadays, static magnets contained in bandages or rugs can be applied to the horse for home treatment. We are exposed to a natural magnetic field every day (Earth's magnetic field), the strength of which is measured at about 1,000 Gauss. This exposure is reduced when we are inside or in a car. In the same way, a stabled horse with a thick rug will not receive as much magnetic energy. Magnets can be either bipolar or multipolar, and both are effective. It is wise to chose those measuring 1,000 Gauss or less to mimic the natural level in the atmosphere (although the rug or boot encasing them will absorb some of the effect).

Osteopathy

Osteopaths concentrate on the whole body to correct misalignment problems between the bones, muscles, ligaments, and connective tissues. They aim to correct deformation and misalignment of the skeleton. What may seem at first glance to be a problem specific to one area of the horse's body may actually have a

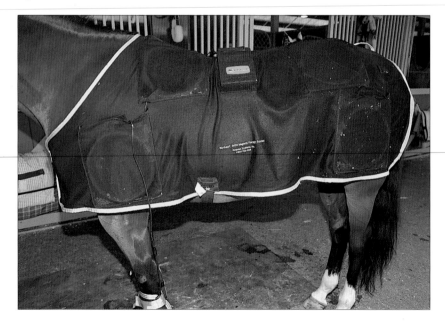

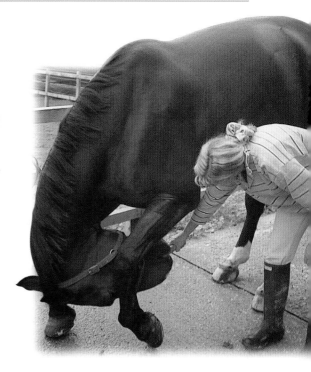

dramatic influence on other parts of the body. Osteopaths work to release tension and improve blood flow. On horses, this is carried out by manipulation of the head, neck, limbs, pelvis, and tail and may be administered under sedation or even anesthetic to allow for more penetrative handling to target deeper muscles. Cranial osteopathy concentrates on the skull and can be beneficial in the treatment of heads hakers.

Physiotherapy

Physiotherapists work in conjunction with a vet and are often used in a preventative capacity as well as for treatment of injuries. The physiotherapist assesses conformation, balance, stride, and type of work undertaken by the horse to work out where possible stresses and strains may occur, for example by a horse overcompensating to alleviate pain caused by injury or deformity. By designing a specific program of stretches and exercises to develop muscle tone and to balance skeletal forces, the aim is to reduce the likelihood of injury and prolong the horse's working life.

Above left: Neck flexion will stretch the horse and make him more supple. Stretching the muzzle around to face the tail will flex the complexus and splenius muscles in particular.

Above right: Stretching down between the forelegs flexes the neck and spine. These exercises are achieved by encouragement with a carrot!

Electrotherapy and heat treatments may also be used in conjunction with this program. Treatment may take weeks or months to complete.

Radionics

An American physician, Dr. Albert Abrahams, conceived a theory that the abdomen could absorb and transfer energy and that a healthy surrogate human could be used to diagnose different diseases in another being by simply holding a sample of their blood or hair. He discovered this when he was examining a patient's abdomen and heard a dull note which could not be explained. He later found that this

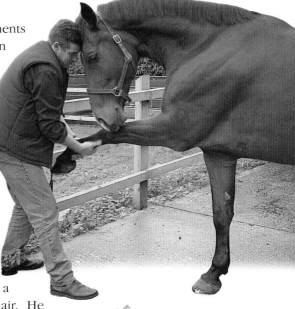

Above: A physiotherapist will develop a program of exercises to restore normal musculo-skeletal function.

 Above: *Reiki healing aims to alleviate physical pain and emotional imbalances and stress. The hands of the practitioner do not actually have to touch the animal for energy to flow between the two of them.*

Right: *Reiki can be both an uplifting experience and a calming influence as harmony is restored. It helps to revitalize the body's own healing system and to restore energy levels within the body.*

66 Some horses find a session of Reiki relaxing, whereas others find it stimulating. **99**

same resonance was achieved in a surrogate – a healthy person holding the diseased tissue in their hand. He mapped out a plan of the abdomen with different regions relating to different diseases. He found that the use of electrical instruments could enhance the energy transference by identifying resistance and normalizing the radiations.

It is popular because, as with kinesiology, diagnosis can be made at a distance, by using a hair sample from the mane or tail. The diagnostic testing dictates which treatment should be used to aid healing, with acupuncture, homeopathy, or even color therapy among the options.

Reiki

Reiki is a form of hands-on healing that aims to activate the body's own healing forces, reduce stress, and promote relaxation. It works on four levels: spiritual, mental, emotional, and physical. To restore energy levels, the therapist will either place his or her hands on the animal or a few inches above the surface of the skin to balance and restore harmony to the horse's body. With this method, therapists are able to alleviate physical pain and psychological and emotional imbalances and stress.

Some horses find a session of Reiki relaxing, whereas others find it stimulating. It is an excellent way of releasing stress and depression in horses. Some physical conditions which have benefited from Reiki are COPD, melanomas, and allergies.

Shiatsu

Shiatsu practitioners use the same meridian lines and theory of healing as practiced in acupuncture. Instead of using needles, they use finger pressure, manipulative massage, stretches, and rotation of the limbs, neck, and tail to balance energy and promote health.

The body is thought of as containing 14 pathways or meridians that relate to specific organs and which trace a long circuit around the body. They serve as channels for the body's natural energy (or Qi).

The meridian lines are used as a map. The practitioner lays one hand on the horse's body for balance and to feel for any sudden movements by the horse. The other hand traces the pathway of the specific meridian, feeling for tense knots and hot and cold areas. The horse may lower his head and appear relaxed or feel agitated if a sensitive area is touched, which may need further massaging or manipulation to release the flow of energy.

Supplements

This heading covers the supplements, usually added to a horse's feed, which profess to have regenerative properties or help maintain good health in the horse. These may be derived from plant, mineral, or even animal or fish sources. Although all the substances listed here have been found to be beneficial in some way, we should bear in mind that horses, as herbivores, are very unlikely to eat anything of animal or marine origin. Therefore animal- or fish-derived substances are not natural supplements for a horse. It is possible that they could cause adverse effects of which we are not yet aware. Always read the list of ingredients, and check with the manufacturer if you are unsure about their suitability.

❏ **Biotin** Very well-known sulfur-rich vitamin which is helpful in promoting a healthy hoof structure. Often used in conjunction with zinc and methionine to aid absorption.

❏ **Cider vinegar** Made from apples, this provides a good natural tonic and source of potassium, phosphorus, sodium, calcium, iron, and other trace elements. It is useful in promoting overall good health and has been found to be beneficial to joint suppleness.

❏ **Cod liver oil** Used to aid joint mobility in horses with arthritic conditions and to improve overall skin and coat condition. High in vitamins A and D.

❏ **GAGs (glycosaminoglycans)** These complex carbohydrates can contribute to cartilage repair in stiff or arthritic joints.

❏ **Kelp/seaweed** Contains a broad spectrum of vitamins and minerals and enhances coat and skin condition.

❏ **Linseed oil** Made from oil extracted from the linseed plant. It is a digestive aid and coat conditioner.

❏ **MSM (methylsulfonyl methane)** This is organic sulfur. It is very useful in maintaining healthy connective tissues in the hooves and skin and also as an anti-inflammatory agent.

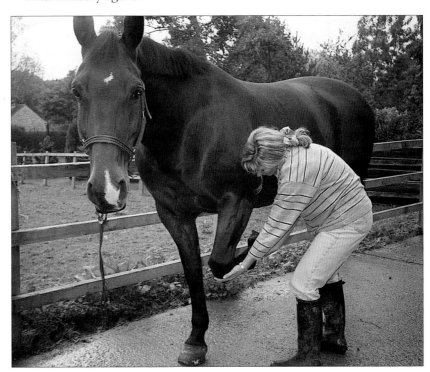

❏ **Shark cartilage** As its name suggests, this is processed shark's cartilage which can be used as an anti-inflammatory in the treatment of joint problems.

❏ **Yeasts, enzymes, and probotics** These are beneficial for horses with digestive problems as they encourage the growth of

MINTS

Mild colic can sometimes be eased by feeding the horse half a packet of sugar-free (hard) mints. The mentha has an antispasmodic effect on the digestive system and the saccharin acts as a mild laxative.

Above: *Shiatsu literally means "finger pressure" in Japanese. The technique generally uses one hand as a support while the other applies fingertip or palm pressure to rebalance energy.*

🐎 **Below:** *Linda Tellington-Jones shows how the Shoulder Lift and Shoulder Release movements help the horse to let go of tension. Using massage can help create a bond with the horse.*

🐎 **Right:** *Here Linda uses light pull-and-release signals to encourage the horse to lower his head as she does T Touch circles on his poll. Working around the acupressure points on the ears is useful after a shock.*

🐎 **Above:** *Monty Roberts, one of the best-known horse whisperers, has a great understanding of horse psychology and the art of communicating with equines. He was one of the first people to promote the mental welfare of horses as well as their physical care.*

good microorganisms in the intestines of the horse to help break down food and aid absorption of nutrients.

For analysis of vitamin and mineral supplements and their function in a horse's body see Chapter 7, "Nutrition The Natural Way."

Tellington Touch – TTeam

TTeam (short for Tellington Touch Equine Awareness Method) was developed by Linda Tellington-Jones, a renowned horse expert and animal behaviorist, who has incorporated her Feldenkrais human body work training with her knowledge of the physiology and mental/emotional adaptation of animals. In her own words, "TTEAM enfolds touch, movement, body language and instructional techniques into a form that permits the animal to heal and learn in a painless and anxiety-free environment. With TTEAM, a human/animal bridge is formed in a communicative partnership that culminates in joy, understanding, and honoring of the animal's spirit."

It uses massage techniques and exercises to relax the horse and improve its comfort and coordination. She has also developed a series of groundwork exercises using a grid or labyrinth to improve the concentration and athletic ability of the horse. Some of the main TTouches are the Clouded Leopard, Python Lift, Tail Pull, Ear Work, and Leg Circles.

Clouded Leopard A circular movement which can be used all over the body to increase circulation or relieve tension or stiffness in the muscles. Your hand should rest lightly on the horse's skin with fingers just slightly curved. Keeping your hand spread out slightly, draw a circle of one and a quarter rotations, allowing the fingers to push the skin. Try different pressures, and watch the horse's reaction.

Python Lift Used to relieve muscle spasm and improve circulation. The flat of the hand is laid over the horse's skin above a muscle. The whole area is lifted slightly by gripping gently with the palm and fingers, held for four seconds, and then released.

Tail Pull Tail manipulation acts to release tension in the neck and back. The tail is held gently but firmly in both hands, flexed by gentle rotation, and stretched by leaning back slightly and using your own weight to pull the tail into alignment.

Ear Work Ear work is useful in helping a horse to relax and release tension. It can be useful after a shock to lower pulse and respiration rates. Lower the horse's head. Work on one ear at a time by using your fingertips to stroke and squeeze the ear gently working from base to tip. There are many acupressure points in the ear. Working on the tip of the ear can be helpful for horses that have undergone a traumatic experience. Be aware that some horses do not like their ears being touched at first.

Leg Circles Excellent for warming up cold limbs before exercise and improving circulation in a stabled horse. To perform this movement on the horse, a leg is lifted slightly and flexed (forward or backward) and moved very gently in a circular pattern and then put back down on the ground.

Whisperers and Spiritual Healing

This is not really a treatment but more of a "consultation" between horse and human. Horse whisperers tend to have a talent for understanding and communicating with their equine patients through actions or a kind of telepathy. They may be useful in determining the root cause of a problem and may reveal past experiences or mental and physical disorders not apparent in other forms of diagnosis. By understanding where the dysfunction lies, a more suitable treatment can be implemented.

Useful Contacts

American Academy of Veterinary Acupuncture
Box 419
Hygiene, Colorado 80533-0419
Tel: 303-772-6726
www.aava.org

American Association of Equine Practitioners
4075 Iron Works Parkway
Lexington, Kentucky 40511
Tel: 859-233-0147
www.aaep.org

American Holistic Veterinary Medical Association Directory
Lists practitioners/associations in all countries
www.altvetmed.com

American Horse Council
1700 K Street NW
Suite 300
Washington, DC 20006
www.horsecouncil.org

American Horse Defense Fund
11629 Deborah Drive
Potomac, Maryland 20854
www.ahdf.org

American Quarter Horse Association
P.O. Box 200
Amarillo, Texas 79168
Breed registry
Tel: 806-376-4811

American Veterinary Medical Association
1931 North Meacham Road
Suite 100
Schaumburg, Illinois 60173
Tel: 847-925-8070
www.avma.org

Bach Flower Remedies
The Dr. Edward Bach Centre,
Mount Vernon,
Bakers Lane,
Sotwell,
Oxon OX10 0PZ
Tel: 01491-834678
Fax: 01491-825022
www.bachcentre.com

Equine Research Foundation
P.O. Box 3356
Santa Cruz, California 95063
Tel: 831-662-9577
www.equineresearch.org

The National Federation of Spiritual Healers
Lists details of healers in the UK, USA and overseas
Old Manor Farm Studio,
Church Street,
Sunbury-on-Thames,
Middlesex TW16 6RG
Tel: 01932-783164
Fax: 01932-779648
www.nfsh.org.uk

United States Dressage Federation
7700 A Street
Box 6669
Lincoln, Nebraska 68506-0669
Tel: 402-434-8550
www.usdf.org

United States Pony Clubs, Inc.
4071 Iron Works Pike
Lexington, Kentucky 40511
Tel: 606-254-PONY (7669)

USA Equestrian
4047 Iron Works Parkway
Lexington, Kentucky 40511
Formerly American Horse Shows Association
Tel: 859-258-2472
www.ahsa.org

Glossary

aids Can be natural, e.g., hands, legs, voice, seat or artificial, e.g., spurs, whip.

azoturia Painful condition of the muscles causing reluctance to move during or after exercise – the result of lactic acid affecting muscle fibers. Often seen in horses on a high-energy diet exercised after a period of rest time; hence the slang name "Monday Morning Disease."

backing Accustoming a horse to being ridden, i.e., the first few times of being mounted by a rider (see also breaking).

barn sour Miserable while being stabled.

barn sweet So accustomed to stable confinement that unwilling to leave this environment.

bars (of mouth) Part of the upper gum behind the incisors and the premolars where there are no teeth. A bit lies in this area.

bascule Pivot from a central point. The term is used to describe how the horse's body describes an arc as it jumps over a fence.

bit A metal (usually iron) bar (sometimes jointed) that fixes to the bridle and sits in the horse's mouth to assist control.

bitting Using a bridle or headpiece with metal bit attached (or rubber bit in the first instance) to go in a young horse's mouth to aid control.

box walking A compulsive disorder of pacing around the stable, due to boredom and the frustration of confinement.

breaking (a horse) see "backing" but also used in the term "breaking a horse to harness" when accustoming a horse or pony to being driven in a trap/cart.

bridle A headpiece made of leather (or webbing) straps which holds a bit to which reins are attached.

capped hock Fluid-filled swelling on the central joint of the hind leg between the thigh and cannon bone usually caused by bruising. Does not generally impair movement.

cavesson noseband A wide, flat basic noseband which fixes under the jaw, lying approximately 1.2 in. (3 cm) below the cheek bones.

coarse mix A nutritionally balanced feed containing a variety of cereals and grains, peas, oils, alfalfa, etc.

colic Pain in the abdomen, usually caused by blockage (impaction) of food in the gut, accumulation of gases or twisted intestine causing spasms of muscle in the gut wall, sweating, pawing the ground. Veterinary treatment needed.

colostrum Milk secreted by the mare's mammary glands at the birth of a foal which is high in protein and antibodies.

conformation Anatomical appearance and proportion of parts of the body. Distinguishes between different breeds and types and whether a horse may be predisposed to lameness or more/less suitable for a particular job.

cribbing A behavioral problem known as a "vice" but usually caused by stress, often through boredom. The ritual of holding on to something by the teeth (usually seen as chewing on the stable door) releases endorphins which calm the horse. More freedom, stimulation, and equine contact lessens the problem, but once it has developed, it often becomes a deep-seated habit.

cool feed Food providing slow-release energy usually from fiber and oil sources, the term usually means that there are no oats in the ration.

COPD Chronic Obstructive Pulmonary Disease. Caused by hypersensitivity to dust antigens found in hay, straw, mould, etc. causing coughing, wheezing. Similar to human asthma. Most frequently associated with stabled horses.

cross-country A series of rustic-looking fences and ditches over a pre-determined (usually timed) course over fields and through woodland, i.e., across country.

cross training Teaching your horse a variety of techniques and disciplines in many spheres, e.g., show jumping, dressage, schooling, hacking, hunting, gymkhana, which will help with fitness, agility and mental stimulation, even if you only compete in one field.

curb groove The area behind the horse's lower lip where the chin begins. A bit fitted with a curb chain uses pressure here.

dressage A series of ridden patterns and movements performed in a measured arena, the "tests" becoming more complicated and elevated as horse and rider progress. Sometimes these are performed to music.

drop noseband This is positioned slightly lower down the horse's nose and passes below the bit rings. It is generally used with Fulmer or full cheek bits where the shanks may catch on a normal cavesson noseband.

eventing Made up of the three components: dressage, cross-country (sometimes with a road & tracks course beforehand) and showjumping. Shows versatility of horse and rider as well as a good degree of fitness and stamina. An event is usually held over one or three days.

fetlock The joint of the foreleg or hindleg where the cannon bone, pastern and sesamoid bones meet.

flash noseband A noseband with two straps, one fixing as per a cavesson noseband and the other coming down at an angle from the front of the nose, in front of the bit and fixing at the chin, behind the horse's lower lip. It holds the bit central in the mouth but does not allow the horse to open his mouth or his jaw.

flatwork Schooling a horse using circles, forward, backward, and lateral movements as a precursor to dressage or to improve lightness and paces generally. On the flat, i.e., no jumping.

Flehmen response When the horse holds his head high and curls the top lip back exposing his teeth to give greater smelling sensation. Seen in stallions trying to identify if a mare is in season and also by many horses when encountering an unusual or strong scent or flavor.

foal Young horse or pony from birth through weaning (weanling) to one-year-old (yearling).

foal slip A small halter made of webbing or leather for leading a foal.

forage Any high-fiber herbage including fresh grass and plants or dried hay, haylage, chaffs, etc.

forehand The front of the horse. The term "on the forehand" is often used to mean the weight of the horse when ridden is predominantly carried by his forelegs, giving a feeling of traveling downhill.

4-H events These include jumping, barrel racing, trail riding, pole bending, and showing, both English and Western. 4-H is the U.S. equivalent of the Pony Club in England, promoting good horsemanship to young people and being split into regional clubs holding shows and summer camps.

free radical Compounds of oxygen which affect cell activity and can be very damaging. Injury, stress and excessive exertion can lead to the production of higher amounts of free radicals. Their effects can be neutralized by antioxidants including vitamins A, C, and E.

frog A triangular-shaped spongy area of the undersurface of the hoof used to absorb concussion and for weight-bearing in unshod hooves.

gelding A castrated male horse.

getting cast Becoming stuck while lying down or rolling, usually against a fence or in a stable or confined space. Usually involves the horse being manhandled into a position to allow him to get up again.

grackle noseband This consists of two straps but rather than lying one on top of the other, they cross at a pad in the centre of the horse's nose. One strap then lies just below the cheek and the other lies in front of the bit. It is often used in an effort to increase control but clamps the jaw shut and should never be used with anything other than a snaffle bit.

grass sickness A condition of the alimentary canal (often fatal) associated with grass but more likely caused by a virus living in pasture which causes paralysis of the gut leading to dramatic weight loss and depression.

hackamore bit A bit which does not sit in the horse's mouth but instead uses pressure on the nose, leverage from two shanked arms (to which the reins attach), and a curb chain for pressure on the chin. It can be used as an alternative to a traditional bit in preference to putting a bit through the mouth and useful for horses with both sensitive or deadened mouths.

halter An adjustable headcollar made of leather, or nylon webbing or rope which loops over the poll and around the nose to give control when leading in hand.

hands (hh) The measurement used (before metrication) to determine the height of a horse or pony. 1 hand = 4 inches. It is measured from the ground to the top of the withers. Derived from the approximate width of a man's hand.

Harbridge Two straps with elastic ends which fasten from the girth, between the horse's front legs and to each bit ring. It encourages the horse to work from behind and hold itself in the "correct" outline and, because of the elastic, rewards when the desired position is achieved. It should only be used for short periods.

hard feed The portion of a horse's ration made up of concentrates, i.e., pony nuts, mixes, straight cereals, etc., as opposed to the forage part of the diet.

haylage Semi-wilted cut grass, usually vacuum-packed in plastic sheeting.

heating/non-heating food Most commonly used to convey the energy level of a feed; a heating feed is likely to contain oats, maize, and barley to give an instant energy boost for a hard-working horse rather than a higher fiber:cereals ratio in a cool mix. The term is misleading though as cereals are digested quickly and produce little "heat" whereas the process of eating fiber, such as hay, which takes longer for the body to digest, will warm a horse.

hocks The central joint of the hind leg between the thigh and cannon bone at the same height as the horse's knee on the foreleg.

hydroponic Culturing plants without soil. Hydroponic grass is grown in a machine using water but no soil which means that the whole plant including the roots can be fed.

kimblewick A type of bit with "D"-shaped cheeks which uses leverage and a curb chain in a similar action to a Pelham but with only one rein. Often used on strong horses.

laminitis Inflammation of the laminae (blood vessels) lining the pedal bone in the hoof causing lameness and an

obvious "leaning back" stance in severe cases. Most often associated with ponies fed on rich pasture or concentrates. Although it can be effectively treated by drugs and farriery care, it is often recurring.

leadrope The rope which attaches with a clip to the halter with which to lead a horse.

leas Areas of land under a temporary crop of grass, in contrast to permanent pasture.

lunging Exercising a horse in a circle around you using a long webbing rope attached to a ring on the front of a lunging cavesson halter and encouraging the horse to go forward in a circle by flicking a lunge whip, although rarely touching the horse with it.

lymphangitis Inflamed lymphatic vessels and lymph nodes usually apparent by hot, painfully swollen legs caused either by infection or excessive feed upsetting and overloading the fluid balance.

manège An arena with a firm but cushioning surface, e.g., sand or rubber chips, usually enclosed by fencing or walls, ideal for schooling horses.

manger Feed trough.

Market Harborough Similar to a Harbridge as it passes from the girth, up between the front legs and then divides into two straps which pass through each bit ring and are attached by clips to each rein. As there are elastic inserts, it only comes into effect if the horse pulls or raises his head too much. It should only be used with a snaffle bit and only for short periods.

martingale A leather device with a loop that passes over the horse's neck and a strap that starts at the girth and goes between the front legs and either fixes to the back of the noseband or divides into two straps with a ring at each end, through which the reins are threaded. It is used to prevent a horse from lifting his head in the air. Unfortunately, it is often adjusted incorrectly, causing a constant downward pull on the reins (and therefore the bars of the mouth) and interrupting the straight line from hand to mouth. Because of incorrect fitting and the effects of long-term use, it often fixes the horse's neck and causes stiffness and resistance in the neck.

navicular Adhesions to the bone behind the coffin bone and deep

flexor tendon causing pain and lameness (often intermittent) generally caused by concussion or conformation such as upright pasterns.

over-reaching The action of overstepping with the hind leg so the hoof steps on or grazes the heel of the foreleg on the same side.

Pelham bit This can have a jointed or straight bar going through the mouth with long shanks. One set of reins is fitted to the top rings and another set of rings used on the rings at the bottom of the shanks, which has a levering action on the poll and brings into action the effect of the curb chain. It is useful for horse and rider combinations who are not suited to a double bridle and is also fitted on short-necked animals to help bring their nose in to the perpendicular.

poaching (grass) Ground which has been cut up by hoof prints, usually waterlogged, causing rutted and muddy areas, e.g., in gateways.

pole work Schooling over poles to improve gait and as a precursor to jump training.

poll The area behind the horse's ears

quarters The flanks, hindlegs, and back end of a horse.

quidding Dropping food out of the mouth when eating, usually caused by missing teeth or sores in the mouth resulting from sharp hooks on teeth puncturing the cheeks.

scurf Flakes of dead skin and grease removed when grooming horses.

short-chop Fiber including straw or alfalfa which has been machine-cut into short lengths. Used to bulk out short-feeds or as a hay replacer fed from a bucket or manger.

short-feed A term used for any ration fed from a bucket or manger, given in addition to forage.

snaffle bit There are many variations of snaffle bits with straight or jointed bars and fixed or loose rings, but generally speaking a snaffle is a fairly mild bit which is used with only one rein and which works on the corners and the bars of the mouth.

splints Bony formations on either side of the cannon bone, often seen in youngstock caused by a knock, or deficiency of calcium or vitamins.

stifle The upper joint of the hindleg formed where the upper end of the tibia and lower end of femur meet.

straights Feeding individual cereals, e.g., oats, barley, rather than a more nutritionally balanced mix of cereals and vitamins.

succulents Fruits and root vegetables, e.g., apples and carrots, enjoyed by horses and fed to increase the moisture and vitamin content of the diet.

sweet itch A type of eczema or allergic reaction to biting insects causing much irritation usually to the areas of the mane and tail which can be rubbed raw by the horse in an attempt to relieve the itching.

tack Equipment used to facilitate riding and handling the horse or for protection, e.g., saddle, bridle, numnah, brushing boots, etc.

turnout 1) An area for free exercise and relaxation for horses with/without grass.
2) The appearance of horse and rider including tack and clothing to suit a particular event or show class.

warmblood The largest sector of modern horses, mainly derived from pure or part bred Arab or Thoroughbred ancestors as opposed to draft-type horses or "coldbloods." The term is often used for breeds associated with sports horses or dressage, e.g., Hanoverian, Trakehner, Danish, or Dutch warmbloods.

weaning Gradually taking away a foal's dependence on its mother's milk until it ceases drinking and eats a diet of forage and concentrates to gain its nutrition. Naturally occurs at about ten months old when mare will discourage suckling but is usually done at about six months old with domestic foals.

weanling A newly weaned foal.

weaving A nervous condition of shifting weight from one foreleg to the other and swinging head and neck from side to side (usually above a stable door), generally caused by boredom and classed as a "vice."

withers The top of the shoulders, seen as the highest point where the neck joins the back, formed by the 3rd-9th thoracic vertebrae. The height of a horse is measured from the ground to this point.

youngstock Term used to describe immature animals usually older than foals but generally too young to be ridden, normally refers to one- to three-year-olds.

Index